YVONNE

YVONNE

An Autobiography

Yvonne De Carlo
with Doug Warren

St. Martin's Press
New York

Design by Giorgetta Bell McRee/Early Birds

Library of Congress Cataloging in Publication Data

De Carlo, Yvonne.
    Yvonne.
    1. De Carlo, Yvonne. 2. Entertainers—United States
—Biography. 3. Moving-picture actors and actresses
—United States—Biography. I. Warren, Doug.
II. Title.
PN2287.D354A3   1987   791.43′028′0924   [B]   86–26290
ISBN 0–312–00217–3

First Edition

10 9 8 7 6 5 4 3 2

This Book Is Dedicated to
All the Kings, Princes, Lords, Millionaires,
and Truck Drivers I Have Known.

With appreciation to the late Hector Arce

Yvonne De Carlo wishes to especially thank Ken Ross Mac-Kenzie and Howard Neujahr for their assistance. Also: Robert Hussong, Marie Middleton, Bruce Morgan, Helen Morgan, Michael Morgan, Robert Morgan, George Shdanoff, Melva Wickman, and thanks to you, Djounam.

PART ONE

The Road to Hollywood

Good times and bum times
I've seen 'em all, and my dear,
I'm still here.
Plush velvet sometimes
Sometimes just pretzels and beer
But I'm here.
I've stuffed the dailies
In my shoes
Strummed ukuleles
Sung the blues
Seen all my dreams disappear
But I'm here.

Chapter 1

It was a very warm Sunday afternoon in August of 1940. The spectators gathered around the runway were baking in the sun, but the cool ocean breezes chilled me as I waited to join the others onstage. Part of my shivering was from fright, as I anticipated parading in front of hundreds of people, and part was from fear: By today's standards, I was dressed for the street, but the red bathing suit I was dressed in was just about as sexy as anyone then could get . . . and stay out of jail.

This was the Miss Venice Contest, a preliminary to the Miss California contest, and later to the Miss America Pageant. In those days, beauty contests weren't the extravagant productions they are today. This contest was held at the Venice Beach Pier as nothing more than an added attraction to bring people to the park. The sprawling acreage had a huge midway with dozens of rides including a giant roller coaster, games of chance, fortune tellers. There was something for everybody at Venice, and it was just about the same a mile or so up the road at Pacific Ocean Park in Santa Monica. Both places had giant dance pavilions where name bands played nightly, and each park struggled to win the same customers.

I would have loved being at either place on a Sunday, but not *this* Sunday. Our scruffy little apartment in Hollywood wasn't much, but that's where I wished that I was. My mother had gotten me into this, and then couldn't even be with me for moral support. The problem wasn't so much that I was shy—which I certainly was—but that I couldn't conceive of myself as being beautiful. I had nice shapely legs, thanks to my years of dancing, and I was either blessed or cursed by ample chest measurements, but to me that wasn't enough—especially when I looked at the other thirty-eight contestants, of whom at least twenty were gorgeous. It took a lot of nerve for me to be there, and I hated every minute of it.

A sea of faces stared from the sand looking up at the runway built just for the contest. As I strutted out trying to look graceful in my spike heels, I saw frowns, leers, expressions of scorn from a variety of adults, and there were children interspersed among them with hot dogs and Popsicles, caring not at all about what else was going on. I also recall that one of the judges was none other than the dignified British actor Sir Cedric Hardwicke, if you can imagine that incongruity.

I could hold my own in the talent requirement, and I wasn't scared. I chose a tap number to a popular tune of the day, something I was sure the orchestra could accompany easily, and after it was over I was shocked to find myself among the ten semifinalists. I assumed it was a mistake until I made the next cut as well. A major miracle occurred when I was chosen first runner-up to Miss Venice. I had won second place in the contest, and a check for twenty-five dollars—a small fortune.

Almost more important than the money, which was more important than you can imagine, was the fact that a booking agent took note of me. He cornered me after the contest and said to report late the next afternoon to the Earl Carroll Dinner Theatre. They were auditioning dancers for openings in the chorus. When I told my mother, Marie, about it, she somehow came up with enough money for me to have my hair done the next morning, and for good luck she let me pick out a new white bathing suit for the audition. Today, almost every young girl has drawers full of cute dance warm-up outfits, leg warmers, and such, but not then. It was customary to show off your figure in a swimsuit, and for rehearsals the girls wore slacks or shorts, or whatever else they could improvise.

Marie was more conscientious about my work than about her own. She had landed dozens of jobs, some lasting a week with good luck. But at this time she was a waitress in a small restaurant near the old Fox Studios, where the workload was light and the tips were good. What pleased her most was the clientele, which included film moguls and celebrities. Among her special customers were George Burns and Gracie Allen. Every night after work, Marie would regale me with the latest gossip regarding stars she had seen or served. The inside scoop on George and Gracie was that he loved apple pie, and that she used tons of pepper. So Marie, trying her best to keep the job alive, had consented to work that Sunday. But now that something had come from the beauty contest, her job became a secondary priority. There was no way on earth that Marie would fail to get in on my audition for Earl Carroll's.

We arrived at the appointed time at the art-deco theater on Sunset just east of Vine Street, and passed beneath the famous lettering: Through These Portals Pass the Most Beautiful Girls in the World. The sign didn't encourage me at all.

There were a few tall and shapely girls inside and a rather young man who seemed to be in charge. Marie tapped him on the shoulder to announce our arrival. The man gave me a cursory glance and mumbled, "She's probably too short."

"Too short for what?" Marie asked, testily.

He looked me over again, his eyes lingering over my bust line. "Mm, she might be okay," he said. Then, to me: "Are you willing to show off your upper assets to Mr. Carroll?"

I stared blankly, but Marie jumped in. "Why would she have to do that?" Marie asked. "The dancers wear clothes, don't they?"

"Not very much," said the stage manager, "and it's Mr. Carroll's policy to take a look to make sure nobody's cheating, if you get what I mean." We sat down, and one of the girls pointed out that Mr. Carroll was very businesslike in examining the girls, and there was never any hanky-panky. "There's nothing to it," she said cheerfully.

There might have been nothing to it for that girl, but there was plenty to it for me. I had been self-conscious about my "upper assets" since I was thirteen, when I'd started wearing C-cups. "I won't do it," I whispered to Marie. "We might as well leave."

If Marie had insisted, I might have gone through with it, but she didn't. My grandmother had instilled in me the fear of God and a moral code that was impossible to break. Since Marie had left me so frequently in my grandmother's care, she had to know that her mother's teachings would have made an impression.

As we left the theater, Marie said, "I've already missed work. Let's make another stop before we go home." Marie started to flag a cab, but thought better of it. This day had cost enough already. We crossed the street and walked past the glamorous new Hollywood Palladium, and went north on El Centro to Hollywood Boulevard. We walked a couple of blocks east, and Marie pointed to the big square building across the street. The sign identified it as the Florentine Gardens, another popular

Hollywood theater-restaurant, but not as posh and sophisticated as Earl Carroll's.

"We might as well give them a try," Marie said.

"You mean, audition?" I didn't like the idea, but I already felt guilty about my behavior at Earl Carroll's.

"If you're lucky. I spent a week's tips on you today. We can't let it go to waste."

We went through the deserted barroom and found the large multi-tiered dining room, with aisles converging at the stage. There was a grand piano and music stands on the stage, with the initials P. W. on each stand. On the bass drum in the center was lettered PAUL WHITE-MAN. There was a small table down front at which a man was seated looking over some papers that were lighted by the beam of a gooseneck lamp.

"My name's Marie Middleton, and this is my daughter, Yvonne. She's a wonderful classical dancer and she would like to see the person in charge."

The heavyset man looked at me over his horn-rimmed glasses. He was chewing on a dead cigar.

During the brief pause, I drew in a breath and said, "I like the looks of your place. I might consider working here." As shy as I was, I always amazed even myself that I could bluster like that when it came to business.

The man flashed a brief smile. "So, you'd really consider it, would you? I guess we're pretty lucky, huh?"

That was all the cue Marie needed. As always, she went into an oversell that would embarrass an encyclopedia salesman. "My daughter dances like a prima donna . . . sings like a bird . . . and she's so alluring onstage . . . look at those beautiful legs. . . . Show them off, Yvonne," she said, hiking my skirts. "Now, it would really be an asset to you and your—"

"Hold it, hold it," said the man, waving his hand. "You're wasting your breath. I'm Dave Gould, the choreographer here. N. T. G. is the man you have to sell, and he won't be around until about seven to-night."

"Perhaps you'd make an appointment for us," I threw in, still playing Miss Haughty of 1940.

"Not necessary. Show up about eight and ask for N. T. G., and I'll make sure he's expecting you. One tip though, wear a bathing suit under your dress. And, for what it's worth, Mr. Granlund's favorite color is red."

My new bathing suit was white but the other one was red, and if that was N. T. G.'s favorite color, red he would get. Marie and I went home, made the change, and looked through our sheet music for a good audition song, just in case.

What had been dreary caverns by afternoon were transmuted into a sparkling wonderland by night. When I saw how elegant the Florentine really was, I lost much of my earlier bravado. We were admitted backstage and told to wait near the wings of the stage. Minimally clad showgirls scurried about, seeming very blasé and professional. Dave Gould finally came over to us and took us aside to meet the tall, thin, middle-aged proprietor of the club, Nils Thor Granlund. He was known publicly as N. T. G. and personally, I would soon learn, as Granny.

"You must be the little baby Dave's been raving about." He took both of my hands. "Can you dance, kid?"

Marie elbowed in with her sales pitch, and N. T. G. was very patient with her. He then took us both to a vacant dressing room, where I was asked to show my legs. I lifted my skirt, which was red, to the edge of my also red bathing suit. He gave a quick nod of approval and asked me about myself: Where was I from; why did I want a career; where did I study dance; what was my experience? He almost asked me my age, but it was obvious that he would just as soon not know. Had he asked, and had I told the truth, it would all have been over, because I was considerably underage. Before leaving the room he said I should strip down to my bathing suit and be ready to perform, just in case. Marie gave him the lead-sheet for "Tea for Two," also just in case.

A short time later, Marie and I were standing in the wings, with N. T. G. nearby. He gave me a wink as he awaited his cue from the orchestra. There came a drum roll, and an orchestral crescendo, and N. T. G. went out to open the show. Marie and I stood aside to make way for the backstage bedlam. It was a kaleidoscope of false eyelashes, makeup, mesh stockings. There was a tinny clatter of shoe taps against the boards as the girls hurried to their places. The show opened with a big production number, with all the girls onstage. While it played, N. T. G. told me to listen for his cue when he went back on. I had no idea what he had in mind, only that I was supposed to be prepared. But for what?

After N. T. G. went back onstage to the microphone, I heard him say, "Now, folks, I want you to meet a little girl who thinks she wants to be in our show. I don't know if she sings or dances or stands on her head, but I'm going to let you decide if she gets into our show. Here she is, Miss Yvonne De Carlo."

I ran out to join him with pasted-on grin and trembling legs. He put an arm around my shoulder. "All right, baby," he said, giving me a squeeze. "Show us what you can do." He gave a cue to the orchestra, and abandoned me. The pianist played "Tea for Two," the orchestra added rhythm—and I may not have been Ginger Rogers, but I wasn't bad either. I showed the audience every tap step I knew, made sure the smile stayed put, and soon it was all over. N. T. G. came back, gave me another hug, and said to the audience, "Well, folks . . . is she in or out?"

It was a Monday night and the house was far from filled, but those in attendance gave me a rousing round of applause, with whistles and cheers. "Okay, little girl," said N. T. G., "you've got the job." I was never quite sure if it was my dancing or the red bathing suit that got me hired, but I always remembered to wear red whenever I had something special to ask of the boss.

I spent several days under the guidance and tutelage of Dave Gould, and was woven into the show's chorus line. If I worked hard, I was told, there was always a possibility that I could get a specialty number, which would elevate me from the chorus ranks.

My starting salary was thirty-five dollars a week, which made me practically wealthy by the standards of the Depression years. It was more than men earned for fifty hours of hard factory work, and more than twice what Marie earned as a waitress. When I think back on the milestones in my life, I can't remember feeling any prouder, or more successful, than I did on that August day of 1940. I felt that all the years of hard work had finally paid off, that neither my family nor I would ever be poor again. It wasn't far from the truth, as it turned out.

Chapter 2

I recall the sense of independence I felt when I proudly turned over my first Florentine paycheck to Marie. The rather symbolic gesture marked a great change: from that point forward it was no longer a matter of little Peggy being led by Mama. From here on I had a voice of my own. She said, "I've always known, Yvonne, that you were the brains of this outfit. I'm just the skivvy."

I was never sure quite what was meant, but it acknowledged my new status as Marie's equal. And it *was* that way—sometimes.

The Florentine Gardens was always a popular nightclub and became even more so when the war started, but when I began working there a couple could have a complete evening for a ten-dollar bill—much less if they didn't drink those expensive fifty-cent cocktails. If I'm not mistaken, the dinner and show cost two dollars a person, and I don't recall the price increasing more than fifty cents during the war. Of course, this was in the days when a fancy lunch at Melody Lane on Hollywood and Vine was going for seventy-five cents, including beverage and dessert. Some people had to save up to have their evening at the Florentine, but everybody had a good time. The Florentine was less tony than Earl Carroll's. At Carroll's the girls wore costumes that were filmy and lacy, in the Paris mode, while we at the Florentine were more likely to be dressed in fringe and spangles. It was the caviar crowd at Carroll's, meat and potatoes at the Florentine. Each place was a variation on the same theme, and both, in their own way, did extremely well.

As master of ceremonies, N. T. G. communicated with the regular joe more successfully than with café society. His jokes were raunchy, and his double entendres tended toward the obvious. Granny actually ran the Florentine for a man named Frank R. Bruni, but Granny was so much a part of the restaurant's success that everyone assumed it belonged to him. He was rough-cut but gentle, and I never knew him to hurt a living soul. His act was an interplay with the audience, almost in the style of today's Don Rickles but without the bite. Nothing pleased him more than a good dirty joke; he was forever picking up dinner tabs, and helping anyone who needed it. Born in Swedish Lapland, he had been transplanted to the New York slums as a child and had somehow found a niche in show business after starting as a press agent, radio announcer, and talent scout. He was a close friend of Texas Guinan, the famous speakeasy matron, and was pals with many of the Roaring Twenties gangsters. One of them, Owney Madden, backed Granny in his first New York nightclub. He opened another in Long Island, and later had great success with a place called the Paradise Café in Manhattan. It was there that he helped the careers of Barbara Stanwyck, Joan Crawford, and others. He hadn't been at the Florentine Gardens very long before I started there, but he was a rousing success.

Granny had a special girlfriend in the show, Sylvia McKay, who played the dumb blonde in gaudy clothes with expensive furs and jewelry, but she was no dummy. Granny's name for her was Miss Unconscious, on and off the stage. I felt I had arrived when he nicknamed me Dingbat. It may not have been especially flattering, but coming from Granny it was the ultimate compliment. To be addressed by your real name meant he didn't especially care for you.

I started in the back chorus line, and I really worked hard with Dave Gould to improve my work. It must have showed because Granny took me aside. "I've been watching you, baby," he said. "Don't you ever get tired?"

"I just want to get ahead," I said.

"Never lose that hunger, kid," he told me. "That's the way to get places in this town. I've seen plenty of girls come and go, and I know what I'm talkin' about."

It sounds like a Warner Baxter sermon to Ruby Keeler, but that was how it went and I clung to every word. I spent hour after hour practicing on my own time and then attended the regular rehearsals. In a short time I was moved to the front line and was getting more specialty numbers.

One afternoon I was on the stage practicing ballet all by myself. Granny came in and out a few times, and finally came over to me. "Why do you do that junk?" he asked, looking at my feet. "Nobody likes toe dancing. Go take a rest—your toes are bleeding." I did as I was told, but I had been doing what my mother had been drilling into me since I was eight, so the next day I was right back at it again, more strenuously than before. I had been promised a featured dance spot and in my imagination I saw myself stopping the show with my skills in classical ballet.

The day finally came, about four months later, when Granny broke the news. I would be featured, and rehearsals were to begin the next day. I was there an hour early. I was given my costume, a pretty thing with chiffon veils, and in the dance I would gracefully cast each one into the breeze as I leapt across the stage. When I was down to nothing but a couple of well-placed pasties and a G-string, balancing a huge head-dress—a crashing music crescendo would sound. That was the cue for the entrance of my dance partner—a huge, growling gorilla. He met me center stage, killed the Sultan for whom I was supposed to be dancing, thrust me over his hairy shoulder, and carried me off into the wings. That was it, the wonderful ballet number I had been practicing for so long. My big moment.

On one occasion, my G-string panties broke at the seam, baring most of me as I was flung over the gorilla-man's shoulder. It gave the audience an additional laugh as I covered the naked section of my anatomy. There was extra applause that night, some of it coming from Henry Fonda, who was in the audience. The King Kong number was only the start of my solo routines. There would be many more, most with a Middle Eastern motif, for the simple reason that it gave them an excuse to bare plenty of skin. In the movies even a girl's navel had to be covered, so we were going pretty far.

One day several of us show girls were told to bring our harem costumes and report the next morning to a movie studio near Melrose and Gower. I was to be the lead dancer in a movie. A movie—me? But it wasn't really a movie-movie. It was what they formally called "featurettes," but were known more generally as soundies. These short features were very popular for a time. A big jukebox-type machine would offer a number of these features for a quarter each. In this one I was "The Pearl of India" and I did the number I was doing every night at the Florentine. Before I got into real motion pictures, I did several of these, and I must admit that there were quite a few afternoons when I would disguise myself and go to the Radio Room Bar on Vine Street to take a look—the first peeks of myself in movies.

My career really flourished during this first engagement at the Florentine Gardens, when you consider I was only a kid in my teens, and I could think of nothing better than to hang on to the good job as long as possible. As it turned out, it wasn't my decision to make. That same year I was wondering what to buy Marie for a Christmas present when a pair of stern-looking characters came into the dressing room at the club. I hadn't had experience in such matters, but I somehow knew a cop when I saw one. "I want to talk to a Margaret Yvonne Middleton," said one of the men.

The name didn't register with the several other girls in the room, but I recognized it. "You . . . want to see . . . me?"

"I'm from the Department of Immigration," said one of the men, flashing his badge, "and you have overstayed your visa."

I was given twenty-four hours to leave the country. It's hard to imagine that two men would be sent out to nail a single teenager from Canada, but that was then—and they meant business. Actually there were only a few people who knew I was Canadian, because I told most people I was from Bellingham, Washington. I think it must have been one of the other dancers who did a number on me.

I tearfully explained my plight to Granny, who was as sweet as could be. He promised to pull every possible string to get me out of Canada, but could do nothing to prevent my deportation. Needless to say, I departed on the next train northward. Marie, whose papers were in order, remained behind.

Being separated from my mother was no novelty. In fact, since I was quite small we'd spent more time apart than together. When I returned to Vancouver, it was like coming home to my real family. My aunt Connie and my grandmother were more mothers to me than Marie, and I was happy to see them again despite my disappointment at having to leave the Florentine.

I had always dreamed of a triumphant return to Vancouver with banners and brass bands, but on this occasion there was no one at all to meet me at the train station. I took a taxi to my grandmother's house, and she, Connie, Cousin Ken, and I had a warm and wonderful reunion. Ken was like a younger brother, and now that he had reached high school age I felt even closer to him. I had never really warmed up to my grandfather, but it was great now to see him because he was family and I had come home.

Another person very close to me was June Roper, at whose academy

I learned to dance. On the days when I went to check with the Department of Immigration, I would stop at the school and spend hours with June, who was as interested in my welfare as any member of my family.

My calls to the immigration office told me what I already knew. To return to the United States I had to have an American sponsor and a full-time job. But it wasn't that simple. I had to be employed in a field where I was uniquely qualified. I wrote Granny several times explaining how much I wanted to return and what was required for me to do so. A week passed without a response, and then a letter came reassuring me, saying that the wheels were already in motion.

With Canada a part of the British Commonwealth, there was active involvement in the Allied war effort. June Roper suggested that meanwhile I volunteer to entertain the Canadian troops, which I did gladly. I did impromptu shows at all the nearby canteens and military bases, and in helping the morale of the military men I lifted my own as well.

The Christmas holidays came, and as nice as it was being with my family I was getting worried. Then in January I finally heard from Granny again. That started a small avalanche of letters and telegrams, all with the same goal. The plan was to make my entry into the United States a permanent one, as a resident alien. In the long run this was far better than a limited work visa, so the waiting time was well spent. Here is the telegram that seemed to influence the immigration officials:

> You are a unique and splendid performer. See no reason why you should not work for me for a long time. I can assure you I will use you in many shows no matter where I play. Letter confirming the telegram follows. Hope to see you soon. Have found no one in Hollywood or New York who can equal you in beauty and dancing ability. Believe you can have a splendid career in America.
>
> Best wishes,
> N. T. G.

His follow-up letter named my weekly salary as forty dollars a week and included other details regarding our contract. When I presented this to the immigration officer, he said, "If you are all the things he says you are, why is he only paying you forty dollars a week?" I had no answer for that one, but giving my best response wouldn't have mattered. The official either was tired of seeing me or had a soft spot somewhere in his heart, because my legal immigration was stamped and approved. I was free to return to Los Angeles whenever I wished.

In the following few days, I spent as much time as I could with my

Vancouver family, and savored the city as well, because I had the feeling it would be a while before I would see any of it again. I at least knew that I wouldn't be thinking of Vancouver anymore as my home. Now was really the first time that I thought that way of Hollywood, California.

Chapter 3

As I reflect on my childhood in Vancouver, I definitely remember climbing the dizzying heights to my father's knee, and I can recall crawling over the floor to my father's feet, waiting to be picked up. That's it. It's strange, I think, for these recollections to be so vivid while there are no others to accompany them. I suppose I desperately wanted to remember my father, since he was only around until I was three. The remainder of my memories from my early days are what others recall: my mother, my aunt Connie, my grandparents. Their memories have become my own. For that reason my father is something of a ghost conjured up by others. As far as I am served by my memory, I had no father, and there was never a time when I took the void lightly. I craved a father deeply, and would cling to any man who would allow it.

My mother tells me how, as a toddler, I would try to cross the floor with hands clasped behind my back as my father used to do, and would frown as though in deep thought. But, as I say, these are other people's memories.

I guess it was my grandmother who told me about the terrible quarrels my mother and father had. I remember nothing of that. He left us quite suddenly, and from what I've been told it wasn't entirely his own idea. I think he was one step ahead of the police, who were anxious to confront him about one of his recent business transactions.

I guess a more appropriate word would be "swindle."

I was told my father had piercing eyes of pale blue, and a wealth of straight black hair. My grandmother thought he looked like the movie star Edmund Lowe. What got him into trouble was the sale of stock in a wireless burglar alarm; the idea was good, but unfortunately the thing didn't work. There were other deals: one having to do with threshing machines, and another in which he failed to keep his promises about a proposed ballroom. My grandmother used to say, "He could sell iceboxes to Eskimos."

When he made his hasty departure, he promised to send money for my mother and me, and later to send for us. By this time, however, my mother had lost faith in the man she married and held no doubts that the outward-bound four-masted schooner was carrying William Shelto Middleton out of her life forever.

My mother and father had met through Kenneth Ross MacKenzie, a steamship purser who was engaged to my aunt Connie. My mother, obviously, was as charmed by Middleton as were his unfortunate investors. Within only a week or so of their introduction, they ran off to Alberta to get married, but after a couple of months of poverty the young couple trudged back to Vancouver and moved into the home of her parents.

Marie's parents despised Middleton, especially my grandfather, and by this time they weren't all that thrilled with my mother, who had become a wayward and rebellious teenage girl. Marie's goal was to become a dancer, so she had dropped out of high school. Since there were no opportunities for dancers, she became a milliner's apprentice, but it didn't take long for her to realize that this wasn't her calling. And with no training in anything else, she was pleased to meet an eligible bachelor. Since Middleton was also handsome and obviously rich, her worries were over—so she thought. One good reason for the newlyweds' return was that Marie had found herself to be a bit pregnant.

On the evening of August 31 that year, three days after her own birthday, Marie was having five-minute contractions. She was taken to the public ward of St. Paul's Hospital, where she went through a difficult labor. I was born the following morning amid the tumult of the season's worst thunderstorm. Marie's doctor hadn't arrived, and the delivery was made by a pair of floor nurses. They confirmed afterward that as she was being shifted to the delivery table she was shouting, "I want a girl. It must be a girl. I want a dancer!"

With the thunder crashing, and sleet and hail assaulting the windows of the delivery room, I emerged. According to my mother I was born with a double cord wrapped dangerously around my neck. I guess a doctor happened into the room at that exact moment, and completed a successful delivery. The nurse came over and said, "You got your wish. It's a girl." Over the years, Marie told me many times that at the moment of my birth a clap of thunder accompanied my first cry of life. I've never known if that helped form my personality, or if it was simply a warning of storms to come. There have been plenty of those, and I think I have always been able to shout down the thunder when necessary. So, who knows?

I was named Margaret Yvonne—Margaret because my mother was very fond of one of the derivatives of the name. She was fascinated at the time by the movie star Baby Peggy, and I suppose she wanted a Baby Peggy of her own.

What happened to my father is anyone's guess. All my mother ever heard were rumors: that, posing as a widower, he married two women subsequently and had children by each; that he ended up in silent movies and once played the role of a lawyer; and that he was killed at sea aboard the four-master *City of Alberta.* None of the rumors checked out, and no further word was heard from him. My own assumption is that he died before he had the chance to discover that his Baby Peggy had become a Hollywood actress, or I think he would have tried to contact me.

My mother's bad luck on her first go with men had little effect on her outlook. She remained a staunch enthusiast for men all her life; the only detail she usually avoided was marriage. Even in those rather staid and traditional times, my mother was convinced in her heart that marriage was not necessarily the logical conclusion to romance.

All my life I was reminded, "Your father deserted us when you were three." But instead of turning away from men I developed a strong attraction for just about anything masculine. My perennial dream was to fall in love with a tall, blond-haired man with blue eyes and muscles, and produce a brood of blond, blue-eyed sons. I didn't live out the fantasy. Both my sons, handsome as they are, have brown hair and eyes. There were, however, a few blond lovers along the way.

Marie was having a very difficult time making it on her own. There was too much quarreling for her to stay at home, so she took a job in a shop of some kind, and I was taken off to live with "friends." I still remember looking out the back window of a car and seeing my mother as she waved goodbye. I remember crying. When we were reunited, we lived in a series of different places, never long in one spot, but each apartment was within the city limits of Vancouver and most were rather close to my grandparents. I recall one small flat where we had practically no furniture at all, not even a stove.

Connie had married Kenneth Ross MacKenzie. The year I was five, he was hired for a shipping job in the Yukon, and Connie asked if I could come along as a companion for little Ken Junior, who was two years younger than I. My mother tentatively agreed to the plan, but Uncle Ken, a frosty man with very set ideas, made it clear that one child on such a long trip was already more than he cared to deal with. Two? Never. So that was one adventure I wouldn't experience, and Marie and I were left to continue life in Vancouver on our own.

Things looked bleaker for us in rainy Vancouver than they possibly could for the MacKenzies in the frigid Klondike, but for once fate cracked a faint grin our way. Marie met a tugboat skipper named Jack. He terrified me at first with his thick, black beard, but once I could read the smile beneath the foliage I adored him. He was a gentle man and liked children. I can remember riding on his tug, watching a trailing barge that was loaded with logs. It's as if I can still taste the salt air and hear the chug of the overworked engine. I had many delightful adventures with Jack on and off the tug. On walks along the beach he taught me how to explore nature. It was with him that I touched my first starfish. In my dreams, Jack became my real father.

This episode was truly a highlight of my younger years, and "Daddy Jack" was in our lives, off and on, for quite a while. Then he stopped seeing us. Much later, my mother told me what had happened. Jack had contracted cancer, and it finally killed him. Marie thought it would be easier on me if I didn't know the grim truth. Maybe she was right, but I missed him either way.

My grandparents' home was a huge white frame house at 1728 Comox Street. Marie always hated to return there, but I loved it, because this was where I could live like regular people, where I wouldn't be so lonely, where I would be surrounded by family. On one of our returns to the Comox house, not only were my grandparents there, but so were the MacKenzies, who had returned from Alaska. The house was large enough for the MacKenzies and us to have private quarters, but the food for everyone was prepared in the downstairs kitchen. Frequently Marie would bring our food up to our rooms. This made for better digestion, because it was almost assured that a quarrel would erupt if all of us were at the dinner table.

I enjoyed living at my grandparents' house, but that doesn't mean I liked everything about it. Granny had fixed ideas about everything, and even more so when it came to food. The mainstays were turnips, yellow squash, pumpkin, and carrots, all of which I found disgusting, but I was expected to clean my plate at every meal. I devised what I considered an clever plan, which worked, at least for a while, when we ate upstairs.

I would wait for Marie to turn her back and would then dump the vegetables in the darkness behind the steam radiator. I had amassed quite a pile of garbage before a dead-cat odor led Marie to my cache. I got a resounding smack for that, but it was worth it.

Marie's methods of discipline were probably the result of her father's treatment of her. Papa De Carlo—I always called him Papa—was a simple man of Sicilian heritage. He was of medium height, swarthy, and had a mean and explosive temper. He would lash out first and ask questions afterward whenever his rules were disobeyed. He treated Marie and her brother, John, that way, so he thought nothing of slapping me or Kenny across the mouth. My grandmother, who was far gentler, had long since stopped trying to change him. Why risk a stroke for a lost cause? Papa De Carlo was a difficult man to communicate with. There was his broken English, of course, but that wasn't all of it. He simply had no patience with children. If I was subconsciously seeking a father figure in him—forget it. It was not to be.

Marie's brother, my uncle John, ran away from home at fourteen and joined the merchant marine. He occasionally visited home, and I adored him with his seaman's worldliness. What I didn't know until much later was that Uncle John was hopelessly addicted to drugs and alcohol, and would eventually end up a skid row derelict. The last time I saw Uncle John was in Vancouver. Connie and I met him at English Bay to see if we could help him. It was a terribly sad encounter for Connie and me. But John was satisfied with his bum buddies, his alcohol, and his free way of life. He was to die soon after that reunion.

Papa was born in Sicily, where he spent most of his childhood. When he was in his teens his family migrated to Nice, France. There he found a job as groom and gardener on the estate of a Lady Hull. And there he met my grandmother, Margaret Purvis, a domestic in the home. Lady Hull was very fond of this Scottish teenage servant and warned her against an involvement with the low-bred Michel. My grandmother was reared as a sheltered Presbyterian, while Michel De Carlo was of peasant stock and a Catholic. Lady Hull could see no future for such an alliance.

They did marry, however, in 1897, and had four successive children. Stanley died of cholera as an infant; next came Connie, and two-and-a-half years later my mother was born. They had moved to Cannes by the time John was born a couple of years later.

Having been convinced by a doctor that Canada offered a much healthier climate to rear children, Michel and Margaret moved there. That was in 1912. He found himself a job as a driver and mechanic for a Vancouver bakery. The transition from Cannes to Vancouver was a difficult one for Connie. She saw the rainy summers and cold winters of Canada as a poor trade for the tropical splendor of southern France, and she hated the Vancouver school, where, because of her French accent, she was called Froggy. My mother, on the other hand, adapted to Canada with ease and within a few months behaved as as if she had lived there all her life.

Marie idolized a lovely girl friend named Suzanne because she had attended a Swiss finishing school and learned ballet. Marie tried desperately to emulate her friend, but Suzanne was so far advanced that Marie gave up and contented herself with admiring Suzanne in all of her performances before school audiences. It established Marie's passion for classical dance and would be the basis for her ambitions for herself, and later for me.

The lessons at home started out fairly subtly. Marie first demonstrated the Charleston and other popular dances when I was about six. It was fun. She would show me the step, and I would try my best to imitate her, to the music of the Victrola. Soon the lessons became more serious, and far less fun. Over and over, Marie would say to me, "Wouldn't you like to become a ballerina, and wear beautiful costumes, and be famous?" I answered yes because that's what was expected of me, and I always tried to please my mother. She was usually a fun-loving, happy-go-lucky kind of person. But not when it came to my dancing.

At the time I was devoted to drawing, or playing with my dolls. I didn't play what I guess were the conventional doll games, however. Instead, I would cast the dolls as characters in original playlets. One pastime was to play grocery store with them. I would spend hours alternating between shopkeeper and customer in the improvised dialogue. I also played school with the dolls, in which I would provide my doll pupils with small pencils and notebooks, and heaven help the ones who misbehaved. I would smack them around unmercifully, or slap their palms with straps, maintaining strict discipline at all times in my classrooms.

My penchant for discipline carried over into my interplay with Cousin Kenny. Being two years older, I got away with bossing him around for some time. He was my faithful follower at that early age and frequently suffered equal punishment with me for mischief I had initiated.

My grandparents were very religious and on Sunday mornings would either drag us off to church or hold services in our parlor. Occasionally Kenny and I would be trusted to go off to church on our own, with coins in hand to drop into the collection plate. That was a mistake. I could see no reason on earth to waste good money on church when it would buy penny candy. I would persuade Kenny to spend those Sunday mornings with me in Stanley Park, where we would find plenty of places to buy the candy.

Kenny was also my accomplice in a more serious scam I had dreamed up. It involved the neighborhood grocery store, where Kenny's role was to ask the grocer for something we all knew was in another part of the store. With the attention off me, I would grab handfuls of candy and stuff them into my bloomers. Kenny would then tell the grocer that he forgot to bring the money for the item, and we would scamper off to a safe place to eat the loot. I actually had the audacity to pull the stunt several times, until, one unhappy day we were caught. As I was stuffing my bloomers on that fateful occasion I felt a hand on my arm. I was caught, you could say, with my pants full. The grocer called my grandmother, and it was awful. The sound thrashing both of us received was nothing compared to the ranting and raving that accompanied it.

But another punishment wasn't earned, at least to my way of thinking. I was always staging plays in the house on Comox Street, and was in constant need of materials for props. I'd written a play that needed a fireplace, a gravestone, and a coffin. Kenny and I went down to the local drugstore for large cardboard boxes to make our scenery. We found several and set about dragging them home. Kenny carried a couple of the smaller ones, and I handled the big one myself. Since it was too big to hold, I poked holes in it for my eyes and wore it home. As I trudged up the hill to the house, with only my spindly legs showing beneath the box, all seemed well. But at the house we were met by a very angry Uncle Ken. "What the hell do you think you're doing?"

I told him we were just bringing home boxes for my play, but that didn't help. He took the box off my head and threw it angrily over the fence into the backyard. Uncle Ken didn't have what could be called a cheery personality, but I had never seen him this mad before. Aunt Connie tried to explain it to me later, but I still didn't understand. I thought the lettering on the box spelled out Kleenex, when it had actually said Kotex.

If that incident was baffling, I was doubly confused by what happened a year or so later. On the way home from school one sunny afternoon, a classmate called Bubbles caught up with me. He was a really cute boy with blond hair and bangs, a Buster Brown haircut. I guess I was about ten at the time, and hadn't given much thought to boy-girl relationships. He took hold of my shoulders and kissed me on the mouth. I remember looking up at the sweeping branches of a weeping willow as I tasted the sweetness of his kiss. With the mission accomplished,

Bubbles was gone, but the memory of the incident didn't die. I couldn't wait to tell someone—anyone—about this curious event.

"Granny," I exclaimed, as I bounded into the room. "Guess what just happened to me!"

She was busy cleaning a lampshade. "What?" she mumbled.

"My classmate Bubbles just made love to me under the willow tree!"

Somehow the words seemed right to me at the time. I watched as my grandmother very nearly fell into a dead faint. She gasped, fanned herself, and blinked, as though wondering if her ears were playing dirty tricks on her. "He *what?*" Granny aimed a trembling finger at me. "That's evil, Peggy . . . wicked! The wrath of God will be on your head. Don't you ever, ever do anything like that again!"

Then came a relentless grilling, and I started crying. I told her exactly what happened, but it didn't help. It was still evil, and I was sent to my room. I cried for hours, wondering what had been so wrong. In the first place, I didn't do it to him, Bubbles did it to me; and in the second place I couldn't see what was so terrible about it. How could anything so nice be so bad?

There was no danger that Bubbles would repeat the act. Every afternoon thereafter, I was met at school by one of the adults in the family. I learned very early in life that to kiss and tell is not the best idea in the world. If I had kept my big mouth shut, Bubbles and I might have gotten a thousand more kisses in before the end of the school term.

Chapter 4

Although Papa De Carlo always held some sort of job during the Depression, there were times when money was very tight. Not that he ever confided such a deficiency, but we learned to judge our affluence by the number of rooms that were let out to boarders. Sometimes there were none at all, and at times we shared the house with as many as three. One such guest in the house was an old codger named Anderson. He was the only boarder at the time, and for some reason I rarely crossed his path, except perhaps in the hallway in the mornings. But one night, when I was about sixteen, I saw much more of him than I wanted.

Marie had gone out on a date, and I was alone in bed sleeping. I wakened to make out the form of Mr. Anderson standing over my bed. I was horrified but didn't cry out. I couldn't; I was too scared, and too shocked by what I saw. The old man was totally naked. Without a word he took hold of himself and began to urinate on me. That brought me to action. With a scream of horror, I leaped out of bed and ran downstairs.

By the time my startled grandfather got himself organized enough to investigate, Mr. Anderson had long ago taken refuge in his room. The elderly midnight stalker was no longer a part of our household when I returned home from school next day. The sad upshot of the episode was that from then on I had to go with Marie when she went out on dates. She didn't think she should leave me alone, but she wasn't about to forgo her social life.

The routine was that I would ride along to the roadhouse with Marie and her date, and before they went inside I would be bundled up in the back seat of the car and told to go to sleep. It wasn't always possible, and more often than not it was the sound of my own mother's voice that woke me. I remember one hot night, when the roadhouse windows were open, the loudest voice of all the revelers belonged to Marie. "Whoopee!" she kept shouting. "Whoopee, whoopee!" I was only a kid, but not too young to be embarrassed.

Marie was one of those persons who have practically no capacity for alcohol; one drink and it was lampshade-on-the-head time. Her drinking frightened me as a child, and it was good news for everyone when she decided to give up alcohol altogether.

I recall many wonderful days with her. Whenever she could be sidetracked from my dancing lessons, she tried to broaden my experience. In the summer, she would enthusiastically take me to the beach almost every day. We'd go to nearby English Bay, or occasionally to Second and Third Beaches, and there was also Crystal Pool. I was never deprived of sunshine and swimming. I think I was born to swim. And my mother couldn't swim a stroke.

When fall arrived I didn't dread going back to school, as some children did—I loved it, and was always a good student. I do recall a time when Marie and I lived alone in a very simple apartment near Third Beach. I knew none of the circumstances, but Marie was having a rough time of it financially. One morning at school the teacher said: "Everyone in class whose parents are on relief, please stand. You are to report to the principal's office." I stood up obediently and looked around. I was the only one standing. I could feel the eyes of all my classmates follow me to the door. It was one of the most humiliating experiences of my life.

But the good times in school far outnumbered the bad ones. I remember, for instance, the time we students were assigned to write a poem that started out: "As I was walking down the street." The best poem would be submitted to the poetry contest being sponsored by the Vancouver *Daily Sun.* At the signal, my pen darted across the page as though my muse had just been waiting for this moment. The next day the teacher announced the winner. "And here is the winning poem, "A Little Boy," by Peggy Middleton."

This made up for any heartaches that I may have had before. I couldn't have felt prouder if I had won the Nobel Peace Prize. Then, to top this, my poem won first prize in the newspaper contest. I was given a check for *five dollars!*

A Little Boy

As I was walking down the street
A little boy I chanced to meet.
His clothes were ragged as could be;
He had a cut upon his knee.
I called him over to my side,
Behind a tree he tried to hide,
For he was shy as shy could be,
And dared not venture nearer me.
I called to him again and said,
Is your name Robert, Jack or Ted?
He didn't answer me at all,
But kept on playing with his ball.

When I tell this story I usually add an *s* to the last word just for laughs, but I can assure you there was nothing funny about my success back then in fifth grade. I quite seriously thought I had "arrived" as a poet, and fame would soon follow. As it was, the five-dollar prize was a small fortune to me, and was the first money I ever earned.

I had always composed playlets, which my family let me stage in the living room or wherever I chose to put them on. A highlight of my junior playwriting career came with my adaptation of Charles Dickens's *A Christmas Carol.* It was a hit on the block, and practically all the neighbors came to see it. Of course, most of the neighbors' kids were in the show, which might have helped.

Marie didn't encourage any of this extracurricular activity, because it took time from my dancing and she was still hell-bent on my becoming Vancouver's answer to Pavlova. But she was a good audience, and bragged to her friends about her gifted little girl.

I guess I was really a contradictory child in many ways. I seemed bold enough when I was in charge of my plays, and later on I could get up before people and perform without overpowering stage fright, but I was really very shy. I dreaded getting up before the class in school, and tried not to attract attention to myself. I went a long time without much-needed eyeglasses because I didn't want to stand out from the flock.

I felt especially miserable when Marie insisted on showing me off to people. It was her habit to scrimp and save so she could dress me up in cute little outfits and show me off to anyone at all. I would be dragged along the sidewalk under a continual barrage of commands: "Look up . . . hold your head up . . . walk straight . . . smile at the lady . . . pick up your feet." She would yank at my arm angrily and fairly drag me along. It was hard for me to look these people in the eye at the time, and it would be years before I would overcome the problem.

At times, when Marie would be otherwise occupied on a Saturday, I would be given a dime for the movies and an extra nickel to spend. That was where I was in my element, alone in a movie theater where I could watch those great musicals over and over and over again. Sometimes I would stay from the first matinee at noon until well after dark. I would use my nickel to buy Spanish peanuts, because you could get a lot for the money and they were easy to ration out, one at a time.

I adored the movies of Fred Astaire and Ginger Rogers, and was equally impressed with Eleanor Powell and Ruby Keeler. But I loved all movies, and especially the spooky ones. I knew every movie star's name, and had a mental catalog of each of their movies. With my eyesight so poor, I discovered I could see better when I pulled at the corners of my eyes, making myself into a movie-house Asian.

I think I always fancied myself a singer, and I earned my first praise during those impromptu Sunday services held in our parlor by my grandparents. I would sing out on "Rock of Ages" or "The Old Rugged Cross" while the rest of the family nodded and smiled in approval of my gusto. Later on I became a steady member of the church choir. I was told, even at an early age, that my voice had good tone and timbre, and that was all the encouragement I needed to spark my ambition.

I had the solitude to let my fantasies run their course, because most of the time I was alone, or with Kenny, or possibly with one other person. I was never part of a clique and never joined a club. My friendships were always on a one-to-one basis. I was unable to mix in groups; it was impossible—I felt stifled, penned in by them. My classmates must have sensed this, because they never tried to rally me into group activities. It's true that I loved my church choir activities, but even then I was probably just doing solos—in unison.

Five days a week I was required to be home after school for my dance lessons, and Marie was very strict on that score. Then one afternoon Marie made the casual announcement that she was going to Los Angeles. After learning that I wouldn't be going along, I thought immediately of the daily dance lessons. Would all that be over? Nope. I would be staying with Aunt Connie, who was usually easier about such matters, but Marie made her promise to keep up the lessons. Connie kept her word, but she was no taskmaster. I was allowed to take things pretty much at my own pace, and as a result of the freedom I became quite creative. I choreographed little numbers, and had fun.

Connie and Marie didn't get along. I guess they were just too different. Marie had her daydreams and her lovers, along with a reckless, hedonistic approach to life. Connie was more serious-minded. She worked all through the years as a telephone operator, and during the years of her marriage she was content to spend her off-hours at home being a mother and a housewife. I was always content staying with Connie while Marie was away because she headed a happy home and was always kind to me. At this time, the MacKenzies were living in a nice old house at 3330 West 42nd Street in the Kerrisdale section of Vancouver.

It was during this time with the MacKenzies that I became aware of the growing friction between Connie and Uncle Ken. Her favorite way of escaping the household tension was to rent a horse at a nearby stable and ride for hours. Connie took me along on many occasions, and taught me how to stay on an English saddle. I have since adopted riding as my own form of therapy, and have always been grateful to Connie for that.

I learned much later the details of Connie's breakup with Uncle Ken. Both she and my grandmother heard about the other woman, whom they referred to as "that Clary woman." It was my grandmother who, uncharacteristically, advised Connie to go and confront the home-breaker on the issue.

Connie called on the woman and tried to reason with her. She said that her marriage was solid in every way including sex, and if she didn't believe it she could come and see for herself. The woman, who had been given quite a different story, accepted the invitation and showed up the following Sunday morning. My grandmother let the woman into the house and escorted her upstairs to the MacKenzie bedroom. She opened the door, and in an instant "that Clary woman" saw her lover and his wife in a solid embrace. Uncle Ken snatched a sheet. "What the . . . You bitches!" he shouted as he fled to the bathroom. The Clary woman got down on her knees and begged Connie for forgiveness. Nevertheless, my aunt and uncle were divorced about a year and a half later.

There was no word from Marie except a noncommittal postcard or two, so when Christmas approached Connie got an idea: Why not drive down to Los Angeles and surprise Marie? Even Uncle Ken thought the idea was great. So the week before Christmas we set out for a place called the San Fernando Valley. We traveled for several days, and it was cold. There was no heater in the car. Connie suggested that we put our feet into paper bags. It worked!

I was eleven by now, and Kenny was nine. It would seem that by this time we would have learned how to behave while traveling with Uncle Ken. Not true. We were cold and tired and grouchy, and got into one battle after another.

It was a cold, drizzly night when we finally arrived in the San Fernando Valley, passing miles and miles of citrus groves before we arrived at the address on Verdugo Avenue. Tired and bedraggled, we went to the designated address and rang the bell. After the second ring, Marie came to the door and let us in. She was delighted to have our company; she gave Ken and me a big hug and asked how we'd been. It was as if she lived down the hall from us. Our family was never terribly demonstrative, and somehow this moment stands out in memory.

The trip was really a great adventure for me, this being my first trip out of Vancouver. We saw Beverly Hills and Hollywood, and got a map that showed where many of the stars lived. Some of the mansions were far grander than anything I could have imagined.

We also visited the Los Angeles Zoo, Forest Lawn Cemetery, and a place called Busch Gardens. All of it impressed me, and in a way I was sorry to have to leave, but as our week came to a close we had to head back. Marie had gone to Los Angeles to be with a boy friend, but, curiously, we didn't meet him during the visit. She told me she would be seeing me soon, and we parted company. I didn't believe she really meant that, and maybe she didn't at the time, but sure enough, Marie did return to Vancouver about two months later. I asked what had changed her mind about staying in Los Angeles. She said that she still believed that L.A. was the land of opportunity but our time had not yet come and that we would have to work much harder on my dancing (Oh-oh!) to bring me up to professional standards. When I was good enough to compete, she and I would try our luck. I wasn't anxious to get back to the bloody toes, but it was more exciting now that we would be going for a brass ring. Marie had never said anything about going professional, or at least not in so many words. Now, with all of this said, I was enjoying a new sensation. Was it ambition?

Chapter 5

It was back to the old routine with Marie in town, and this time she was more demanding than ever. While she was away, Connie had turned me loose at a couple of church events in which I danced and tried to sing, and Marie wanted to hear all the exciting details. It pleased her that I had performed before audiences for the first time, and she was glad to hear that I hadn't been afraid. She promised that I would be getting much more exposure in the near future.

Since Marie still believed that ballet was my forte, Vancouver presented a problem. At that time there was no bona fide school of ballet in the city. Beyond that was an even greater shortage of places to perform. Still, over the next several months Marie continued drilling me in the basics of the dance and set about trying to raise funds to finance my further training.

It required about six months, but somehow Marie came up with a travel stake. One afternoon she called me into the kitchen and had me sit down. "The time has come," she said to me. "We're going to the United States."

"Right now?" I asked. "What about school?"

"Don't worry about school," she said. "There are good schools in the States. We have to go while we can."

It was a month before the end of the spring term, and when I spoke to my teachers about the change they were as upset as I knew they would be, but the final consensus was that little would be lost if I missed the last month of the term; they concluded, however, that it could be a problem if I didn't return for school in the fall. It didn't really matter much what any of the teachers said, nor did the expressed misgivings of the family have an effect. When Marie made up her mind, it was made *up.* We were packed within an afternoon and boarded a southbound bus the following morning.

It soon became obvious that Marie had no well-thought-out plan, nothing specific. We stopped in Seattle and checked into the red brick Moore Hotel on Second Street. While Marie checked the city for job opportunities, I lounged comfortably in the hotel swimming pool. What luxury! But upon Marie's return there was always that minimum of one hour's dance practice. Apparently Marie came up dry, because within a few days we were busbound again; next stop San Francisco. On the trip, Marie told me she had a strong hunch that the City by the Bay would be our land of fortune. As for myself, I was saving my crystal ball for later.

Trudging up and down the hills of San Francisco for hours in search of a decent economy hotel, we finally found a place that would do and settled in. Marie quickly lost herself in the study of help-wanted ads. Within only a few minutes she came across one that confirmed her earlier hunch. A family needed a housekeeper and governess of French background. It was for a film producer, his actress wife, and two children. Marie was as giddy as a child; she acted as though God had taken the evening off to give her personal guidance. She called the number immediately and spoke with the "actress wife." Marie mentioned her French birth, and it was a clear path from there. The woman wanted us to come to Oakland the next day to meet her and her husband.

We were at the fog-shrouded ferry landing early the next day and took the ferry to Oakland. I loved the ride. It reminded me of Daddy Jack and the tugboat outings. In Oakland we were met by a chauffeur who escorted us to a black Packard limousine. By now I was convinced that Marie's hunch was on the money. We rode as on a cloud through the rolling hills of suburban Oakland, past expansive green lawns and sprawling mansions, until we turned into a circular drive that delivered us to one of the finest houses we had seen that day.

After a short wait in a massive foyer, a very attractive youngish woman came down to greet us. She led us to a sunny dayroom with windows along two walls and invited us to be seated. The visit lasted for a long while as the woman collected background information about my mother. I knew Marie was manufacturing much of what she said, but I also understood that a little embroidery was probably necessary in job interviews. The big obstacle, as I saw it, was how Marie was going to handle the French language requirement. It was true she was born in France, but unlike her sister Marie had retained no more than a few simple phrases of her native language.

The lady, Mrs. Frazer, was impressed with Marie and laid out the terms of employment. We would be given room and board and Marie would receive a modest salary. What I think clinched the deal for Mrs. Frazer was Marie's promise that as a bonus I would give her daughter free ballet lessons. I was asked to demonstrate my dancing skills, and I dutifully complied.

We had the job, except for a small detail. Mr. Frazer would have to give his approval of the hiring. He would be home in the evening, but we were meanwhile welcome to look about the grounds. Then we would have dinner in the kitchen, and since it would be late by this time we were invited to spend the night in the quarters that would come with the job.

The living quarters assigned us consisted of two large rooms, cheery and beautifully furnished. Marie and I had lived in several flats, but we had never had a place as nice as this. It appeared that our luck had very definitely changed for the better. That night, as I lay on soft, carefully ironed bedsheets, I tried to picture myself living in such grand surroundings. The picture just didn't develop.

Marie was in the kitchen the following morning fixing us breakfast when we met Mr. Frazer for the first time. He was an attractive man, and friendly, if a bit pompous. He said he had hoped there would be a *Mr.* Middleton to help with maintenance and yard work, but he would overlook this shortcoming since Marie had a command of French, which she could impart to his children. With that said, the interview continued in the French language. At least his part of it did. Marie's mouth dropped. She nodded periodically, and tossed in a "Oui" or two, but she was hopelessly lost and he knew it. "I am very sorry," said Mr. Frazer, back to English. "But my children must have someone who speaks perfect French." That was it . . . end of job. We were driven to the ferry and left once more on our own.

"I knew all along that Los Angeles was the place," Marie said as we were checking out of the hotel the next morning. "Someday I'll learn to follow my hunches."

Marie slept through most of the twelve-hour bus trip, which suggested to me that she hadn't had much sleep the night before. During the bus trip, I mused over the life that might have been. Since that time I've often wondered what turns our lives might have taken had Marie remembered a little more French.

It was late afternoon when the bus pulled into the Greyhound Terminal in the center of downtown Los Angeles. Once more we were lugging our suitcases in search of a room. It was obvious that Marie was not herself, but I assumed she might be depressed because of the Oakland fiasco. Then I sensed that the problem could be physical. She seemed drained of all energy and walked in short, stiff steps. She took less care than usual shopping for a room, and settled for a cheap women's hotel. She tried to find a listing for her brother John in the phone book, but was unsuccessful. I asked Marie if she was sick. "I'm all right," she said. "But what you have to do is find the May Company department store. Aunt Jean works there in the linen department. Tell her where we are."

Marie gave me some pocket money, and I hurried off in search of the department store before closing time. I knew it was important to find Aunt Jean tonight instead of tomorrow. After several inquiries I found the store, and got inside just as the doors were about to be locked. I found the linen department, but no one was there. I started to head toward the down escalator when a rather sad-looking lady came out of a back room and walked toward me. On a chance I asked, "Do you happen to know where I can find Mrs. John De Carlo?"

"Why, I'm Mrs. De Carlo," she said, almost suspiciously.

When I explained who I was, she smiled and gave me a hug. I told her all about our trip, and the trouble we had finding a phone number for her and John, and then I told her about Marie's apparent physical distress. Aunt Jean came to the hotel with me, and my suspicions were confirmed. Marie was experiencing extreme menstrual hemorrhaging. She had to be hospitalized at once.

That was my introduction to our new life in Los Angeles. Marie was in the hospital, and I shared a scantly furnished apartment with an aunt I didn't know. She was very nice to me, but since she seemed rather depressed I tried to be as unobtrusive as possible.

During the days while Jean was working, I happily occupied my time at the Los Angeles Public Library, which was only a few blocks from the apartment. At that time, my great reading interests lay in Greek mythology, and astrology, and at this magnificent institution I could have kept on reading for years. If the gods hadn't been very generous with Marie, they were treating me just fine. I had everything I needed.

I was experiencing a strange mental clarity at this time. I felt as though I was outside the earthly plane in some way and was getting a glimpse of a greater truth. It came as a flash as I was walking home from the library one afternoon. I didn't hear a voice, but the message was clear. I saw myself rising above the crowd. "You will one day be famous," I was told. "Don't worry. Your time will come." The glow remained with me for at least an hour, as though to reassure me that the experience was real. Much later, I would wonder why I didn't trust this psychic message when I found myself confronted with problems along the way. I should have.

Marie was discharged from the hospital, and we found a small apartment of our own near Aunt Jean's. It was shabbily furnished. Our only bed was so battered that when we lay down at night I would be wedged flatly against the wall. Marie had to prop a chair at the outer edge to keep from rolling off onto the floor. It was dreadful, but it was our home for a week. Then Marie found a clean and comfortable rooming house for us in Hollywood. It was, after all where she really wanted to be from the start.

Marie was about thirty at this time and quite pretty in a bubbly way. She was acutely aware of the passage of time, however, and demonstrated her youthfulness at every opportunity. She was very proud of her legs and would show them off on the least provocation. After lifting her skirts and striking a few poses, she might surprise everyone by dropping into the splits. On these occasions she would more than likely have had the help of a drink or two.

Marie was on the hyper side to begin with, so with the help of alcohol she almost functioned in shorthand. At times she could be great fun and truly the life of the party, but just as frequently she would try too hard and make a fool of herself. With my own shy nature, Marie was frequently the source of great personal embarrassment. But that was only when she was drinking. Luckily, she didn't drink all the time.

Marie had the kind of moxie that would probably have served her well as a performer, but never once did she pursue a show business career of her own. Her desires in that area were transferred to me.

When Marie started to look for a job, she found one right away. She had little trouble finding jobs; holding them was the problem. Once she was hired to work at the candy counter of Graumann's Chinese Theatre. She was supposed to show up at nine A.M., but spent so much time getting pretty for the public that she was late for work. She was fired before she could start.

Later the same day we took a walk along Hollywood Boulevard. I was really enjoying myself, because for one thing I had captured my first glimpse of a real movie star, Pat O'Brien riding past in the back seat of a limousine. I was thrilled.

Marie missed the event entirely because she was busy studying a store-window advertisement which spelled out a promise to Make a Star Out of Anyone's Child. I was dragged inside. The man in attendance let loose his spiel to Marie, and she listened attentively. He said the agency would not handle just anybody, but he could see that I was really special and he'd use his influence to convince the boss. Marie asked if there was any charge. He said there would be minor charges for photos and publicity materials. It got down to his asking Marie outright how much money she had. She told him she had fifty dollars to her name.

The man looked at her, and then at me, and shook his head. As he ushered us to the door, he said to Marie in hushed tones, "Look, honey, save your dough. This is nothing but a gyp joint. I could lose my job for this, but I don't want to cheat you." The man practically pushed us out on the sidewalk, and I think Marie was disappointed; she so wanted to believe him. I'm sure she would have emptied her pocketbook if the man had asked her to.

Within a few days Marie landed her first job as a waitress, and it was not a vocation for which she was well suited. She found it impossible to juggle plates gracefully and had great difficulty remembering orders. If she wasn't spilling coffee in someone's lap, she was carrying off half-finished meals. She went through several such jobs in succession. The times she held a job more than a few days were when the management was impressed by either her personality or her shapely legs. It was nice while it lasted: Marie bringing home pocketfuls of change which we converted readily into hamburgers, malts, and french fries. But it never lasted long.

While Marie worked, I walked. Each day I would expand my orbit to include as much of the Hollywood environs as possible. My trails eventually widened enough to include the expansive Griffith Park. Once I found it, I knew it was exactly what I'd been looking for. Day after day I would explore the lush hills and dales, starting from Ferndale, a charming little park that abounded in flowers. I climbed the steep trails for more than two hours, but the results were worth the effort. There above me was the Griffith Park Observatory, a place where I would at last have a direct experience with outer space. The exhibits were wonderful, the lectures superb, and occasionally, at night, I was given actual glimpses through the telescope of the pockmarked moon.

In those days the trails that wove through the trees and foliage, up hills and down ravines, were uninhabited. It was like being thousands of miles from civilization, and the wonder of it was my freedom to explore it all. Marie didn't know what I was up to; nobody did. But in those days it didn't matter. They were simpler times, when the only dangers were of accidents.

The summer came to an end, and Marie enrolled me in Le Conte Junior High School. My greatest memory of that experience was meeting Hal Belfer, who would be a brief heartthrob but more importantly a solid lifelong friend. Otherwise, I wasn't there long enough for much else to be remembered. With no warning at all, Marie announced one day that we would be packing up and heading back to Vancouver. So much for my second trip to Los Angeles. I had fun, but very little had been accomplished by either Marie or myself. What now?

Chapter 6

This return to Vancouver was a kind of interim. It gave me time to pass through puberty, and I also changed from amateur to professional performer, although my professional debut was nothing spectacular—not even so-so.

The W. K. Gardens in Vancouver's Chinatown was a popular tourist place with a sign that promised Famous American Artists. They pretty well kept their promise with well-rounded vaudeville entertainment and popular name performers.

Just a block away was the Mandarin Gardens, whose competitive pride prompted an even bigger sign that said A Stellar Revue with Imported Acts. I don't know how she did it, but Marie convinced the Mandarin management that her daughter, a top dancer and singer, was available after a successful tour of Los Angeles and San Francisco theaters and nightclubs. I was given a week's booking.

When Marie told me the news I nearly collapsed. I had no act. I had no costumes. What possessed my mother to do such a thing? I tried everything short of amputating a leg to get out of it, but Marie was adamant. This would be my big break. Aunt Connie was elected to create an appropriate costume, and it was up to me to improvise an act. The only thing I could think of was to do an impression of some dancers of the day. I tried desperately to come up with clever patter, but with the opening date upon me I knew I couldn't deliver. Marie suggested a ballet number from *Swan Lake,* but we both knew the clientele of the Mandarin would never stand for that.

If I had been nervous about the church social a year or more earlier, I was in a state of cardiac arrest on opening night at the Mandarin Gardens. I vaguely recall tapping and smiling and whirling to the sound of the loud, tinny band. All the tables were filled with people far more interested in their food than in me, which was a godsend. When the music stopped I made my way offstage and braced myself for a tongue-lashing from Marie because I had committed a cardinal sin: I hadn't waited for my applause. Then, it occurred to me that I was all right, because there *wasn't* any applause. My opening night at the Mandarin Gardens was also my closing night.

Marie insisted that I go back to work on my dancing at once to ensure that I wouldn't fail again. The practicing work did indeed go on, but at this time in my life, other considerations began to bombard my consciousness. Maybe this poem of mine will give a clue:

> *Romance, romance is in the air,*
> *Romance, sweet romance, it's everywhere.*
> *It hides in the treetops,*
> *It plays in the dewdrops,*
> *And pierces young hearts with love.*

My poetry may have been flawed but its message was clear. I had started to notice boys. I had noticed boys before, certainly—Allan Rhodes, for instance, way back in the Comox Street days. I would watch from my secret tower safe-place at hours when I might expect to catch a glimpse of my handsome, blond, across-the-street neighbor. But that was preadolescence and I wouldn't have known what to do with my Prince Charming had I captured him.

I had something of a crush on Cecil Alton in the ninth grade. Since he played the piano we planned to team up for an act, but my heart started to beat to a different song. I wanted amour, not a business deal. Then Jacques came along: tall, handsome, and a popular member of the senior class. To win him would have really catapulted my stock at school. We flirted over lunch and walked hand in hand along the school corridors, and finally he invited me to a school dance. We went and had a wonderful time, with the feel of his body close to mine on the dance floor and kissing on the way home.

I was certain I was eternally in love with Jacques and was glad to be able to reciprocate on the dance invitation. I had been invited to what promised to be a spiffy beach party and asked if he would come along as my date. He agreed. He came to my house at the appointed hour, and we started off together along the shoreline to the party. As we reached the place where the party was supposed to be, a horrible realization came over me. This was Saturday night; the party was Sunday. I was a day early. I had never been so mortified. Anyone with brains would have apologized and made the best out of an honest mistake. Not me. I was so afraid Jacques would misconstrue the situation, that he would think I had planned this just to get him alone—I snappishly insisted that he see me home. I apologized for the mistake but refused to replan our Saturday evening. He must have thought I was a bit weird, I guess, because I didn't even ask if he wanted to go to the party the following night. I saw him in the school hallways and we spoke to each other casually, but the big romance was over. I was probably too intense at the time for him to feel comfortable. Who knows? I only know I climbed back into my shell and didn't object at all when my mother casually announced that it was time for us to try our luck again in Hollywood.

Marie had a specific plan for me this time. She had learned about the school of Fanchon and Marco, the famous brother-and-sister dance team. The team, with their brother Roy, had not only established a school but produced road shows and offered booking services as well. The building at 5600 Sunset Boulevard housed the rehearsal halls, five of them, and the booking agency—and they even had their own library. It was big business, and their prestige at the time couldn't be matched. Among the stars that were seasoned here were Judy Garland, Betty Grable, Cyd Charisse, Jackie Coogan, and many others.

I think Marie liked the idea of the booking office being part of the package. "When the doors of opportunity open, you'll be ready to walk right in," she told me again and again. If I could align myself with Fanchon and Marco, the doors of opportunity would be right there on the premises.

Marie rarely confided in me regarding our finances. I never knew if she was carrying five hundred dollars or five cents, but the odds definitely favored the latter. When we walked into the Fanchon and Marco reception room, I figured she must have come into some money; it was obvious that they wouldn't take on students without a fee. When the receptionist confronted Marie, she insisted on speaking only with the proprietor.

Following a brief wait, we were shown into the office, where we were met by a striking, immaculately groomed woman: Madame Fanchon's daughter, Faye Emerson, would begin a career a few years later at 20th

Century–Fox. The elegant lady explained that students could sign up for classes as money and time permitted: they could participate full-time, or by the day, or by the lesson, and could leave for jobs and return again after the job had been completed. The only condition was that the student be talented enough to learn new steps quickly. The charge was one dollar per day. Marie proceeded to oversell me, much to my embarrassment, but the woman was as gracious as could be. Before we left I had been signed up for classes the following morning.

With this behind us, Marie ushered me across the street to a small restaurant. Just as I was wondering where she was getting the money to pay for my dance lessons, I was in for another shock. In the restaurant she again insisted on speaking with the proprietor. Soon a weathered-looking woman emerged from the kitchen, eyeing us suspiciously. "Is there a problem?" the woman asked, wiping her hands on her apron.

"No problem," Marie said firmly. She straightened her shoulders, her head held high. "I'd like you to give my daughter and me a full, blueplate lunch. I will wash dishes to pay for it." If Marie hadn't clamped her hand on my arm, I would have dashed out of the restaurant. Then I was astonished to see the restaurant owner's face soften. "Okay," she said. "Go sit down."

My God—it worked. I was no longer anxious to get away; I was too hungry. We had our dinner, and our benefactor joined us. She asked about us, and Marie filled her in between dainty bites of chicken-fried steak. She was a woman alone, trying her best to care for her talented daughter who was struggling for recognition as a ballerina. She told about my enrollment at Fanchon and Marco's, and by the time dessert was served Marie had a job.

The deal was that Marie would work for the usual small salary and tips, and since I was part of the package the woman agreed to provide daily meals for me. It seemed too good to be true, and I, pessimist that I had become, knew it was too good to last. But for the moment all was well. Now all we needed was a place to stay. We had come directly from the downtown bus station to Hollywood. Our suitcases were still checked there.

The restaurant owner gave Marie a list of streets nearby where she had seen FOR RENT signs recently, and we set out. Of course our situation required more than finding a place to stay, because it was obvious Marie had no money. She had to find a place where the landlord would trust us until payday.

Marie was on a winning streak. On our third stop she landed us a very pleasant room with kitchenette at a cheap price—on credit. It was on a good street, with huge palm trees reminding us of where we were.

"I like palm trees," Marie said to me. "They suggest an oasis—a land of plenty."

Things went well at the school, and I liked it, at least some of it. Acrobatics, which I hated, was a required subject, and I was also in a constant press when it came to money. Sometimes Marie could spare a dollar, and other times she simply didn't have it. Some of Marie's craftiness rubbed off on me. I soon learned that by paying a special compliment here, or with a hug and sweet word there, the male instructors would sometimes "forget" to punch the daily ticket. That meant that the same ticket would get me through two days of classes.

I ran into my old Le Conte school friend Hal Belfer at the dance school one afternoon. He told me he was attending Professional High School, which enrolled child movie stars and others who had either talent or money. He also mentioned that he was in love with a girl named Doris. I guess he tossed that in, in case I wanted to resume our previous junior high school crush, but I didn't actually. During adolescence a couple of years makes a big difference.

This was a time when the part of my sex drive that hadn't been sweated out by hard dance practice was sublimated by writing. I fancied myself a Pearl Buck, I think, or some other famous author of the day, and I had to write, write, write. Late one afternoon I was walking along the school corridor and spotted a small, unoccupied office with a typewriter sitting there beckoning. I closed myself into the room and started pecking away. Time dissolved; it didn't exist. When I finally emerged from my creative cloud and went into the hall, I found myself in darkness. I called out, but my own voice echoed back. I tried the side door that I often used, but it was locked. So were all the others. Panic time! I had been locked inside the Fanchon and Marco school building for the night.

The thought occurred to me that a call to the police would require calling Madame Fanchon, or else they would have to break into the place to get me. Marie couldn't get in either. What would I do?

Finally, by stacking three chairs I found my way to a high window. The drop of eight or ten feet to the alley seemed as high as Pike's Peak to me, but I had no choice. I shinnied down a drain pipe a few feet, and then jumped to the concrete surface below.

The restaurant across the street was closed for the night, and when I reached our apartment house I found Marie pacing back and forth in front of the building. When she saw me she planted her fists on her hips and tapped her toe in impatient anger. She laid into me when we were inside. She had been moments away from calling the police. I was reminded of the sacrifices she was making in my behalf. The scolding continued until I promised to work twice as hard on the dancing, and that I would give up my writing. I kept my promise pretty well after that, but I put my heart and soul into my diary entries a couple of years later.

I stayed on the straight and narrow from then on and tried to live up to Marie's expectations. I worked hard, and my dance instructors started to reward me with special attention, such as teaching me specialty dance steps. Just as I was beginning to feel at home in Hollywood and optimistic in my work, the inevitable occurred. Marie broke the news that it was back to Vancouver again. By this time, it was the early summer of 1938.

After returning to Vancouver, a name kept cropping up in show business discussions. "Your daughter should enroll at June Roper's," or "June Roper does wonders in classical dance." Once Marie heard this, we were on our way downtown. This was exactly what Marie had been seeking in Vancouver and what had heretofore been nonexistent, a legitimate classical dance school. June Roper was a former Texan who had studied under Ernest Belcher in Los Angeles and performed in stage and club revues across America. She expanded her conquests to London, Berlin, and Paris. In Paris, she studied under Preobrajanska, and with de Valois in London. She was appearing in a stage revue in London in 1929 when her mother's sudden illness forced her to return to America. She and her mother moved in with June's sister in Vancouver, and June took an early retirement from dance. Finally, with a need to nourish her aesthetic appetites, she established the British Columbia School of Dance. It was located in a two-room studio next to the Orpheum Theatre. The school was just coming into its own when we returned this time to Vancouver.

Marie made a mistake in regarding June as a relative fledgling in the dance business, and acted a bit haughty because of my experience with Fanchon and Marco, but June accepted none of her nonsense. She made it clear that there would be no interference from Marie, or I would not be accepted by the school. It would cost fifty dollars a month for private lessons, or thirty-six dollars for group. Six lessons would cost four dollars, or we could pay a dollar per workout. Marie accepted the group setup and didn't even flinch at the prices, but I knew she had no money at all.

I have no idea where Marie came up with the first month's tuition, but she did. I had long since stopped trying to second-guess her, and I also knew better than to sell her short. With all her faults, Marie somehow got things done, and I, of course, continued to adopt some of her tricks. In this case, when the month ended and I was reduced to a daily lesson fee, I learned to show up just after the session had started. I would hide behind a curtain in the rehearsal hall and sneak peeks to get what was being taught. After Hope, the secretary, collected the daily fees, I would mingle with the girls. I was proud of the deception and got away with it for several weeks. Then the day came when June put her arm around my shoulder and walked me into her office.

"Do you think I'm a fool, Peggy?" she asked.

"No . . . of course not."

"I'm glad of that. Because if I were a fool I could never succeed in business. Then you and all the other girls would be deprived of some very worthwhile training."

I got the drift. I was saddened by the turn of events, not just because of being found out a cheater, but because I loved June and was really enjoying the classes. After I had missed a few days, June called Marie in for consultation. It was agreed that I would pay for the workouts when possible and could earn my lessons otherwise by teaching basic tap to some of the younger students. Just before my very first teaching lesson, Marie issued some practical advice: "Don't teach fast. Take your time. Get what I'm saying?" I got it.

June and I became very close friends and were to remain so all our lives, but back then our affinity came about gradually. One afternoon she called me into her office and asked about my childhood, and for the first time I really opened up with an outsider. June inspired that kind of confidence. When I came to a pause, she leaned forward and grasped my hands. "Peggy, you have had a very difficult life. That is all the more reason for you to work harder."

"But I do work hard," I protested.

"Not hard enough. To become successful in ballet requires tremendous dedication. It demands an extra strength from inside. You are not giving enough of yourself in classes. I want you to work harder."

I was so in awe of this woman her words were like Holy Writ. I repeated the words over and over until they were ingrained, and I did work harder.

Chapter 7

Despite my increased dedication, ballet was a losing battle. I never seemed to get limber enough to get through the grueling exercises without agony even though I could perform other dances with grace and confidence. Ballet was *harder* than all the rest, of course, the hardest of all disciplines. It wasn't until the 1970s that I discovered I'd had a form of arthritis in my back since I was fifteen years of age. No wonder all the limbering and stretching was so painful for me. I always just thought that my will wasn't strong enough.

June eased me down in gentle steps during our increasingly frequent personal discussions. She explained that toe dancing success came only after classic ballet training of from five to fifteen years, requiring a minimum of two or three hours of daily work at least five days a week, under the relentless tutelage of a master. That alone made my mission impossible. We never had money enough for that many lessons, and June couldn't take time away from her paying students to help me. I continued studying but accepted my limitations.

A fellow student told me I'd never succeed because my arms were too long. June assured me that this was nonsense. "Someday," she said, "you will see for yourself."

In later years, I realized that it wasn't my arms but my ankles that did me in. They were always too weak to support me on point. Had June advised me of this early in my study, it could easily have ended my dance career. But instead she guided me in new directions. I remain eternally grateful.

June rented the Strand Theatre for two days each term as a showcase for her dancers, and to acquaint them with audiences. I took part in a couple of the "Stars of Tomorrow" shows with relative success, but I really came to life in the shows next door at the Orpheum Theatre. June made a deal with the management to stage shows whose theme matched that of the movies that were playing. My debut was in "Waikiki Revue," in which I did a routine with Ken Mayhew. The audience loved it. I helped with the choreography, which made the occasion a double victory. There were other thrills too, such as my crush on one of the cute Tahitian dancers. We would flirt backstage, and compound the misbehavior by sneaking out to a nearby bakery to devour forbidden glazed donuts.

I had an almost concurrent romance with King Edward's High School's star rugby player, Gordy Noel. He was aggressive on the field and off, with a penchant for daredevil driving. Fortunately Marie never learned of Gordy's driving habits, which included traveling along a city sidewalk at sixty miles an hour. I was scared nearly to death but thrived on the thrills. It's a wonder either of us survived.

I couldn't have been busier with high school and dancing school with all of its extra activities, but I made sure to find time for the St. Paul's Church Youth Group. Singing was my love, even more important than boys, so I would always look forward to the Friday-night choir practice.

By now I was maturing in many ways, some more obvious than others. I hated the wolf whistles, and it was hard to get used to the open stares of strange men when I was alone on city streets. As a result, I would walk with my arms crossed over my chest and dressed in clothes that covered as much of me as possible, but that helped very little. It's hard to believe that I would be posing for cheesecake just a couple of years later.

I wasn't terribly mature in my relationships with boys. I was well aware of my inner stirrings but dealt with them obliquely rather than head-on. What I did was pour my sexual energies into work. I would work until I was so exhausted that only sleep appealed to me. Marie laid out a couple of lectures on the facts of life when I was in puberty, but general information wasn't what I needed. What I did need was a less exhausting way to douse the sexual fires.

A new nightclub called the Palomar opened in Vancouver with great hoopla. A month before it opened, I made an appointment to see the manager and haughtily informed him I had just completed an engagement at the Los Angeles Biltmore and was home visiting relatives. I said that for the sake of keeping active I might consider taking a job in the new club. He asked me to demonstrate a few dance steps, which I did, and, surprisingly, I was hired. I went home thinking I was pretty tricky.

This was an important date for me in another way. Marie and I discussed it at length, and decided that Peggy Middleton just wasn't right for me. Marie thought my name should have a more exotic sound. We tried on all sorts of names before the obvious occurred to us: why not stay with Yvonne, my middle name, and use Marie's maiden name, De Carlo? So that was it. From then on my professional name would be Yvonne De Carlo, and that was how I was billed at the Palomar.

I had no idea what the Biltmore Bowl might have paid me in Los Angeles, but at the Palomar the pay was twenty dollars a week, and I was booked for one week. I did my routine in which I emulated dancing stars, and for this big occasion I wrote myself some fancy patter to go with the dance:

> *When you go to a picture show*
> *to see "Forty-Second Street,"*
> *And the reason why you go*
> *Is to see those dancing feet.*
> *Now you may like Woolsey and Wheeler,*
> *But just give me Ruby Keeler . . .*

At this point I would break into dance doing a Ruby Keeler routine.

> *Ginger Rogers and Fred Astaire*
> *Make an ideal dancing pair,*
> *Doing a dance that's always new,*
> *A dance with pep that pleases you . . .*

Here I did Ginger Rogers . . . and so it went.

I included Eleanor Powell, then closed with Mae West. The audience applauded with some enthusiasm and I finished the run, but I wasn't held over for a second week.

My next job came from an ad in the newspaper. A promoter named Lindsay Fabré was coming to Vancouver and needed a pretty girl for "A Special Onstage Performing Spot." When I met the man I was hired on sight, and he offered me the astounding salary of thirty-five dollars for the week's run. All I had to do was pretend to be refereeing a boxing match between a man and a kangaroo. He said I was really in the act as decoration, because the bout was carefully choreographed. I was game. What he didn't know was that I would have fought the kangaroo myself for that kind of money.

The money didn't come quite as easily as I was told, naturally. First of all, the kangaroo smelled something awful. He and the trainer boxed around for a bit and then really started mixing it up. Then the kangaroo let go with a haymaker that sent the trainer to the canvas. My simple task was to step in and raise the kangaroo's paw in victory, but the kangaroo had other ideas. He pogoed around behind me, plunked his paws on my shoulders, and he started to make a meal out of my pompadour hairdo. I let out a yelp, much to the delight of the audience, but nobody came to my aid. After what seemed an interminable pause the trainer sat up, shook his head, and finally got up to shake hands with his opponent. I was led to believe that the antics of the kangaroo were entirely ad lib, but the ad libs were included in every show throughout the week. A sensible person would probably have quit, but I wanted that paycheck and felt I had earned every cent of it.

Just as everything was going nicely Marie stepped in again. By now I could read the look in her eye. "We're going back to Los Angeles," she told me. In remembering those times, it occurs to me that I rarely demonstrated against Marie's orders. That would make me seem a very obedient child, and I think I really was; a hell of a lot more obedient than Marie had been at my age.

In a final consultation, June Roper suggested that I continue with Fanchon and Marco but asked that I try to get in with her former master, Ernest Belcher. He was a specialist in formal ballet but was also a noted instructor of Spanish dance. She said she would write him about me. "Yvonne," she also said, "you should carefully consider going into movies. I think you might have a good chance there." I thought this an unusual statement from someone so dedicated to the classics and the stage, but when it came to my career Marie made all my decisions for me. Since Marie had never so much as mentioned the possibility of movies, I assumed she didn't want that for me.

It was nice to see the bright sunshine of Southern California again despite all my misgivings, but I wasn't thrilled with the shoebox Marie found us to live in. It was located near glamorous Hollywood, but the tiny apartment was actually in a tacky part of Tinseltown. It seemed as we were regressing. I signed on again with Fanchon and Marco, and after a lengthy interview I was accepted for special study with Ernest Belcher. Belcher was a strange-looking man, regal and stern with ram-rod posture. He was an unrelenting disciplinarian, and heaven help the student who failed to follow his specific instructions. I remember my pride when he complimented me on my fouettés; from then on I would do them at the drop of a hat. Belcher was instructing his daughter at this time, a cute teenager who would later become famous as the distaff side of the team of Marge and Gower Champion. Belcher also had Eduardo Cansino, the father of Rita Hayworth, as one of his instructors in Spanish dance.

Having previously proved myself with Fanchon and Marco, I was now qualified to work in their five-a-day shows that were booked at the downtown Paramount, the Manchester Theatre in southwest L.A., and at the Mayfair and Baldwin theaters. Hal Belfer and I would vie with the others to land the second half of the week, because that meant four days' pay instead of three. In addition to the theaters, we would sometimes play other random dates, such as at the Hollywood Masquers Club. I was adopting the blasé attitude of the seasoned trouper with all these bookings, but the pay was terrible even by Depression standards. Marie, who bounced from one bad job to another, often depended on the generosity of her boy friends to help us pay the rent.

Amid all this activity, I was diligently studying French at Hollywood High School and had started to get my first cheesecake modeling jobs. One such job involved five Fanchon and Marco girls who were hired by a press agent to publicize "Golden Days in Real Estate." I was costumed for the event in gold lamé tights with formfitting blouse, and it struck me as a joke that people would actually spend money for girls to appear in scanty costumes. It didn't take long for me to stop worrying about my bust measurements, either. I guess it was just a matter of getting used to my new adult equipment.

Marie hadn't given up her own efforts in finding bookings for me. Once she got me a job in the farming community of Bakersfield, about ninety miles north of Los Angeles. I bought my roundtrip bus ticket, did the strenuous solo tap dance performance, and collected my paycheck. It was one dollar short of the price of the bus ticket.

Another booking in which Marie had a hand was the "Imogene the Horse" act. I was hired to do a tap routine as the two-man horse cavorted about on the stage. The act consisted of two men, one very tall and one very short. The short one had a libido ten times his size. His hands were all over me whenever I would turn my back. During rehearsals he was always suggesting that we limber up together. "Lie down," he would say, "and let's have a warm-up." I lay down and did a few bicycle kicks, and Shorty was all over me. He said it was my leg muscles he was massaging, but his hands knew no such limits. I gave him a smack in the face and warned him, but he never really gave up. I wanted to keep the job, because Leo Carrillo, a very famous movie star of the time, was master of ceremonies, but all it led to was more of Shorty—the horse's ass.

Ken Mayhew, another June Roper disciple, came to Hollywood and we worked together trying to improvise some kind of act that might impress the booking agents. We auditioned again and again without a glimmer of interest, and it was starting to get quite discouraging when my mother got the idea of entering me in the Miss Venice Contest.

There had been a couple of previous beauty contests for me and I hated them. On one occasion I was the happy winner of a Miss Something-or-Other contest and came home with a brown bag full of canned goods. At least the Miss Venice contest might lead to something more. I was amazed when I came in second and was even more surprised at the check for twenty-five dollars, and that was the start of the chain of events that led me to the Florentine Gardens.

I've already described my first stint at the Florentine, which lasted until the Immigration Department nipped my career in the bud. Thanks to Granny, as I've said, my deportation didn't last very long. I was glad to be back, and with my involuntary vacation in Vancouver behind me I was ready to get back to work.

Chapter 8

Granny greeted me as a long-lost daughter when I showed up for rehearsals at the Florentine, and I lost no time in getting to work. I had to prove myself worth the forty dollars a week to which Granny had committed himself.

Whenever talk started about a new revue, I would dream up a routine that was compatible with the theme and try to sell it to Dave Gould and Granny. Sometimes they would go for it, other times not. This time, my idea for a dance to Ravel's "Bolero" made the grade. I dreamed up a slinky black beaded dress that gave the illusion of total nudity underneath. The routine was exhausting. Each night I'd stumble, panting, into the wings and the girls would taunt me with remarks like "Passion Lily is finished with her 'specialty.'"

Another routine I invented was a tarantella number using a gypsy costume and a tambourine bedecked with multicolored silk ribbons. I also created an Indian dance, a modified war dance of sorts, in which I wore a costume made of feathers. I was ecstatic over the freedom given me by Granny and Dave. The more they praised me, the better I performed, so *I* thought.

My biggest number of all at the Florentine Gardens was my "Babalu" number. The song was in Portuguese and I had no idea what the words meant, but the music brought out the best movements I'd ever done. I just went for it and it worked! The audience actually thought I was Spanish and the song remained a showstopper for me during my entire Florentine period.

There was a segment of the Florentine show that I despised. At a given point, Granny would bring men out of the audience to dance with the showgirls. Some of the men were so drunk they almost fell off the stage and most were crude and fresh, but they could do no wrong as far as Granny was concerned. The audience loved this feature and since Granny believed in pleasing his customers, that was that. Sugar Geise, the dance captain, always admonished us to smile before we went on. We were expected to act as though we were enjoying it as much as the hicks who were pawing us. That's acting! I recently came across some flash pictures of me and three other chorus girls with a few of the visiting firemen. The other girls were beaming as though this were the highlight of their young lives. Me? I was wearing a look that could kill.

Granny was constantly trying to find outside work for his girls, not least because the more we earned on the side, the less we would ask from him. It also created publicity for the Florentine Gardens, and, of course, for Granny himself. For one date, several of us appeared for a week with Granny at the majestic Orpheum Theatre in downtown Los Angeles. We often had shows of this kind to do. There were also appearances at auto shows, fairs, and expositions, and for those of us who could ride there were rodeos. For the latter occasions we would dress up in cute cowgirl outfits and join in on some of the less violent events in the show. We would also do our share of local parades, sometimes for pay, sometimes not. I always volunteered for the riding dates, because I loved it, and so did Granny.

He owned three horses, and I think it was my riding skills that endeared me to him from the start. I could, of course, thank Aunt Connie for that. She taught me to ride English style in Vancouver, but it was easy to switch to Western when the need arose. Granny always rode his horse named Chief, and my favorite was Kickapoo, a spirited chestnut stallion, part Morgan, part Arab, who would buck at the top of every hill we'd race up. I'm proud to say that I managed somehow to stay on. My girl friend, Pat Starling, whom Granny had met in a riding event somewhere, rode a horse named Little King. Pat was a beautiful blonde from Kentucky whose warm sense of humor endeared her to everybody. We have been closest friends all through the years and back then we would ride for hours, with and without Granny.

Granny had frequent parties in his rambling home above Franklin Avenue, near the Greek Theatre. The party room was a beautiful rathskeller decorated with expensive prints of hunt scenes. His guests were from all castes—New York high society, down-to-earth vaudevil-lians, and all the gradations in between. The parties were all co-hosted with his special girl friend, Sylvia McKay (Miss Unconscious in the show). When I first saw the fabulous buffet spread, standard fare for Granny's parties, I was moved to joke, "Hey, Granny, could I have a pound of butter to take home to my mother? You've got plenty." Thereafter, whenever I ate there, he would hand me a plate of butter for my mother, no matter who else was present.

I was still quite an innocent teenager, so I didn't mind having my mother serve as a buffer between me and "the real world." But there were times when her interference angered and hurt me. One night backstage, I happened to overhear Marie saying to a showgirl, "You wouldn't want Yvonne at your party. She's a virgin, she just wouldn't fit in."

The girl, one of the few friends I had in the group, shrugged and walked off. "Mummy!" I cried out. "How could you?"

She turned in momentary surprise. "You weren't supposed to hear that," she said, dismissing it.

"But I did, and I don't like it at all. You'd better keep your nose out of my business. I don't want you ever to say such personal things about me . . . to anyone."

She gave me a stern look, as only Marie could do. "Sometimes it's a good idea to go directly to the mark," she said. "To let people know exactly the way things are. Suppose I had just let you go to that girl's party, and suppose . . ."

"Stop it!" My mortification was growing. "Don't you ever do that again. Just leave me alone . . . I can take care of myself." I said it, astounded, and secretly proud of myself.

It was true, of course, that I was still a virgin, but in my present society that was not exactly something one bragged about. There were times when I wanted to tear off my "good girl" badge and throw it away, but I couldn't seem to do that. It was understandable that Marie was overly protective, because I told her everything. I would mention it when some old geezer would make a pass at me, and I would some-times criticize the behavior of the other girls. I would hear backstage gossip about topaz rings, fur stoles, the promises of Tommy, Bruce, or George. I would also see how some of the girls came back after the breaks between shows, with hair disheveled, clothes in disarray, lipstick gone. If I came into a dressing room suddenly, the conversation would halt. I learned to cough before entering hearing range of the girls' confabs so they could change the subject. I would have liked to be one of the gang, but I wasn't.

Outside the nightclub I remained my silent, introverted self. One young man paused during our dinner conversation to say, "You remind me of a monkey."

That woke me up. "A monkey?"

"Uh-huh. They can never look you in the eye either."

I never dated him again, but I remembered what he said. What he told me was true, but I wasn't aware of it until then. I found it almost impossible to face a man directly.

The pretty girls in the show attracted lots of men to the club, and many of them were among the town's most eligible bachelors, including Errol Flynn and Bruce Cabot. This was a couple of years before Flynn's first entanglement with the law, but his reputation was already well established. The girls who went out with Flynn and his friends knew pretty well what would be expected of them, and plenty of them went. I simply wasn't among them.

The celebrities I learned to trust were Franchot Tone and Burgess Meredith. Their table was always a place of gaiety and laughter, and before I met them I envied the girls who were included in their fun. Then one night a note was brought backstage. "Dearest Yvonne," it said. "You are wonderful. Please come over to our table." It was signed, "Doc Tone and Burgess (the Creep) Meredith."

Burgess Meredith was known as Buzz by his friends, and just about everybody qualified for that distinction. He was consistently witty and gallant, and a joy to be with. Our relationship was always platonic, and he never made an overt attempt to change the status. He hinted, of course, and made it clear that he was available for the heavier stuff, but let it rest there. I went out with him many times, to parties—at George Cukor's home, for example—and to late suppers at his home, where I met friends of his such as William Saroyan and Artie Shaw. I didn't mix in very successfully, but I appreciated being given the chance. I think one reason Buzz may have let me off the hook was that even then he was dating Paulette Goddard, whom he would wed a few years later.

Franchot Tone was another matter. With his charming, crooked smile and patrician good looks, he attracted women readily. By now he had ended his marriage to Joan Crawford, and was trying to make up for lost time. He may have been on the make, but he was so urbane that he was never offensive. It was a strain being around Franchot, because all a girl had to do was lower her guard once, and POW!

One night Franchot took me to a party where he tried his best to get me to stay the night. He said there was an extra bedroom and that nobody would bother me. I had heard that one before and had no intention of setting myself up. He slid his arm around me, kissed my neck lightly, and murmured sweet somethings in my ear.

"Are you proposing to me?" I whispered back at him.

"Huh?"

"When I go to bed with a man," I said, "I want it to be with the man I'm going to marry."

That was our brief moment of truth. From then on Doc devoted his attentions to other, more available girls in the show. It wasn't long before a new one caught his roving eye. I don't know what her formula was, but Jean Wallace became the second Mrs. Franchot Tone.

Another star who showed interest in me was red-haired Van Heflin. He was a serious man and a gentleman, and took much time to give me advice about my acting. "Observe," he told me. "Be aware of everything that goes on around you. If it's a car accident, a drowning, or the joy of a wedding—watch people's reactions and store the pictures in your mind."

I thought that good advice, and I remembered it. He also suggested that I fashion myself after his friend Katharine Hepburn. Easy to say. Van and I were to have a fling of sorts, but it would be about a decade before the circumstances were just right.

In my attempt to become "one of the gang," I joined the whole cast in an outing at the Circle J Ranch near Newhall. There was riding, swimming, a restaurant on the premises, and a scattering of motel-type cabins. It was a favorite recreation spot for Western actors and stuntmen, and could sometimes get a little raunchy. I, as always, found myself roaming around alone, while the others were busy dancing and drinking. I ran into a screen newcomer, whose face I recognized. The macho-looking young man said, "Hi, my name's Tony Quinn."

"Hello," I said.

"Don't you have a name?" His black eyes had a hypnotic effect.

"Yvonne," I stammered.

"Lovely name, Yvonne," he said, grinning. "I'd love to get to know you better. I'll see you later, right?"

It was after dark when we ran into each other again, and the free drinks were taking their toll.

"Oh, there you are," he said, taking my hands in his. "I've been looking for you. I wanted to tell you that I adore your long, wonderful legs."

His self assurance was disarming, and those eyes—oh those eyes!

"Thank you," I said, shyly.

"I have something to ask of you," he went on. "I want to place you on a pedestal, where I can worship you hour after hour."

I looked at him blankly—I'd never heard this one before.

He continued, "With your goddess-like figure you should *never* wear clothes."

I just listened.

He flashed me a wide grin. "Now," he said, clutching my hand, "let's take a walk in the desert moonlight."

"Oh, I'd love to, but someone is picking me up in a while."

"How about a swim, then . . . and then a nice shower in my room?"

"Not interested," I said. "Sorry."

That was it . . . all of it. Without one more word, he left me and mixed in with the crowd. I must admit that I played the scene substantially differently from my girlish fantasies. He was easily the sexiest man I had met since coming to Hollywood, and it's just possible that if he had been a bit more believable I might have gone along with him. But, alas, I didn't. My status as a Hollywood virgin remained unchanged.

Around a cozy campfire later that night, I happened to overhear Quinn talking to Lili St. Cyr, a well-known exotic dancer in the forties and fifties. "You have wonderful Egyptian eyes," he told her. "Come with me into the desert moonlight." The last I saw of either of them, they were walking off into the desert—hand in hand.

Another of the Florentine bachelor customers was the then slim and handsome wunderkind of the movie business, Orson Welles. His *Citizen Kane* had just been released, and he was the talk of the land. When Buzz Meredith introduced him to me, I clung to his every word, hoping, I suppose, that some of his genius would rub off. But his conversation was mostly small talk. When the time came for him to leave, he arose, kissed my hand, bowed, and said goodnight. I had given him my phone number, and he said he would call, but I didn't believe it. Yet within a couple of weeks he did.

Orson called for me at the stage door on the appointed night and escorted me to a huge black sedan. As we drove through the Hollywood streets, he asked me all about my background. I got so involved in my own dull story, I lost track of the miles we seemed to be covering. "Aren't we going to eat?" I finally asked.

"At my place," he replied, "and here we are now."

I didn't know if it was Bel Air or Brentwood, but it was definitely in the high-rent district. We climbed a long trail of stone steps to a compact but lovely home. By this time my virgin alarms were clanging loudly. Oh-oh, here we go again, I thought.

When we were inside the snug and cozy home I started talking. "My, what a lovely library," I said, dashing over to examine a book. He came up behind and rested a hand on my shoulder. I moved from under its clasp and pointed out another book that caught my eye. When he closed in again I crossed the room. "Oh, look at that," I said, pointing to a painting. "Isn't that a . . ."

"A Degas," he said.

On the move, I went through Manet, Monet, and a pair of Chagalls, and worked my way into a corner, where I was trapped. He clutched me gently, and eased me into the softest couch I had ever known. There were art books on the coffee table, which he leafed through with one hand while his other arm drew me close to him. He went into a discourse on the Gallic artists, and I flattered him, joked and cajoled —anything to ward off the inevitable. When that failed I was on my feet again. I found a magnificent sculpture, a Ming horse. I think it was brass, but I know it was heavy. I weighed it in my hand, poising it in a way that conveyed a message to him. "My, this is heavy," I said.

The game played on for at least an hour, with Orson regaling me with adventure stories, one of which impressed me particularly. He told me he had once contracted leprosy on a journey through the Far East. It occurred to me that this wasn't the most seductive line to give a girl, but maybe he had given up on me by that time. When he ushered me into his bedroom to show off his Oriental prints, I told him it was late and I wanted to go home. I could tell he was furious, but he held his temper. What he did was excuse himself to make a phone call. Within a few minutes the doorbell sounded. It was a taxi driver who had been called to take me home. How humiliating. But how relieved I was! My dinner consisted of an egg sandwich—after I got home. Orson wasn't as friendly to me from then on.

I mentioned that my dream men were consistently tall, blue-eyed, and blond, so you might imagine how my heart pumped when Buzz Meredith introduced me to Sterling Hayden. "How do you do," I said in a nervous squeak.

He gave me a nod.

"Sterling's in movies," said Meredith.

"I know," I said. "I saw you in *Virginia,* with Fred MacMurray and Madeleine Carroll."

I felt proud to have managed a whole sentence under the circumstances, but no matter how I tried no small talk was forthcoming. I was grateful to Buzz, who filled the vacuum as only he could do. I was relieved when the time came to get ready for the second show, because I was sure I had struck out with this handsome Scandinavian giant. I felt badly about it, because I was really attracted to him. I had more or less dismissed him from my mind when he surprised me with a note delivered backstage. "Are you busy after the show?" said the note, which he signed, "Sterling."

I sent the note back with "No" written on it, and included the backstage phone number. When the phone rang I nearly dropped it, I was so nervous. He said he would meet me on the corner of Hollywood Boulevard and Bronson Avenue thirty minutes after the show. I said I'd be there.

I'm not sure if it was my nervousness or a dirty trick being played by the gods, but I somehow managed to get the meeting place fouled up. I stood on the corner of Hollywood Boulevard and *Gower* Street for an hour and a half. Had I stood on a corner that long today, I'd have been arrested. Even then, I would never have waited so long for anyone else. But this was the man of my dreams. I finally gave up in total despair. I was sure I had been stood up.

My shattered world mended quickly the following night at the club. Jessie, one of the nicer girls, told me Sterling had called twice the night before. She said she thought Viola had taken a message. By this time Viola had had plenty of time to give me the message, but hadn't. She was in the enemy camp, a hateful kind of person who was continually showing her disdain for me. So when I went into her dressing room I was ready for mortal combat. I asked if she had taken a message for me. She shrugged and continued adjusting her pasties.

I pulled her around to face me, and would have flailed into her if one of the other girls hadn't grabbed me. When Viola saw the murder in my eyes, she delivered the message. It was that he would call again.

Well, Sterling did finally call and the misunderstanding was soon explained. We made a date for dinner, and I can't remember ever feeling more in awe of a man. Over candlelight, he spoke and I listened. His great love was sailing, and much of the conversation was devoted to that. He had bought his first vessel three years earlier, when he was twenty-two, won a fishermen's race on the East Coast, and finally lost the ship in a storm. Now he owned another sailboat, which he docked in Newport Beach. Originally from Montclair, New Jersey, Sterling had broken into movies after modeling in New York. We had several dinner dates together, and I missed none of the information he bestowed on me during those magical evenings.

After each date he would politely escort me to my door and lean down from his six-foot-five frame to kiss my forehead. Of course I had a reputation for being a prude, but I was ready to make an exception in his case.

Then the time came when he invited me to come with him to spend a day at his boat site. I had worked late the night before but was dressed in pedal pushers, a peasant blouse, and sandals when he called for me at six in the morning. I also had a seductive nightie tucked away in my satchel—in case!

Sterling revealed even more of himself on our drive to the boat harbor. He discussed his liberal political views and expounded his contention that the U.S. would sooner or later have to go to war against the Axis powers. He revealed his abhorrence for material things, such as jewelry and furs, and for those who were influenced by them. He said that he had put Madeleine Carroll straight on many such issues. Her name came up far too frequently to please me, and I would quickly change the subject when the conversation returned to her.

Sterling had a cozy cabin near his boat dock, and asked me if I'd like to cook breakfast for us. I would have done it to please him—anything. But I didn't know how to cook breakfast, and I could tell I lost big points when I told him so. He attended to the task himself, and did it very well. He later had to do to some chores on his boat and suggested I take a nap while he was gone. I lay on his couch, arranged my long tresses over a pillow, and struck a seductive pose. The dream was that he would charge forward, see how beautiful and sexy I was, sweep me into his arms, and dash off to the nearest Justice of the Peace to get married. I was really tired but knew I wouldn't sleep. I was too keyed up—too stimulated. I lay there with eyes closed and waited for his return. I waited, waited, and waited, squinting through my eyelashes at the slightest outside sound. Finally he returned, and I could feel his presence as he stared down at me. I was saying silently, "Take me. . . . Take me." I could imagine the expression of adoration on his face as he stared down at me, and after a long while I stirred and opened my eyes to catch him at it. It was then I discovered that he wasn't standing over me at all. He was seated across the room at a window seat trying to untangle fishhooks from a snarled line.

The remainder of the day was spent on his boat, walking along the beach, enjoying the lovely weather with casual conversation. But time was running out. I had to work that night, and it was nearing time to start back. In the orange glow of a setting sun, Sterling took my hands in his and smiled down at me. "Yvonne," he said, "you're a very nice girl and I want you stay that way. Keep away from all those phony Hollywood playboys. Wait for the right guy."

What a letdown. He drove me home, and at the door I got another of his Uncle Sterling kisses on the forehead. That was it with Sterling Hayden. We wouldn't cross paths again until after the war, by which time he'd become quite a different person. As it turned out, he and Madeleine Carroll would make *Bahama Passage* together and then marry. I pined over him for more than a year.

Chapter 9

It was the fall of 1941, and I had a fairly successful career going. I was doing specialty numbers at the Florentine, I had done several more Soundies film shorts, and I had even made my debut on network radio in a brief routine with Edmund Lowe and Victor McLaglen, a condensed version of a scene from their Captain Flagg–Sergeant Quirt series. I had even bought myself a fake fur coat, so I should have felt happy with myself, but I wasn't feeling well at all.

The possibility occurred to me that the malaise I felt might be physical, so I went to a doctor. My physical complaints were chronic headaches and an annoying bout with a stiff neck. I had a strong hunch that my ailment was something simple—like a brain tumor. The doctor plunked my knees with his rubber hammer, used his mirror to peer into my eyes, checked my heartbeat, and took my temperature. Nothing turned up.

After learning more about me, the doctor advised: "What you need to do is go out and live . . . be happy, understand? Go and . . . be happy." Later, I figured out what he was trying to say. He couldn't just come out and say it, I suppose, but what he meant was: "What you need at your age, young woman, is to go out and get laid!" But this was back in the 1940s, and sex was almost never dealt with directly.

Burgess Meredith was the one to introduce me to yet another eligible bachelor. This time it was one of the country's hottest bandleaders, Artie Shaw, just coming off marriage number three to Lana Turner. He had made recent headlines by his remark to the press that "All jitterbugs are morons." Artie Shaw was darkly handsome, but there was more than that to his attraction to women. There was a masculine intensity about him that was almost overpowering, and he was remarkably bright and articulate. Our friendship was helped by our mutual interest in riding, swimming, and music. I think I was audacious enough at the time to consider myself an intellectual, but he was light years ahead of me. I never dueled with him in sparkling conversation, so I wasn't really tested. What I did—which probably endeared me to him more than anything else—was listen.

My nickname by this time was "Icebox De Carlo," and Artie was exposed to the chill on our very first date. He was determined to get me into bed, and he was accustomed to getting his way. But he hadn't reckoned on the brick wall of the De Carlo virginity. Once he learned of my state, he tried no more. It was back to the old routine. He freely discussed the other women in his life and philosophized about his requisites for a wife. The girl had to be neat and attractive, have a sense of humor, and above all be intelligent. Actually, his standards were so high he could never find a girl to meet the requirements, and he never did—for long.

One night over a late supper at Mike Lyman's on Vine Street, I confessed my singing ambitions. "I'd really like to be a singer," I said.

His train of thought was derailed. "Don't you realize you can't just *be* a singer. It takes study, my girl!"

I regretted my remark, especially when I saw how it soured his mood. Over dessert he said to me, "Tell me this—how do you expect to get anywhere working in a dump like the Florentine Gardens?"

I decided my best bet was to keep quiet.

"Look," he said, "you're not just in a rut, you're in a hole. In a rut you can at least move in one direction. I advise you to quit—right now."

Quit the Florentine? Me? The notion terrified me. Had someone else advised it, I'd have shrugged it off, but coming from Artie Shaw, who knew just about everything there was to know—and let you know it— well, it was disquieting at the least. And he didn't let it rest. "Look, kid," he said. "I know you can't afford to be out of work, so I'll make a deal with you. Quit your job, start studying singing, get yourself a movie agent—and I'll pay your salary for a month." He must have read my mind, because he added, "No strings attached, I promise."

I don't know why I let him talk me into it, but I did. I guess it shows how impressionable I was at the time, and trusting. The worst thing was my treatment of Granny. I just walked out; I didn't even give notice. That would have forged enemies for life in most circumstances, but not with Granny. He just wanted me to promise to keep coming to his parties, and to remember our riding dates. He gave me a warm hug, and said, "Just remember, Dingbat, there'll always be a place for you at the Florentine if you ever need it. I hope you won't."

I lost no time in getting an actor's agent. I signed with Jack Pomeroy, who was a friend-of-a-friend of someone my mother knew and was known to be young and hungry, having recently gotten into the business. He proved this almost at once by getting me into my first feature. It was a dreadful B movie called *Harvard, Here I Come,* but I didn't know it was dreadful.

I played a bathing beauty who was used in a classroom test of student responses, and who gave Slapsie Maxie Rosenbloom an excessive pulse rate. My single line of dialogue was "Nowadays a girl must show a front." This, coming from the same girl who used to fold her arms to hide her breasts. The film was shot at Columbia, and my pay for the day's work was twenty-five dollars. It may not have been much, but it was a start, and it got me into the Screen Actors Guild. I was certain I was hell-bent for stardom.

Unfortunately, my string of successes stopped at one. I plummeted from euphoria to despair—well, not quite, but almost. Artie Shaw kept his word about the month's salary, but now Artie was off somewhere with his band and was no longer a factor in my life. I faced a moment of truth and considered crawling back to Granny, but I didn't have to, thanks again to Jack Pomeroy. He heard Earl Carroll was hiring girls and suggested I give it a try. This idea seemed more appealing than admitting defeat to Granny, so, despite my misgivings a couple of years earlier, I was now ready to pass through the famous portals.

I was prepared this time for the chest inspection, and, thanks to a shade more sophistication, I wasn't worried about it. I stepped into a small room where Mr. Carroll sat waiting for us to come in one by one. It was really painless, though a bit embarrassing. I was fortified, however, in the fact that I had company. I undid my blouse, took off my bra—took a deep breath, and gave him a quickie look. He thanked me and I was hired. It was that simple. At my moment of hiring, I became one of the "Most Beautiful Girls in the World" who passed through those portals. It would be ironic, but a few years later I would receive the same title—all to myself.

I don't know what I expected, but working at Earl Carroll's was a bit intimidating. Granny treated his girls like family; Mr. Carroll treated his like strangers. There was none of the camaraderie between troops and management, and the atmosphere was stiff and constrained. The dining room was a huge multitiered place decorated in the Ziegfeld tradition. While the restaurant was one of the most popular in Los Angeles, it was seldom filled because of its size. Beryl Wallace, a beautiful brown-eyed brunette, was Earl Carroll's girl friend and served as MC for the shows. She didn't do much other than that since she couldn't dance. But she made a magnificent impression with her beaded gowns and feathery fan and soft, sweet voice—and, fortunately for all of us, she was just as sweet as she seemed.

All the girls had to wear white body makeup to make us look alike, and the result was that we looked like studies in white marble. That took some getting used to, but it wasn't nearly as challenging as the part I was given to play. There was a Busby Berkeley-type number with a human pyramid of alabaster girls. There were steps that we mounted to effect the illusion, and I—vertigo and all—was placed on the step next to the top. At the very top was a very tall showgirl, and I could never figure out how she did it every night. I was only thankful that I wasn't placed there. I was traumatized every night by that part of the show, but somehow I lived through it.

Marie struck no friendly chords with Mr. Carroll. I learned of their disharmony one morning over breakfast. "Yvonne," Marie said, "I was at the theater last night."

"Oh?"

"Yes. I was sitting at the bar having a drink and watching the show, and I saw Mr. Carroll."

"Oh-oh," I said to myself.

"I told him I was your mother and asked him if you didn't look just swell up there on the stage."

I was choking on my orange juice. "Uh . . . what did *he* say?"

"He said, 'Please be quiet, I'm trying to watch the show.' Can you imagine that?"

I could.

The girls were allowed to do outside publicity layouts only if they were first approved by Mr. Carroll, and we were not permitted to freelance on our own. I was aware of the rules, but when a bit part in a major Paramount film came my way I simply had to risk it. The movie was *This Gun for Hire,* starring Alan Ladd. I couldn't pass it up, and I didn't dare risk asking permission for fear it would be denied. I reported to the studio, said my line, "Cigarettes, sir?" in the Neptune Club scene, and was free at an early hour in the day. The only problem was my fascination for watching the stars perform. I stayed on to watch the beautiful and temperamental Veronica Lake doing some of her scenes. I wondered if all the stars were as loud and demanding. Then I wondered what I would be like in the same situation. When I was finally able to tear myself away, it was well past dinnertime, and there was no time to go home to change. I went directly to the restaurant. I was on my way backstage to the dressing room when a hand clamped my shoulder. "Where do you think you're going?" said a voice that needed no introduction.

"To the dressing room, Mr. Carroll," I said, innocently. "I'm not late, am I?"

"What is that you have on your face?"

I was wearing the telltale orange-colored panchromatic makeup that was used in black-and-white films. I tried to conjure up a lie, but it was hopeless.

"That's motion picture makeup," he snapped. "You have violated your contract with me. You're fired!"

No reprieve, no special consideration for a first offense. I was scuttled, dumped, banished forever. I ran home in tears and poured out the sad story to a sympathetic and attentive Marie. "Well, we'll just see about that." she pronounced.

I went directly to bed, too tired and miserable to eat. When I was finally able to get to sleep, I didn't wake up until morning. Marie was awaiting me with a glint of triumph in her eye. "I fixed Mr. Carroll," she said. "I went to see him last night. I told him in no uncertain terms that he'd better rehire you. I told him that if he didn't do so at once, I would make a stink the whole town would hear about. I let him know that he'd hired an underage performer in his club."

If I hadn't been miserable before, I surely was now. I couldn't eat, and that night I couldn't sleep, not at all. Early the next morning I went to see my agent, hoping to repair some of the damage. He had already heard the news through the Hollywood grapevine: I had been blackballed all over town.

Marie got me into it, but it was she who also got me out. Through a friend of hers, an official at the Motion Picture Relief Fund, the right strings were pulled to have the ban lifted. My first instinct was to board the next bus to Vancouver and forget about Hollywood, but I realized by now there was nothing for me up north. That had been my sanctuary in the past, but now I had a new refuge, the good old Florentine Gardens. I went to see Granny, told him my sad tale, and hoped for the best.

"Dingbat," he said with a hug, "the Garden hasn't been the same without you. You're welcome as the rain in August, if you'd like to come back."

"I do want to, Granny," I said, fending off the tears.

"Tell you what," he said. "Take the rest of the week off, on salary, of course—and report for work next Monday."

My head and neck pains had recurred after leaving the Florentine, but now they lifted as though by magic. Just to know I had a friend like Granny was probably what did it. I fell back into the two and three shows a night routine without difficulty and worked harder than ever before. By this time, I was looking to the movies as my goal.

Business had begun to drop off at the Florentine as it had almost everywhere else. We were obviously going through a depression of sorts, to accompany the Depression we already knew. To bring the customers back, Granny produced a whole new revue called *Glamour Over Hollywood,* featuring the Paul Whiteman orchestra. It worked for a while, then business dropped off again. One day, Granny and Dave changed the show's content by featuring the exotic superstar, Lili St. Cyr. This brought people into the restaurant, but we still didn't come close to the kind of business we had known a year earlier. I started to feel grateful that enough business remained to keep us all in work.

One Sunday morning in early winter I woke drowsily and joined Marie for a cup of coffee in the kitchen. I was picking over the Sunday *Los Angeles Times,* when strange sounds played into the kitchen from the outside courtyard. Windows were being lifted, and voices mingled in a kind of breathless chatter. Marie opened the door to see a group of neighbors clustered around an open window across the way. A radio was blaring from within the apartment. "What's going on?" Marie called out. "Is something the matter?"

Our next-door neighbor, a heavyset man with a face that was redder than usual, replied, "Yeah, there's something the matter, all right. Turn on your radio."

We did, and within moments learned that the Japanese had bombed Pearl Harbor. We were at war.

PART TWO
The Movie Years

I've slept in shanties
Guest of the WPA,
Danced in my scanties
Three bucks a night was the pay
But I'm here.
I've stood on breadlines with the best
Watched while the headlines did the rest
In the Depression was I depressed?
Nowhere near
I met a big financier
And I'm here.

Chapter 10

With the advent of war, the complexion of the city changed almost overnight. Before Pearl Harbor, there were times when a person could walk across Hollywood Boulevard in mid-afternoon without a car, truck, or trolley in sight. There were FOR RENT signs on several houses in each block, for rooms or apartments. When midnight came, most Angelenos were already tucked into bed. Now the studios changed over to war and propaganda themes, and many executives and stars started signing up for military duty. War bond tours began, and the bright lights of Los Angeles and every other coastal city were dimmed "for the duration." And there was real danger. I wasn't aware of it at the time, but there was great fear by our leaders that California might be invaded.

Many of us volunteered to do whatever we could to help the war effort. The girls from the Florentine were constantly putting on shows at nearby military bases. We also did shows at the Hollywood USO on Cahuenga Boulevard, and when the Hollywood Canteen opened we danced there with servicemen. The Canteen was a studio effort, headed by Bette Davis and John Garfield. Every night hundreds of G.I.s would wait in around-the-block lines to glimpse a movie star or dance with a starlet, but many of them just wanted someone to talk with, to help soothe their homesickness. The sadness of war was all around us, but so was the electrical charge of the common cause.

With the USO and the Canteen located within a block of each other on Cahuenga Boulevard, the strip between Hollywood and Sunset Boulevards swarmed with military personnel passing through town on their way to unknown destinations. Honkytonk bars sprang up, storefront photo galleries, pinball parlors, Midway-type arcades, rifle ranges. The old restaurants were packed with new business, and new places opened to profit from the overflow. The struggling Florentine Gardens became a thriving entertainment mecca overnight. The wartime business boom was on; there was something for just about everyone to do, most of it for the war effort.

The racetracks closed down and movie premieres were halted for the time being, but there were still plenty of rodeos going on that included Granny and his girls. We did a minirevue at the Hollywood Paramount Theatre in which I did a vaudeville routine with Granny that he had done ten years earlier with Alice Faye. There were also charity luncheons to attend, and dances to raise funds for the war effort. I got in another Soundie, called *The Lamp of Memory.*

Then my agent started coming up with some studio interviews, one with John Zinn, head of casting at Paramount. As he studied several of my photos that he had spread over his desk, I gave him the old I-might-just-consider-working-for-you routine. Thank God he smiled. "It's possible," he said, shocking me half to death.

"It is?"

"We're doing a Crosby and Hope picture that's set in Morocco, and we'll be needing some harem types." He leaned back to look me over. "You just might fit in, with that olive skin and those slanting eyes."

"Slanting eyes?"

"Sloe eyes, then. Seventy-five a week, and you'll play one of Dorothy Lamour's handmaidens."

"You . . . you mean I'm hired? I can count on it?"

"The job is yours."

I almost ran out of the office clicking my heels. I was told to report for wardrobe March 6, 1942, and then to Stage Ten for Production Number 1333, *The Road to Morocco.*

It was a great joy working on the set with Hope and Crosby, even though David Butler, the director, kept the handmaidens pretty well separated from the principals. There were always practical jokes and high jinks going on to overcome soundstage monotony, and time passed rapidly. The director also made sure we were kept deep in the background in Dorothy Lamour's scenes. The heavy in the movie was none other than Anthony Quinn, and I couldn't wait for him to speak to me. I had all kinds of clever quips prepared in memory of the Circle

J Ranch, but as it turned out he didn't give me so much as a nod throughout the picture.

Paramount must have liked me, because they called me a short time later for the role of fourteen-year-old Ata in the film adaptation of Maugham's *The Moon and Sixpence*. I was given a test for what was described as "a small but showy part," in which I would play the Tahitian wife of Gauguin, played by George Sanders. Everyone said I was great in the test, and I was counting on the part, but it went instead to Elena Verdugo. I would learn to deal with this kind of disappointment in due course, but at this tender age each rejection left a scar. I was heartbroken.

As I suffered over my defeat, my spirits were buoyed considerably when I received a very special phone call:

"Uh, hallo . . . am I, uh, talking to Yvonne, uh, De Carlo?"

"Yes, this is Yvonne. Who's this?"

"Wal, uh, this is Jimmy Stewart, and . . ."

"Yeah, sure it is. Come on now, who is this, really?"

"No, no . . . really. I am Jimmy Stewart. I, uh, saw you a while back at Earl Carroll's, and I, uh, thought it would be nice to get to know you. I . . . uh . . . got your number from a pal, and, well . . ."

It *was* Jimmy Stewart, and he asked me out to dinner. He asked where I lived, but I asked if I could meet him somewhere. The apartment I shared with Marie was a real hovel, and, as phony as it might have been, I just couldn't bear to have James Stewart call for me there. So we met in the lobby of the Plaza Hotel on Vine Street.

He was so cute in his new Air Corps officer's uniform, all six-foot-four of him. I must say I felt proud to be escorted by such a film personality to the fashionable Clover Club restaurant on the Sunset Strip. We had a lovely candlelight dinner, and he was such a perfect gentleman. It was like a scene from one of his movies. And we danced. I can't say that he whispered sweet nothings into my ear, because his mouth and my ear were separated by about a foot, but he made clear his attraction to me nonetheless.

After we left the restaurant and he was driving along Sunset he hinted that the night was still young, and I was thinking to myself that this might be just the night—the *big* night. It would certainly be memorable if James Stewart happened to be your first lover. I was waiting for him to take charge, to drive me to a cozy cottage on the beach or a mountain lodge, maybe, with a crackling fire, but instead he asked where I lived. I decided to tell him, in spite of the humble appearance of my quarters, and that was where we went. Then, in the hallway, he just kind of stood there, on one foot and then the other, waiting for me to invite him in. I didn't have the guts then to explain that my mother was inside, snoring away in one of the two beds in our only bedroom. To break the growing silence, I thanked him for a lovely evening and emphasized my hope of seeing him again. He gave me a kid's kiss on the cheek and bade me farewell. And that was exactly what it was. For days, I leaped at the phone when it rang—hoping. But Jimmy Stewart never called again.

I managed to get a bit part in the Paramount film *Lucky Jordan,* and then in May I shared a bill with Donald O'Connor and his brother and sister on the Eighth Annual Police Show at the Shrine Auditorium. This was followed by a drought of several weeks, which was broken by a part in a dreadful Republic Studios bomb called *Youth on Parade.* I had been feeling bad during the shooting, but by this time I was feeling very poorly. Then Marie started noticing my rundown appearance and called a doctor. The doctor examined me, and I could see him in the hallway talking with Marie. It was like a scene from a Dr. Kildare movie, with the doctor shaking his head gravely. I called out to them. "What's going on? Am I going to die or something?"

"No, it's not that bad," the doctor reassured me, "but we are going to have to put you in the hospital, where we can take proper care of you. You have bronchial pneumonia, and it has to be treated."

I was in the hospital for two weeks before the "walking pneumonia" finally cleared up, and it was depressing to be lying helplessly in a bed when the world was passing you by and the bills were mounting. I made a pest of myself at Paramount after my recovery, determined that this was where I could recoup my losses from the illness. It finally paid off. John Zinn spotted me in the studio hallway one afternoon and called me into his office. "Yvonne," he said with a grin, "are you still willing to come to work at Paramount?"

"Sure," I said, holding my breath.

"Well, I think we can give you a six-month contract."

I saw no need to ask either mother or agent if I should accept the offer. Although it was only for sixty dollars a week, nobody turned down a studio contract. I signed on the dotted line.

On August 19, 1942, the Hollywood trade papers announced the signing by Paramount of six young actresses. The terms were that at the end of seven years each of the salaries would be five hundred a week, but to reach that plateau was too farfetched to even contemplate. As it turned out, the other five girls did much less well than I, but the actress I envied the day I went before Superior Court Judge Emmett Wilson to receive minor's sanction was a Broadway transplant named Nancy Walker. Her starting salary was three hundred fifty a week.

I went directly into a picture after signing, but not at Paramount. They loaned me out to Monogram Studios for *Rhythm Parade*—through no coincidence whatsoever—to play a Florentine Gardens dancer. Granny had requested me for the role, in which I played support to the lead, Gale Storm. From this I went into Paramount's *The Crystal Ball,* where I served only as background. Only my left shoulder survived after editing.

After a few weeks it occurred to me that it would be no simple feat to survive at Paramount, and there was no question but that they expected their contractees to put in work. There were almost daily publicity sessions in the office of the PR chief, posing for cheesecake photographers. There were workouts in the gym under the care of Jim Davies and intensive acting and diction lessons under Bill Russell, head of the talent school. Then we were issued scripts of past Paramount films, from which we were given parts to perform. It was left to us to rehearse on our own, and when we were ready to show our skills we were scheduled for "the room." This frightening place was variously called the "Glass Cage," the "Snake Pit," and who knows what other pet names, but anyone who ever auditioned for Paramount remembers it. The room was intimidating to say the least. It was not large in dimensions, perhaps the size of a small radio studio, and its far wall was a window, behind which was total darkness. You never knew who was on the other side scrutinizing your every sneeze, wheeze, flub, or murmur. It could have been Bill Meiklejohn, the talent head, Cecil B., or who knows? I did many, many scenes there, often with young actors with dreams of making it big in Hollywood. I never saw one who wasn't a nervous wreck trying to perform under those conditions, and even though I was most often there just to throw cues, I was uncomfortable myself.

There were stars galore at Paramount, and it was exciting just being there with them. There were also a bevy of starlets such as Diana Lynn and Elena Verdugo who were chaperoned by ever-vigilant mothers. Fortunately, Marie never established this habit at Paramount, mainly because she felt I could take care of myself. Thank goodness. Another contractee was the shy and sensitive Gail Russell. I felt I had much in common with her, but she was much more vulnerable than I. She confided in hushed tones how she wished her mother, Gladys, had never dragged her to Paramount for her screen test. She despised acting and everything it entailed, especially being put on display before executives and film crews. I sympathized with her misery, but had no soothing words for her. My great concern was holding on to my contract, not getting out of it. There was an actress on the lot, however, who would show Gail how to cope, the good-natured but tough-talking starlet Helen Walker. She took Gail under her wing and introduced her to the tranquilizing benefits of vodka. Poor Gail was only thirty-six when she died in 1961, surrounded by empty liquor bottles.

My mainstay in entertaining servicemen was my tried and true rendition of "Babalu." I did it dozens of times, sometimes with N.T.G. and the Florentine Girls when we entertained at training camps or hospitals, and as part of the Paramount brigade, which was transported to outlying military installations to do shows. As one can easily imagine, I had no difficulty in meeting young men under these circumstances, and I dated several I had met in this way. My diaries chronicled some of the events of those days:

> January 1, 1943. Lt. Wehrer and I went to the Rose Bowl game in an Army car. Then we helped Marie move to 410 Norton . . . dined at Sardi's with five lieutenants . . . I was the only gal! Lt. Wehrer and I went to the fights, stayed til' ten, then went to Radio Room. After, went to Graciosa Drive [our former address] to rescue Mitzie my cat who was stranded. Chuck [Wehrer] then took me home and we made a date for next Saturday. Went to bed in new home.

For my entry of January 8, I mentioned getting a script from Bill Russell, and that later I bought a music box and a doll on Hollywood Boulevard in a shopping spree with Marie. At five-thirty that day I was picked up by my friendly lieutenant and taken to Melody Lane, where I had dinner with him and his Army Depot basketball team. I went with them to their game at the Shrine Auditorium and afterward had a later supper at Sardi's. I was elected the team's honorary captain.

A couple of days later I took the team onto the Paramount lot, where they met Cecil B. De Mille, Loretta Young, and Alan Ladd. Marie and I went to the movies that evening to see *The Moon and Sixpence.*

It was forbidden to make dates after performing at the Canteen and U.S.O., but most of us did it anyway. My pal Pat Starling and I quickly accumulated a sizable collection of pilot's wings and other military insignia, which were given us as remembrances when the men moved out. Some of them wrote letters; most didn't. I've often wondered who, among the many time-blurred faces, made it through the war, but—more poignantly—who did not.

My romances were limited pretty much to show-business figures. There was my big fling, for instance, with Red Skelton. I met Red at an industry gathering of some kind, and when he asked if we could go out together I agreed. A dinner date was set, and on the designated evening, when I was in the final stages of applying my makeup, the phone rang. It was Red.

"Yvonne," he said in anguished tones, "I hate to do this at the last minute, but I'm afraid we'd better cancel out for tonight. I've been thinking it over, and I don't think it's fair to Georgia."

"Okay, Red. Thanks for calling."

It was Georgia Davis he was referring to. He was only dating her then, but a year later they were married.

We shouldn't forget Rudy Vallee either, although in this case I wasn't stood up. We dated on several occasions, usually at the Coconut Grove in the Ambassador Hotel. Our relationship was noteworthy because I was given a rather expensive dress by this celebrity, who was known as much for his parsimony as for his talents. He said he wanted to further my career, and he left no doubt that he wanted to further our relationship, but I simply couldn't summon any enthusiasm. Whenever we met, he would ask me why our relationship never went any farther.

Chapter 11

Politics has always been of utmost importance in the movie business, but I couldn't quite get the hang of it. Or maybe it would be more accurate to say that I didn't *want* to get the hang of it. By "politics" I mean playing palsy with the studio brass, making yourself available, making sure they see you, and when they do making doubly sure you say all the right things.

I was having all this drummed into me at a lunch-hour confab with Barbara Britton and Noel Neill. They had been under contract at Paramount a little longer than I, knew the nuances of studio survival, and convinced me I should try, very much against my nature. It seemed there was no way on earth I would ever pop into an office and say, "Hi, I'm Yvonne De Carlo," but that's exactly what I ended up doing.

The way I handled it was to pretend I was playing a part. I would improvise the scene beforehand and hope that the actual encounter would play fairly close to my projection of it. Oh, there were times when a nasty growl would send me packing, but most often the producers and directors were warm and friendly and liked having pretty girls bother them. I somehow seemed to be most successful with the more powerful directors on the lot. Among those was Sam Wood, then directing *For Whom the Bell Tolls,* who always made me feel welcome on the set.

I recall watching Gary Cooper and Vera Zorina in a scene and a day later seeing another actress appear in her place. It was the new Swedish sensation Ingrid Bergman. I asked Sam what happened to Zorina. He said the short cropped hairstyle made her nose stand out too prominently. Bergman looked great. Since they were still making changes, I asked Sam Wood if there was a small bit in the picture for me. "No, Yvonne," he said, slapping the script in his lap. "I don't think Ernest Hemingway had you in mind when he wrote this novel."

"Maybe you and I could write something in," I said. "I know, we'll write a flashback where one of the characters sees his sweetheart's smiling face—me, of course—just before he's executed." He laughed and said he would think about it.

That was the kind of rapport I had with Sam Wood, and it paid off even on this picture—in a small way. He cast me as one of the cantina girls in a scene with Gary Cooper. This was what the political game was all about, and I was playing it.

On a few occasions, I took calculated risks. After my cantina girl scene Sam Wood asked if I would join him in visits to Gary Cooper's dressing room, and I did. In the scene, Gary entered the bar, gave a girl a swing-around hug, and en route to yet another girl at a table, stopped where I was sitting to give me a tweak on the chin. It was in long shot, and there was an exchange in pantomime, before he moved on. What he actually said was "You look like someone I'd like to see more of."

I smiled, which was in character for the scene. When Wood invited me to Cooper's dressing room, I assumed there had been some discussion between them and that Gary wanted to meet me. That didn't turn out to be the case, but I went anyway and was glad I did. Gary Cooper was warm and shyly charming, but he did have an eye for the gals.

The after-work gatherings took place in quite a few of the dressing rooms on "Dressing Room Row." Dottie Lamour was three doors down from Gary, and her laughter could be heard from behind her closed door. Her dressing room, by the way, was one of the most elegant on the lot. Joel McCrea was a couple of doors down from Dottie, and Ray Milland was just beyond that. Ray's door was always open, and Cooper's as well.

In Coop's (as they all called him) dressing room, you could expect to see his producer, his stand-in, his pal Sam Wood, and you could almost bet there would be at least two lovely girls there. Coop was an adorable flirt, and it was difficult for any woman to resist that boyish charm of his. Years later we rode together in the Parade of Stars at the Los Angeles Coliseum, and Patricia Neal showed up to protect her territory.

Along about this time, I did an audition with Sonny Tufts for the role of Tremartini in *The Story of Doctor Wassell.* I was told a bit later that De Mille liked the test, but when I met him he told me I had bony shoulders, which didn't seem appropriate for a native girl, and there was the problem of my blue-gray eyes. In the end, after days of anxiety, the role went to Carol Thurston.

Ray Milland came into my life at this point. On March 20, 1943, I went to a dance class at Ernest Belcher's, and then returned to join the gang at the studio commissary. "We finished lunch at quarter to two," says my diary. "I spoke to Pomeroy [my agent], and Ray and I walked to his dressing room. He told me he adored me and asked if I would go with him on a trip to Canada someday. He is going away for a couple of weeks. I kissed him goodbye. I really believe he's sincere."

The next day, says the diary, I was at the same lunch table with John Farrow, and Ray told me he was jealous. He must have known Farrow's reputation as a womanizer. That was the day before Ray left for his two-week trip to New York. When he returned he was apparently more fervent than ever, because our dating intensified greatly. By now he was becoming more practical in his out-of-town trip proposals: instead of Canada, it was Lake Arrowhead, only a few hours away. An entry toward the end of April reads: "I talked this over with Marie [the Arrowhead trip], and she wasn't very enthusiastic about my going. She is afraid that I'd be taken advantage of."

On May 31 my diary entry describes Ray taking Marie and me to see him in his Lux Radio Theatre performance of *The Major and the Minor* with Ginger Rogers. I said: "It was a very good show. Ray was swell."

I recall that Marie was not at all happy with my growing involvement with Ray Milland. For starters, he was too old for me by about twenty years, and the fact that he was married didn't enhance the idyll. He was assuring me that the marriage was over except for the final decree, and Marie thought he was feeding me a line. I guess I should have accepted her warning, because if there was anything on which Marie was an expert, it was lines. But I was no longer a little girl; I was a grown woman with a movie contract.

If I wasn't thinking about Ray during this period, I was otherwise agonizing over my career. The *Dr. Wassell* casting fiasco had me in a quandary for weeks. I first thought my chief competitor was Elena Verdugo, because she had dark eyes and her shoulders didn't seem bony. Then Simone Simon came on the scene. She had been tested for the part, and the jury was out for ages on that possibility. Then I heard a rumor that they had decided to dye Veronica Lake's hair black and give her the role, so when an unknown by the name of Carol Thurston got the part it was almost anticlimactic. That was how it went at Paramount. For every part there were a half-dozen girls, and none of us was ever cast in a role without going through all the silly competition—at least not at my level.

I'm not sure who was responsible for it, but I think somebody was being kind to me when I was loaned out for a featured role in a picture at Republic. The movie was a cheapie adaptation of the James Fenimore Cooper novel *The Deerslayer*.

Chapter 12

There have been several movie versions of *The Deerslayer* and this was probably the least memorable, but at the time I was thrilled to be in it. The leading roles were played by Bruce Kellogg and Jean Parker, and I played Wah-Tah, an Indian princess who was on the run throughout the story and made her final escape in a kayak. I had to be taught how to operate the tricky little boat, and although there was some danger involved, I loved it.

There were several pretty girls in the cast, and it was romantic on the moonlit evenings around Lake Elsinore. Since Bruce Kellogg was the leading man and the best looking among the actors, he was the object of all the girls' attention. I might have entered the bidding myself, except that my interests were diverted to a figure *behind* the scenes.

Here's the picture: I had met this tall, lean, rather mysterious gentleman on two previous occasions. The first time was at a party at Rudy Vallee's house, when I was still at the Florentine Gardens. He was introduced to me as Carl Anthony, and I was told that he was a big business entrepreneur with headquarters in Zurich, Switzerland. I found him very unassuming, soft-spoken, and gentlemanly. I asked some questions about his work, but he always turned the conversation back to me. When I told him I was Canadian, he smiled and said that he had lumber holdings in Canada and spent much of his time there. That gave us a kind of bond, perhaps, but from my point of view it was his soft gray eyes that impressed me, and the kind of distant look that occasionally came over his face, as though his mind was constantly traveling. During this encounter he told me that he was interested in movies and had invested in a few. With a smile he said that he might someday produce a movie and have me as the star.

I had more or less forgotten about him when I ran into him again a year or so later, this time at Lucey's Restaurant, a popular spot on Melrose between the Paramount and RKO studios. I had just started at Paramount then, and he said he was having a business lunch with some RKO people. This time he did ask me out, but he was due to leave town two days later and I was busy, so we didn't see each other.

More months passed, and I was really surprised to see him on the Elsinore location. He told me that he was with some of the production people, but didn't explain his interest, if any, in the production.

It was my third encounter with this intensely attractive mystery man, and when I finished shooting, no matter how tired I was, I could think only of seeing him. It was on our third evening together that everything seemed to reach a climax. We found a quaint little restaurant where we had a lovely dinner in front of an open fireplace, and on the drive back to the location Carl asked me to come with him to his rented cabin for a nightcap. That was what we did.

We had a drink, as I recall, but what I remember most vividly was the full moon that could be seen through the multipaned window. I also remember kisses, hundreds of them. I suppose it could be blamed on the moonlight, or the cozy cabin, or, if you want, you can blame it on my youth, but before much time passed I was very much aware of being seduced. And I liked it.

One button at a time, my blouse was opened; it was almost as if I were watching it in a movie. I felt the bra being unhooked, and that was just fine. Then, before I really took inventory of all the contributing moves, I found myself lost in a naked embrace with a man. It was so easy, so neat, and so natural—this thing called sex. I was finally doing the very thing I had been afraid to indulge in all these past years.

There was no self-recrimination afterward, and I didn't try to shift the blame to Carl Anthony. It wasn't that way at all. I was so fed up with my virginity that I was glad to be rid of it. I don't recall the act as being anything spectacular either, but it certainly served as a starting point and I had every confidence that with time and a more stable romance it would get better.

I guess for the sake of drama, my first love scene should have been played with Artie Shaw, Jimmy Stewart, or Sterling Hayden, but it didn't work out that way. My first sexual experience was with a handsome stranger in his early thirties known as Carl Anthony, and that was it. I had every hope my first experience would lead to much more than it did, but as it turned out he went away a week or so later. He wrote brief, loving letters from foreign ports, then one day they stopped coming. I was to see Carl years later in Paris when I was with Aly Khan, but the glow was long dead on my part.

If Marie noticed a change, she didn't say so, and I certainly didn't send out announcements, but from that point forward I found an added element in my appraisal of men. It wasn't so much a matter of dodging their advances anymore; it was more a matter of sizing them up. Not that I admitted it, even to myself, but I think I was already shopping for lover number two. It would not be Ray Milland.

So, what happened with him? Nothing, really. We passed our moment of truth and the infatuation trickled away to nothing. Ray was not exactly Mr. Sincere. He was then married, and he stayed that way.

After all the heartache and suspense with *The Story of Dr. Wassell,* Mr. De Mille tossed me a bone. He gave me the part of—you guessed it —a "native girl," even with the bony shoulders and the blue-gray eyes. I didn't complain, because I wanted to hold Mr. De Mille's respect. I was determined I would one day play a major role in a Cecil B. De Mille movie, and for that he had to like you.

Since the big parts weren't coming my way, I started to concentrate more heavily on my singing. One lunch break I went to the music department to see if I could borrow a piece of sheet music for one of my lessons. I was told I would have to get permission from Victor Young because this was his composition. When I returned the next day I met Victor personally, and I found him attractive. I think he was in his early forties, which was okay, but I also learned he was married, which wasn't. We had long conversations in which he was very instructive about my singing, and he seemed interested in my hopes and girlish dreams. I was honored by his attention and grateful for his help, but I could see where it was leading. As I have so often said, "Men, no matter what their promises, rarely leave their spouses—the louses." When I read that certain look in Victor's eyes, I hit the brakes. I wanted his friendship, and I certainly appreciated his professional counseling, but for once I used my head.

I mentioned that the political rounds had been beneficial to me, and they were. Sam Wood turned into a real friend, and I was on very friendly terms now with De Mille. Another face that was always smiling in my direction was director-screenwriter Billy Wilder's. Billy was just about the antithesis of my lifelong dream man. He was short, round-faced, and definitely not muscular, but he had endless charm and wit, and was consistently flattering. I fell, *kaplunk,* under his spell: he became my mentor, my studio guru, and I looked to him for advice almost on a daily basis.

It all began one morning when I was politicking along the corridors of executive row and said "Hi" to him. He was in conference with his new partner, Charles Brackett, and they both stopped to visit. The contrast in the collaborators fascinated me. Brackett was typical old-guard New York, conservative politically and mild mannered, and he hated the Southern California life-style. Austrian-born Billy was a liberal Democrat, raucous, witty, and very definitely on the earthy side. He and Southern California were made for each other. The team would turn out some extraordinary work, including *The Lost Weekend* and, a few years later, *Sunset Boulevard.* At this time they were coming off their first hit, *The Major and the Minor,* which starred my recent pal, Ray Milland. They did it all, producing, directing, writing, together and apart, and were two of the most important figures on the Paramount lot.

It's impossible to explain the attraction I felt for Billy, but it was there, and it grew steadily. He was separated from his wife, who lived in their home with their daughter, so Billy rented a smaller place in Beverly Hills where he could enjoy his second bachelorhood. It wasn't long before I would become lightheaded just thinking of "my Billy," and looking at his office window as I walked past it on the lot made my heart go pitty-pat. I may have had a girlish crush on Ray Milland, but Billy Wilder was the first big love of my life.

At the time of our closest relationship Billy was working on *Double Indemnity,* and I'm sure it was through his influence that I was called in to test for the part of Lola. It wasn't much of a test really, a zip-zip kind of thing, and nothing came of it. But at least I can refer to that instance where I was helped through someone I knew. There wouldn't be many such examples.

Billy was certainly a help to me in other ways, aligning me with a top talent agency and introducing me to a group of absolutely delightful people, among them Ernst Lubitsch, who would become one of my closest friends.

The relationship with Billy wasn't of lasting duration, even though I hoped it would be. It should have been obvious when I saw him walking arm in arm out the front gate with actress Doris Dowling. They had that certain glint in their eyes that jealous lovers always recognize. As they entered a small bar near the studio, my heart weighed seven tons. I started to wonder then if I would ever be content to accept relationships for what they were. I came up with no answers during this contemplative interlude, nor would I ever.

Since I had been discouraged by Mr. De Mille from aspiring to success in native-girl roles, I was surprised when I was sent to the portrait gallery to pose in sarongs. It was a long shooting session and special care was being taken. Something was up.

The story finally filtered down that Dorothy Lamour was tiring of her screen stereotype and was threatening to walk out. She had refused to play opposite Eddie Bracken in a saga called *Rainbow Island* because she wanted more meaningful roles. That was where I came in.

I was rushed into color tests for the role of Lola, the seductress of a lush South Seas atoll. I was seated on a rattan loveseat in my sarong, and the camera was aimed in my direction. Director Ralph Murphy yelled, "Roll 'em!" and my sensual instincts took over. I writhed and gyrated on back and tummy, and on both sides. My hands were laced beneath my chin, on my hips, or any other place that suggested sensuality. Finally, the director called, "Cut and print!" and I felt good about it. A couple of the crew members told me I had burned up the set, and there were even whistles of approval.

While I was doing my best to smoke everyone's spectacles, I was speculating on my assured stardom. I even saw headlines: "VANCOU-VER GIRL BECOMES SOUTH SEA MOVIE QUEEN." Thanks to the exercise sessions and massages by Jim Davies I was in tip-top shape, and I knew I was in better shape than Lamour. I really believed I had it made. I was set for the role, and only eight days stood between me and my big break. The schedule had me starting work on October 4, 1943.

I heard the news the next afternoon that there was a slight change of plans. Dottie Lamour had thought better of her walkout threat, and was back in the picture. But, not to worry, there would be a part for me in the picture. You guessed it, I was cast again as a handmaiden, and if you have very good eyesight you might just spot me on the TV late show in *Rainbow Island* as I am chased through the jungle by Gil Lamb. You will also see Elena Verdugo, Noel Neill, and Audrey Young. Audrey would later become Billy Wilder's second wife.

Paramount kept picking up my six-month options even though Lamour was back in her sarong and marching the company line. If I was still a Dorothy Lamour backup, it would seem that my services were diminishing in value. I continued to be cast in glorified extra roles, sneaking a swift smile or two as the cameras rolled, but there was another area in which I was constantly kept busy. I was always in the still department, striking cheesecake poses for the sex-starved G.I.s. I dressed in everything from tiny swimsuits to Santa Claus costumes. Once I was a living Valentine. I was named "Sweetheart of the U.S. Mechanized Forces," "The Girl G.I.s in Italy Would Most Like to Read a Map With," and on and on. Photos of me were sent all over the world, and the response from the servicemen was exuberant. That may just have held my job for me over some of the long months of war.

I was still studying French, and I never failed to keep my twice-a-week date with the lads at the Hollywood Canteen, and I continued to do camp shows around Southern California. I was having fun doing all this, but my career was going nowhere. Whenever possible I continued to perform in rodeos with N.T.G., and I loved being included in the Roy Rogers Rodeo at the Los Angeles Coliseum in July of 1944. Betty Hutton was the rodeo queen, Dale Evans was there, of course, and so were Wild Bill Elliott and Gabby Hayes. I rode a beautiful white horse named Wyoming. It was an exciting day. In another rodeo the same year, I was thrown from my horse and had the wind knocked out of me. A hush swept through the stands, and when I finally got to my feet a surging cheer arose from the crowd. It was a fantastic thrill, but not so good for my sensitive back. I threw a hip out of kilter, which severely compounded my chronic neck pains.

Marie moved to New Haven, Connecticut, in mid-1944, but we kept in touch. I also maintained close contact with my grandmother and Aunt Connie in Vancouver. By this time Connie had divorced her husband, and Cousin Kenny was now a member of the Royal Canadian Air Force. My family was very proud of me, even though they had as much trouble as I in spotting my image on the Paramount screens. It was at about this juncture in my "non-career" that Billy Wilder lined me up with a new agent. The relationship had cooled down, but luckily for me we remained close friends.

Billy may have had some intuition regarding my future at Paramount, or he may have had some hard information I hadn't been told about. He suggested that I meet with his good friend and associate Paul Kohner, one of the more prestigious agents in Hollywood, Billy set up the appointment, and I appeared at the offices at the west end of the Sunset Strip.

It was late afternoon, and Kohner was busy with phone calls, as are all agents at that time of day, but he was cordial as we visited between calls. Kohner leaned across his desk, studying me. "Why do you do that with your mouth?"

"Do what?" Was my lipstick smeared?

"It looks like you're biting the inside of your lip."

Oh, boy—now I was nervous.

"What do you think your talent is?" he asked, and that was only the beginning. He asked questions about every facet of my life and show-business background, my attitudes and my ambitions. When he exhausted his marathon of inquiry, he issued a faint smile. "We'll see what can be done."

That was my cue to leave, and I was sure I was expected to walk out and keep walking. I held no hope whatever that anything would come of this, but surprisingly I was called a few days later and was told that the firm would represent me, and that my personal agent would be Jack Fife. My spirits lifted.

But spirits go up and down, don't they? They plunged a few days later when I was called into the Paramount personnel office. I was casually informed that word had come down that my option had been dropped. In more specific terms it meant I was fired. I was told that Paramount was planning ahead to the postwar era, and they were cutting back on production. I was also told that they believed exotic types were now passé.

Goodbye, and good luck.

Chapter 13

"Have you ever played a wolf girl?"

How's that for an opener? If asked if I had ever played a native girl I could have filled some space, but a wolf girl? The interview was with Bob Speers, the head of casting at Universal, and I had to admit that no, I had not played a wolf girl. But I could learn!

My new agent and I had already been to MGM and Warners. At MGM we were given the welcome of a needy relative; at Warner Brothers, I felt lucky we weren't thrown out on the pavement. So to come to Universal and be treated humanely was something.

Universal still liked the exotic types of which Paramount had washed their hands. They had Maria Montez, who was really big then, and they were grooming a girl named Acquanetta, who was more than likely Maria Montez's backup. But Acquanetta had appeared in enough jungle programmers to want better things for herself, so what Universal was probably looking for was a backup to the backup, which would have been fine with me. I guess it was decided that they would chance it with me despite my lack of wolf-girl experience, because they called me back for a test. I was wedged into a tiger-skin costume that was sawed off raggedly at mid-thigh, my hair was teased into a frizzy mass, and with mascara dabbed on my face to accent my "mysterious contours," I was ready for action. It was obvious I was getting the full treatment: everything short of a ring in my nose.

I learned my lines and was introduced to Milburn Stone, who would work with me in the scene and was to become well known several years later as Doc Adams in "Gunsmoke." The script was so bad that even I knew it. Before this, I always assumed a script couldn't be all bad if businessmen were willing to spend a fortune to make a movie out of it. But I was learning.

As it turned out, I would never see myself in this test and would never hear another word about it. I did, however, show up at Speers's office on the appointed day, and as I was sitting in the casting office, a well-dressed, distinguished-looking man passed me on the way to the reception desk. He glanced in my direction and did a double take. The man was admitted to Speers's office, and I waited some more. Finally, the man came out, and it was my turn to see Bob Speers.

"That was Walter Wanger," said Speers, "the big producer. He says he's intrigued by your face, by your look." I learned that Wanger had first been struck by my resemblance to his wife, Joan Bennett, and then it occurred to him that I might be right for the lead in his forthcoming production, *Salome, Where She Danced.* I learned that Wanger had already launched a nationwide campaign to find the perfect girl for the title role. He wanted someone who danced like Zorina, acted like Ingrid Bergman, and sang like Deanna Durbin.

"I can handle that," I said, modestly.

"You dance?"

For a fleeting moment, I wished Marie had been with me. What an answer she'd have given to a question like that. I gave him my background as a dancer, and he was impressed. I told him about all the singing training, and he was overjoyed. I could have told him that he could judge my acting by the test I had just done, but I thought better of it. Speers then said that Walter Wanger had asked that I test for Salome, now, this very day.

That afternoon I was on the Universal soundstage again. The test director sauntered over and said, "Listen, kid, let's do this fast, okay?" Someone slapped makeup on my face, I wriggled into a tattered harem costume, and the cameras rolled. I posed this way; I posed that way; I walked to the camera and away. "Cut!" That was it. It was late, and they wanted to get home or make a stop at the corner watering hole . . . but hey, fellas, this is my big chance! I changed into my street clothes and left.

Once more, I felt as though the parade had passed me by—but the call came. I was asked back to the studio, and the change was incredible. Everyone was treating me deferentially now. Then I learned that Mr. Wanger had personally asked to meet me. Suddenly, I was somebody —for a moment, at least.

We talked in his office for longer than an hour, and he was thoroughly gracious and charming. He explained the concept for the Technicolor feature, and his eagerness to introduce a new and exciting screen personality in the lead. The unknown girl that he finally selected would be billed as "The Most Beautiful Girl in the World." When he said that I started to wonder what part he had in mind for me, but then I remembered that Speers said Wanger was thinking of me for the lead . . . Salome . . . the most beautiful girl in the world? Me?

Wanger ordered a second test and the circumstances were considerably superior to those of the first test. They assigned veteran cinematographer Hal Mohr, and the rest of the technical people were the best available at the studio. My costume was new and specially designed and tailored for me. The wardrobe people fretted over the fittings as though I were Scarlett in *Gone With the Wind.* There were two costumes, actually. One was a burgundy period travel costume with matching bonnet; the other, designed to show off Salome's figure, was a sheer, white beaded chiffon harem-style outfit. Care was taken to make the test as perfect as possible, and with the crew's professional attitude it was a breeze—just "Turn right, Miss De Carlo, now left, now straight on," etc. I was not asked to emote at all; this was purely a photographic test.

Time is relative, of course, and I have a feeling that the people at Universal thought they were breaking all records in getting back to me within a week, but to me those days were like a dozen eternities. I had had so many disappointments over the last few weeks, that I was rehearsing the crawl that would take me back once again to Granny at the Florentine Gardens. I was alone, as Marie was with our relatives in New Haven, and I had no other than Granny to turn to. Then I got the call.

The call was not to tell me that I did or didn't have the part of Salome but to bring me in for a discussion. I went in without delay and learned that Wanger had not made his decision. Despite that, Universal was willing to sign me to a stock contract just so I'd remain available. Well, that was something at least. I would have further tests, and I could brush up on my dancing in a rigorous training program. Let's face it —I signed. The hundred and fifty a week seemed like a fortune to me.

I needed a new place to live, and since I'd be working at Universal,

I started looking in the Valley. I finally settled for a broom closet in a rundown motor court directly across from the studio, with a single bed, a hot plate, and a tiny refrigerator. Each night I would limp home from dance training, make myself a simple meal, and listen to "The Gas Company Hour" on the radio until I fell asleep.

On the morning of September 18, 1944, I got up early with plans to take a walk before reporting to the studio. As I started out the door I stumbled over a stack of newspapers. I had no idea where they had come from, and seeing them there puzzled me. The paper on top was the Los Angeles *Daily News*. I picked it up and read the headline: ALLIES CROSS THE RHINE. I glanced further down and saw the caption: CONTEST WINNER. Then I saw the subhead: MOST BEAUTIFUL GIRL IN THE WORLD SAYS WALTER WANGER OF UNIVERSAL. I didn't dare breathe with the suspense.

I finally came to the small article and the words that said, "She'll star in *Salome, Where She Danced*. The name's Yvonne De Carlo, incidentally."

With my heart pounding furiously, I sat on the stoop and scanned the other newspapers; although the wording differed, the message was the same. I, the little girl from Vancouver, had won the part. I, if you can believe it, was then and there "The Most Beautiful Girl in the World"! That premonitory flash I received those years before as I walked up Hill Street was finally proving true. It had been the idea of the Universal Publicity Department to plant the newspapers on my stoop. They thought it would be a nice surprise—and indeed it was.

After several days, the initial excitement toned down a bit, and I began to wonder how long the Universal people had known I would play Salome. It occurred to me—cynic that I had become—that the studio sewed me up in a low-salaried stock contract, knowing that my price would be substantially higher if I learned I was to be "The Most . . . (you know) . . ." If I thought I was that, I would probably also like to be "The Most Highly Paid Girl in the World." I never learned the machinations behind all of that, but I never really worried about it either. I had finally got a break, and I never really expected Hollywood moguls to act out of the kindness of their hearts.

I had been previously considered for the picture about the wolf girl, and also for an island-type picture. Both assignments went to Acquanetta. As I think of it, her name didn't exactly become a household word. I say this only to illustrate how the fates take command in Hollywood. By accident, I got into bigger and better things. Suppose

Acquanetta had gotten the Salome role. I think both our lives would have followed slightly different trails.

When the congratulations started pouring in, you might guess on which cloud number I was riding. The newspapers in Vancouver gave the story big play, and I was selfishly wondering what the folks back home were now thinking of shy little Peggy. I would have given anything to fly up there and bask in my glory. I heard from my grandmother and Aunt Connie right away, and once the news reached New Haven, Marie made reservations on the next plane to Los Angeles. It seemed that Connecticut didn't promise more than L.A., after all.

I soon learned that Walter Wanger was a wizard at promotion. He had a campaign all planned, with news items to be released strategically and systematically to assure the success of his million-dollar-plus production. One of his stunts was to "leak" to the press that I had been brought to his attention by a Royal Canadian Air Force bombardier trainee in Saskatoon who sent in photos of me. It was not, however, leaked that the mysterious bombardier was also my cousin Kenny. That was just one among countless publicity "dream-ups" that were published.

During one of our encounters, Walter offered sage advice. "Yvonne," he said, "don't take this most beautiful girl stuff too seriously, right? You can't believe everything you read in the newspapers."

I knew what he was saying, of course, and I didn't think there would be any problems in this area, but the impact of the message hit me a couple of weeks later when Granny took me to a party at Rudy Vallee's home. It was a rather big affair with many important people attending, and although I would never have admitted it to a soul I anticipated some attention. A minor commotion and some "Oos" and "Ahs" upon my entrance wouldn't be too much to expect, would it?

I mingled with the guests, assuming everyone knew who I was and imagining that some were happy for me and others envious. They might not fawn, but I certainly expected at least several to comment about my new role or offer congratulations.

Not one word.

I listened more attentively the next time Wanger lectured me, and the occasion came only a week or so later. "You know, Yvonne," he said to me, "you and I are being fed into the studio rumor mill."

"Rumors . . . you and I?"

"The word is that you and I are having a big affair." He laughed. "And we aren't even getting any of the fun out of it."

I was astonished. "Why would anyone think that?"

"No reason is needed. That's simply how it is, and you may as well get used to it. When you're a star, people will talk about you. Gossip is a major commodity in Hollywood." I thought about this a lot afterward. Walter Wanger had never so much as touched me, and yet people were talking about us. When I thought of all my girlish escapades at Paramount, I would have been the talk of the town—if I had been a star.

I'm sure that I have never worked harder in my entire career than I did during the two months of filming *Salome.* My single goal was to prove myself. It would have been no different if I were earning a million dollars for the film; I couldn't have worked harder.

The story line of the film had something for everybody: blend the American Civil War with the Austro-Prussian battlefront in Europe; throw in some bandits in old Arizona; then mix all of it together with the San Francisco Gold Coast for a finale. My song-and-dance menu included an intricate classical ballet number, three songs, and an interpretive version of Salome's famous dance. Also, with no plot justification whatsoever, I did an Oriental routine on a Chinese junk. This dance initiated a procession of scenes in later movies where I'd make my entrance through sparkling, beaded curtains. It seemed I would be forever fighting my way through those damnable bead strands. Later, they would be referred to in the industry as "Yvonne De Carlo Curtains." To cap off the Salome assignment, I had many hard horseback-riding scenes, and love scenes with four different men, and I had to dress in a dozen circa 1860 costumes.

I was so serious about everything, I failed to grasp the satire in the script. It was all right, because satire is best played with serious intent, but I took the tongue-in-cheek dialogue for the straight stuff. Here's a sample:

CLOSE-UP OVER SALOME'S SHOULDER—FEATURING NEWSPAPER

Salome

It's a very bad likeness of me.
Are my shoulders made of iron?

Jim

No, ma'am, I'd say they were
made of sugar and butter.

CLOSE-UP—SALOME

Salome

Which will never be at Count Bismarck's feast.

I soon learned the difference between pleasure riding in blue jeans and riding before cameras in the flimsy costumes dreamed up by the wardrobe department. Since I hadn't reached "valuable property" status, the studio didn't mind letting me do my own riding. The danger came in because most of my co-players were not skilled riders.

In my opening ballet number I was to emerge gracefully from a large, jeweled clamshell, but after the weeks of pounding my toes and ankles in tough rehearsals, I couldn't get on point without terrific pain. Easy to fix—the doctor injected my toes with novocaine. So I did all the dancing on numb toes and was unable to walk comfortably for weeks.

The big day arrived for the shooting of Salome's main dance number. The set was an antique theater in an old Arizona town. Decked out in the highly publicized gold net skirt and jeweled bra, I wasn't surprised in the least by the stares of the crew. It didn't take long to notice that there were other stares, not nearly so admiring, and it turned out they were censors from the Hays Office. They were on the job to make sure no cleavage showed and that my navel was modestly covered. The "Belly-Button Brigade," as they were sometimes called, took every possible measure to protect the innocent public against the world of sin and sex. We couldn't continue with the big dance until my cleavage was more modestly covered.

The scenes were stacking up in the film cans, and all was going well. Then one day on the soundstage I heard a playback of "The Beautiful Blue Danube," which I had prerecorded. There was only one thing wrong: I wasn't listening to *my* voice. After the initial shock, the tears came first in a trickle, and then in a gusher, ruining my makeup. I was supposed to lip-sync the words to the song, but it was impossible. I ran to my dressing room, where Walter Wanger soon paid me a visit. He apologized for dubbing my voice but explained that the music department had said there were notes that I failed to sustain properly.

I would eventually pull myself together and do the scene, but my heart was broken. Singing was too important, and I also thought it had been a shabby trick to slip in the other singer without any warning. Once more, I was learning the ways of Hollywood. Nobody wanted to tell me face to face that my voice had been dubbed, so they let me hear it for myself on the set. So—it was not my voice in *Salome,* but it would be the only time my voice was dubbed in a film.

As Marie was back, while I worked she went out apartment hunting, but without much luck. I was called in to see Stacy Keach, the father of the actor Stacy Keach Jr. He was the studio drama coach at the time. Word had gotten out that their new young star was living in a sleazy motor court and the studio didn't think that was very good publicity. Keach thought a moment, made a call, and found us a nice little house on Laurel Canyon Drive that was well within our means.

After Marie and I moved in, we soon discovered that our next-door neighbor was another Universal player, Susanna Foster. She and I became friends, and as I got to know her I realized I had found someone who hated movie work even more than Gail Russell. Susanna was not happy with Hollywood or picture making, and would prove her point a year later when she walked away from it forever. I have heard over the years that Susanna Foster had one of the finest vocal instruments ever to hit Hollywood, but if you don't like the work, you don't like it. Thank God, I did.

Chapter 14

Walter Wanger turned into a kind of surrogate father. He was consistently kind and understanding, and seemed always to have my best interests in mind, once saying, "You have talent, Yvonne, you'll never have to cozy up to a producer to get ahead." I appreciated the compliment, and the advice, but I didn't have to be told not to sleep with producers. He also promised work in his subsequent productions, but that would never come to pass. I think he may have been too wrapped up at the time with Susan Hayward, whom he had under personal contract. And never once did he invite me to one of the many social events that he and Joan Bennett hosted. There must have been a good reason, but I've always wondered what it might be.

There were a few men in my life; at least I did some dating. Milburn Stone, with whom I had tested for the wolf girl part, and I went out several times. One afternoon he drove me to the hills of the beautiful western San Fernando Valley. We parked on a hill and he pointed out a piece of land he had recently purchased. He asked me if I had ever thought about settling down on a small ranch with a devoted husband. Whoops! We dated very little after that. I don't know why the thought of marriage sent me into such a tizzy, but I just couldn't handle it. Later on, each of the four times I was engaged—to Jocko Mahoney, Cornel Lucas, Robert Urquhart, and Howard Duff—I would look at the ring on my finger and feel trapped.

At a war bond rally I met a very charming chap named Klaus Landsberg. He wasn't my image of male perfection but I liked him as a person and we went out together frequently. He was pioneering in a new medium called television, and we spent hours sharing his dream about the future potential of his brainchild.

Atop Mount Wilson, where his station had its antenna, he painstakingly explained the technology behind the miracle and predicted the day would come when there would be a television set in every home. I listened, fascinated, and accepted his daydream, asking dozens of questions. On one occasion he chose to confess that he had fallen in love and asked if I shared these feelings. Unfortunately, I had to tell the truth. Why on earth couldn't I have loved him? If I had, I could have been Mrs. KTLA, Channel 5 of Hollywood, all these years!

Rod Cameron was my leading man in *Salome,* and he was a fellow Canuck—from Calgary. The studio thought it could get some publicity mileage out of teaming us up, and we went out gladly to studio and industry functions but that was it. As it turned out, six-foot-four Rod and my friend Pat Starling became something of an item, and we sometimes double dated. We once went on a group trail ride, which led Pat and Rod to a romantic niche in the hills. They lost the rest of us successfully, but they didn't choose the best love nest in the world. In a few days they both broke out with miserable cases of poison oak. At other times, Pat, Rod, June Vincent, Edmond O'Brien, and I would go out to nightclubs to give the columnists something to wag about.

Another date set up by Universal was with Turhan Bey, that charming, goodnatured Viennese actor. His Middle Eastern screen image had American girls' hearts throbbing, and he dated just about every glamour girl in Hollywood despite the fact that he lived in Beverly Hills with his mother and grandmother. On more than one occasion he and Lana Turner showed up together for his early makeup call. I remember that dreamy look of contentment on the face of the glamorous blonde —even at six-thirty in the morning. Turhan and I became close friends, even after his return to Vienna, but we were never lovers.

There were also times when the studio paired me off with actors from other studios: Helmut Dantine for example, best known for his portrayals of Nazis in Warner Brothers films. We played the game but it was Ida Lupino he was interested in at the time, not me.

I shouldn't leave out my single date with Rory Calhoun, which was also planned by the studio. There was Rory, his agent Henry Wilson (known for the names with which he used to adorn his male clients: Rock, Tab, Rory, etc.), Marguerite Chapman, and me. Ostensibly I was paired with Rory but it didn't turn out that way. After the photographers stopped snapping pictures, Rory and Henry stood huddled deep in conversation. Marguerite and I weren't even tossed a dangling participle to chew on.

After a while, I said to Marguerite, "Can you tell me what the hell is going on?"

"Don't look now, Yvonne," she kidded, "but I think I'm your date tonight."

I think of that one night out at the Mocambo with Rory Calhoun as one of the least satisfactory dates I ever had. But it was good for a laugh.

Other "musts" imposed by the studio were command interviews for members of the press. There was the press, and then there was Louella Parsons and Hedda Hopper, who comprised an institution of their very own. If there was one thing the studio did *not* want, it was for their contractees to make a negative impression on either of these two. I don't know if their broadside attack would destroy an established star's career, but there was no question that they could make or break a rising star. I think I was lucky.

When I first met Louella, I felt like a fool because of the way the studio had me presented to her. It was one of those hot autumn afternoons in Southern California that could have been the hottest day of the year almost anywhere else. The studio dressed me to the nines, and to establish my full "star" status they bundled me up in a massive full-length mink coat. I was chauffered to Louella's Maple Drive home in Beverly Hills in a rented limousine. I had never felt so ludicrous, and I was honestly afraid that Louella would double over when she caught sight of me. I needn't have worried. Miss Parsons—as I was coached to address her—was as sweet as she could possibly be, and she apparently accepted my costume as standard issue for potential glamour queens. The article she wrote was glowing, and I still have it. It said that I confided to her that "Walter Wanger chose me for Salome, because he knew that I had suffered and lived. . . ." Deeper into the article: "I shall be anxious to see if this girl lives up to Walter Wanger's expectations, and if *Salome, Where She Danced* will do for her what *Algiers* did for Hedy Lamarr and *Arabian Nights* did for Maria Montez."

A few weeks later, a studio chauffered limo drove me to Tropical Drive in Beverly Hills, where I survived a similar confrontation with the other gossip magnate, Hedda Hopper. The interview played well, but she was different from Louella, direct and to the point—no nonsense or small talk. She treated me as well as Louella had, so I was already two-out-of-two. I also had interviews with Sheilah Graham, Harrison Carrol, Jimmy Fidler, and all the others from Hollywood and everywhere.

I became close to Harrison Carrol but that was a mistake, because when I married years later I took the advice of the publicity people and gave the exclusive item to Hedda Hopper. Carrol never forgave me. One has to walk a tightrope when dealing with the big columnists. For the most part, however, I did very well. If I wanted something printed I had only to make a phone call, and presto! it was in the papers.

While the studio pondered what to do next with their new property, the "property" went back to the old regimen of dance, exercise, dance, singing, dance, and—my God!—even piano. I found time for some riding with Granny and Pat Starling, performed in a rodeo or two, and of course kept doing the camp shows and other service-oriented functions.

The movie was yet to be released, but massive publicity gave me my first taste of public recognition. It was a curious sensation. People would look, pause, chuckle among themselves, and then move cautiously forward for an autograph. At first I wondered if I had a run in my nylons, or if my slip was showing. I soon developed a sense that easily distinguished between celebrity recognition and the simple irregularities that otherwise attract attention. As for the loss of privacy, it took quite a while to get used to that.

What soon became apparent was that I was no longer free to behave as I pleased; with my anonymity went my freedom of choice. Universal had invested in me and they expected me to conform to their design —hair, makeup, dress, etc. I was firmly warned that never, *never*, should I walk on the lot improperly dressed. Apparently they had been appalled by my habit of showing up at the rehearsal halls wearing jeans. "Remember," I was told, "you are going to be a big star. Even if you go to a market you must dress like a star." It was always Joan Crawford's name that was brought up. "Act like Joan Crawford . . . you would never see Joan Crawford doing something like that . . . try to imagine you are Joan Crawford." I didn't question their esteem for her, but I sure as hell was not Joan Crawford.

The more I thought about their heavy-handedness the more it got to me, so in a fit of confusion and obstinacy I formed a plan. When I reported one morning for a photo session of "Yvonne De Carlo in a Dance Workout" I was wearing a filmy luncheon dress, white gloves, and a hat with a net. The publicity woman didn't think it was funny and sent me to wardrobe for white slacks and a sweater.

In the spring of 1945, *Salome* was previewed to the press and the reaction was more favorable than anyone had dared hope. *Variety* said, "Miss De Carlo, a looker with lots of talent, should go far with more experience and the buildup which Universal is currently giving her."

Time magazine: ". . . as a woman, especially in her Salome number, brings the house down." Dorothy Manners in the Los Angeles *Examiner* said the movie "marks the debut of a grand honey named Yvonne De Carlo who casts the most torrid shadow in Technicolor of any personality in years. Not only is she completely equipped to inspire wolf whistles, but she is something new in the line of potential stars. Fortunately, she reminds one of no other screen personality." As you might imagine, I was flattered, especially by the last point made by Dorothy Manners.

So I was happy, Universal was happy, Walter Wanger was happy. *Salome, Where She Danced* became one of Hollywood's biggest hits of 1945. Likenesses of me were on the covers of *Pic* and *Look,* and stories were featured in many other national magazines. It seemed as though Peggy Middleton had found her niche. I was already settled into a suite at the Sherry Netherland by the time *Salome* premiered in New York, a kid away from home for the first time. I rattled around in my tastefully decorated rooms, ordering whatever I wanted from room service—not quite like being home and running to the fridge. I finally wangled a few days off from the publicity assignments so that I could meet some of the De Carlo clan in New Haven. Charles Simonelli, the New York publicity representative of Universal, came with me. Every branch of the Sicilian De Carlos welcomed me warmly, and as was their custom they stuffed Charley and me with pasta. To avoid hurting anyone's feelings, we consumed three full-course Italian meals within one day.

Then, thankfully, it was back, expanded waistline and all, to endless radio, magazine, and newspaper interviews. There was a special stunt dreamed up by Simonelli. For my interview with the *New York Times* I wore a conservative black skirt with white blouse, and, as coached, behaved very demurely as the questions were being asked. Then, on cue, someone put a record of *Salome* on the phonograph, and upon hearing it I rose and let my pinned-up hair fall in a sexy cascade over my shoulders. I broke into a slinky, sexy dance around the room to the musical beat. The interviewer took it all in stride, thanked me, and went home, and not a word of my behavior was included in his article. I guess he knew when he was being had by Hollywood.

The next day I was taken to one of New York's most famous restaurants for an interview with Walter Winchell. He was very easy to talk with, and we were having a really good time. Then I said it: "I'm so excited to be here—but where are the zebra stripes?" He laughed heartily, and I could feel my cheeks burning in embarrassment. What could I possibly have said?

"Yvonne," he said. "You're seated in the sacred confines of Club

'21.' What you're talking about is El Morocco—quite a different place." This started a warm friendship and we would go out together dozens of times throughout the years but somehow never to the "different" place with the zebra stripes.

I hoped the lectures had been left in Hollywood, but no such luck. Maurice Bergman, Universal's East Coast boss, plunked me down in his office to recite his version of how a Universal star should behave. His treatise led to the John Robert Powers modeling organization, where the lady in charge asked hundreds of questions and gave me an oral rundown on what the school was going to make of me. I was assigned a humorless female subordinate who stuck to me like glue, and after no more than an hour, I longed for sweet solitude. I hadn't known how good I'd had it alone in the hotel.

"The first thing we must do is correct your posture," she dictated, "especially your walk. Your mind wants you to get places faster than your body can do it. As a result, your head and neck are always thrust forward like a turkey in a farmyard." That was only the beginning. I was also told how to walk, talk, stand, sit, eat, and drink. When I was left alone in the ladies' room I wondered if I should call out for instructions. I soon reached the point where I didn't know who I was, or if I should even admit it if asked. It was awful.

Next, we went shopping—a kind of test run to see if I had absorbed any of this. En route, my shadow informed me how to step down from a curb. Soon I was gliding along as if in suspended animation, not daring to allow my soles and heels to touch the pavement too firmly. In shopping, my tastes led me to the racks that held the happy colors. I was grasped firmly and led to those filled with black. What I ended up with was a black broadtail coat, a black cocktail dress, imitation pearls, a black porkpie hat, and black pumps. I left the shop feeling like an undertaker.

Next stop, the hairdressing salon. Here I was privileged to receive what the stylist referred to as the "VIP do." What this developed into was a teased—I mean teased—beehive mass that stood on my head like a square-rigged sail. There was no way to comb this work of art—so it stayed that way for a good week. Did I complain? No, but I have never gone to an unknown "chic" hair salon since.

It was a company secret, but all this training was to be capped by a coming-out of sorts in the New York social scene. "Make an entrance," I was coached. "Think important—pause in the doorway with one arm lifted and the other gracefully resting on the doorjamb. Then you see somebody across the room. 'Dahling,' you say, and sweep toward them."

"What if I don't see anyone I know?"

"Never fear, our publicity people will be there."

The time finally arrived for me to break in my act; they somehow got me an invitation to a classy Gotham cocktail party. I made my entrance —all in black with the usual string of pearls, of course—and paused in the doorway as instructed. I gave the room a quick scan for the press agent and thought I spotted him across the way. "Dahling!" I called out and did my short-stepped slink across the room, making sure, of course, that my head wasn't pecking forward like a turkey. When I reached the man I realized, in my nearsightedness, that I had never seen him before. So I just kept slinking out the nearest door. I hoped the door would lead to the powder room, or even the kitchen, but I wasn't so lucky. Where I ended up was in a clothes closet. I paused there in the darkness, giving my heart a chance to recover, and burst back into the action. Fortunately, when I emerged from my dark tomb, I found the press agent waiting for me, the only one who had noticed my faux pas.

Universal was spending a lot of money on this grooming program, so naturally they wanted results. I was invited to join my formidable boss in the East, Mr. Bergman, for dinner at Club "21." This time I wouldn't complain about the missing zebra stripes, but I had more than that to worry about. I had been given a crash course in table manners in preparation for this quasi-graduation, so I knew Bergman would be watching my pinky, my small bites, my napkin dabs, with the scrutiny of a pawnbroker examining a piece of questionable jewelry.

I had been taught by the people at John Robert Powers how to sit, how to choose the right piece of silverware at the right time, how to hold a wine glass ("Don't forget the pinky"), everything—including the proper way to eat soup: the spoon goes into the bowl gently, with the sweep of the spoon going outward. Then, without leaning over the bowl, the spoon is brought to the lips. One never makes a sound, of course.

The meeting with Bergman was cordial and I almost relaxed as we chatted over a cocktail, until it came time to order. I had already planned to avoid soup at any cost, but it wasn't that easy. "If you will allow me, Yvonne," he said, "I will take the liberty of ordering for you."

"Oh, how thoughtful of you." (What I was thinking was, I don't need anyone to order for me, you ostentatious bore.)

Needless to say, the order included soup. What did I care if the chicken had been marinated twelve hours in wine and herbs? What did I care about wild rice and mushrooms? All I could think of was the damned cream of leek soup. I tried, Lord how I tried, but every time

I got the spoon to within three inches of my mouth my hand started to shake, sending drops all over the tablecloth. I finally faked it by sipping a couple of quarter-spoonfuls. Then I placed the spoon on the plate beneath the soup bowl, making very sure it was angled perfectly along the right side. It was a long time before I could eat soup without my hand shaking, and I never again ordered it in a fancy restaurant.

My grooming sessions were held concurrently with all the interviews and theater appearances for *Salome.* On April 12, we went to Washington, D.C., for the usual radio and theater appearances, but there was more. I was going to be presented to Mrs. Eleanor Roosevelt in a reception at the Sulgrave Club. I was thrilled because the Roosevelts were my idols, especially Eleanor with her courage and activism. I was nervous, but I needn't have been. The moment we were introduced she made me feel as though I had known her all my life. She was easily one of the most gracious and charming ladies I had ever met, and she had me believing it when she said she would look forward to our next meeting.

I was glowing by the time we held our press conference at the hotel a couple of hours later. Fifteen journalists were present, asking all the stock questions: "How does it feel to be the most beautiful girl in the world?" "Who are the men in your life?" "What will be your next picture? . . . When?" It went on that way for about thirty minutes, and I knew I was handling all the questions well, with just enough subtle humor. I was having a terrific day.

Then something strange began to happen. A reporter got up and left the room, then another. I was giving a response to a question, when, amid whispers and nods, all the remaining reporters rose and began their silent exodus from the conference room. I turned to Charley Simonelli in bewilderment. "Did I say something?" I pleaded. "Did I do something wrong?"

"I don't know," he said. "I'll see if I can find out."

When he returned a minute or two later, his face was ashen. "It's the President," he said solemnly. "President Roosevelt is dead."

We sat in the deserted conference room for a long time, quietly weeping. Later, on the way back to the hotel, we passed the White House, where hundreds of people were standing with bowed heads. We got out of our taxi and joined them.

Chapter 15

Five fast and eventful years had passed since the Miss Venice Contest, and since I had left Vancouver. I returned to Canada for the first time since my deportation with the Eighth Victory Loan Campaign, one among many Hollywood personalities who were invited to help raise funds in a show at Massey Hall in Toronto. We broke all records there and went on to Montreal, where I was treated as returning royalty. The governor asked me to say a few words and, if possible, to sing a song.

At least a thousand people filled the hall, most of them from the Air Force. When I entered the audience arose in a body, and I was so overwhelmed that I tripped over my own feet on the way to the podium. With the audience once more seated, I gave a little speech and then, with the backing of a huge symphony orchestra, I sang in French "J'attendrai." As the audience cheered, I was one happy young woman and proud Canadian.

I was looking forward to our next stop, which was to be Vancouver, but after the Montreal concert there was a telegram awaiting me at the hotel instructing me to report back to Hollywood at once to begin work on my movie *Frontier Gal.*

I got the part because Maria Montez refused to do it. Although I had seen her on the lot a few times, I had never met her, and did not go out of my way to do so now. She had the reputation of being a "hellcat" and a "human buzz saw," and I wondered if one day she would accost me on the set with bared claws. Her reasons for turning down the part were that she didn't want Rod Cameron or Jon Hall as her leading man, and that she didn't like the idea of playing mother to a young girl who might very likely upstage her. The studio knew I would play opposite Rin Tin Tin if they told me to, and would gladly agree to be the mother of the Seven Dwarfs.

But I soon proved that I wasn't quite as docile as I may have seemed. My conflict was with the highly coveted dress designer Travis Banton, who was at Universal as a special consultant. I hadn't had much film experience yet, but if there was one thing I did know, it was how to flatter my figure and deemphasize my short neck and broad shoulders. The costumes Banton cooked up were all wrong for me and I told him so. After several bitter quarrels, I won a few concessions and lost others. Travis Banton never worked with me again, by his choice, but ironically his wife was assigned to accompany me on a later press junket.

I also did battle with the makeup people, who objected to my Egyptian-style eyeliner. I had been doing this for years, and knew it enhanced my eyes, especially onscreen. It also gave me a feeling of originality. (My eye trick would be copied by several other stars, including Sophia Loren, who admitted having fashioned her eye makeup after Yvonne De Carlo. She said she had admired me since she was a teenager. Hmm. . . . Well, I'll take that as a compliment.)

Another issue was the length of my hair. I always wore it longer than most actresses and liked it that way, as a trademark of sorts. They could tease it into a skyscraper if they wanted to, just as long as they stayed away from me with their eager scissors.

On this second Universal picture, I was assigned a terrific hairdresser and a stand-in, both of whom would stay with me for many years. The hairdresser was Olga Collings, who had worked on such stars as Swanson, Garbo, and Shearer. We hit it off from the start, and I've never found a better hairdresser or friend. The stand-in was Marie Bodie, who started in pictures as a dancer when she was eight. She bore a slight resemblance to me, and we formed an immediate team.

Another milestone came with *Frontier Girl.* I was suddenly important enough for them to assign a stunt rider for me. A year or so earlier I had met Polly Burson, an Oregon girl who had been born into the rodeo business. I suggested her for the job, and she was hired. Polly turned out to be a good fighter too. Between us, over the years, we probably smashed and bashed more heads than any two actresses in the movie business.

Frontier Gal was set in a mountainous region of the Old West, so we had locations at nearby Lone Pine and as far away as Sequoia National Park. The routine became fixed: Up at 4:30 A.M. for a 5:30 makeup call, then the trek to the mountain foothills for a long, hot day in the sun. It was Andy Devine who gave me the secret of how to handle the before-breakfast calls. In his gravel voice he said, "Fry an egg, put it between two pieces of bread, add some ketchup, and that'll keep you til' lunch call." It worked.

A few days after the release of *Frontier Gal* the war ended. The streets came alive with celebrating Americans, the lights were on again, rationing would soon be over, and everyone could get back to a normal way of life. The summer of 1945 were glory days in America, and the mood was reflected in Hollywood. I was elated because not only had the war ended, my contract had been renewed and my salary had taken a healthy hike. With the extra money I could buy my first home. I spent weeks searching and finally found what I wanted in a cozy little California colonial house at 12724 Valley Spring Lane in North Hollywood, perfect for me and Marie at the time. It was close to the studio, had a wood-burning fireplace, and it was my own. What a feeling—and such an improvement over the digs Marie and I had shared over the years.

The studio was saying that at this stage of my career every vehicle had to be chosen carefully. That was fine, but what was I supposed to do in the meantime? Why not give me a vacation while the search was going on? To my surprise, they agreed. Now, at last, would come my belated homecoming. I was really anxious to see the old places and familiar faces of my childhood, so, on a September morning in 1945, I flew to Vancouver.

It was the "returning-hero" welcome I had dreamed of. I was met by the press at the airport—which, I must admit, was carefully orchestrated by the studio—and thus began my reunion with family and friends. I directed the rented limousine to 3330 West 42nd Street in Kerrisdale, and was greeted by Aunt Connie and Cousin Kenny, who had just been discharged by the RCAF. We spent most of the night getting reacquainted and reminiscing about the "good old days."

My performance those years earlier at the Palomar hadn't exactly been a world-shaking event, but now the nightclub invited me back. It had to be a publicity coup for the club, but I was delighted with the invitation. On "Yvonne De Carlo Night" Connie and I dressed in our finery and made our appearance. We had barely settled into our ringside seats when a man came over to me and introduced himself as Johnny Meyer. He said he represented Howard Hughes, who wanted very much to meet me. I had heard of the man, but by this time had grown accustomed to meeting important people. I told Meyer that we would be happy to meet Mr. Hughes.

The mysterious Mr. Hughes came to our table looking lanky, underfed, and remarkably sad. I immediately felt my maternal instincts coming out. Not that I was attracted to him in any way; I just felt kind of sorry for him. Strangely, I imagined a fantasy romance between him and my aunt Connie. I guess this was because even though Meyer had said Howard Hughes wanted to meet *me,* his conversation seemed directed more to Connie than to me.

He told us he just happened to be in Vancouver to play a new golf course and heard I would be at the Palomar. What I found out later was that he had piloted his DC-3 all the way from Los Angeles just to meet me. When I was better acquainted with him, he admitted that he became intrigued with me after seeing *Salome* and had watched the movie more than five times. Impressed by my beauty, he wanted to meet me away from the Hollywood scene. When he read about my Vancouver homecoming, he made his move.

My new billionaire friend made a date to see me the next morning so he could meet my entire family. I took him to meet my grandmother, and in the afternoon he took Kenny and me for an airplane ride over the city. Later, in the remaining daylight, Howard took me to see the golf course he had ostensibly come to Vancouver to play. He tried to teach me how to swing a club, and in spite of my lack of talent we had a good time. He *loved* the game. As we left the course, I said to myself, "Yes, I like him . . . I like him very much." He had been charming and very attentive throughout the day, and everything we said and did seemed so spontaneous that I was beginning to believe that he was interested in me for myself rather than for the image projected on a movie screen.

On a mini-shopping spree downtown, Howard bought me an English country-type hat and a leather purse for my grandmother. When I thanked him, he said solemnly, "Yvonne, don't ever thank me for anything material." His disdain for material things suggested one facet of his complex personality, but there would be too many to chronicle. The longer I knew Howard, the less it seemed I really knew about him. It seemed also that his mind operated on a different frequency from regular people, as though his thought impulses were in code.

Howard would frequently send Johnny Meyer on errands to allow us to be alone, but our privacy was seldom of very long duration. Either there would be someone calling him, or he might pop up and run to the phone himself in the middle of a sentence. The calls could be to the next block or to the other end of the globe. His telephone conversations could go on interminably, with Howard issuing very precise instructions to his subordinates, repeating the orders over and over again as though the person on the other end were a moron. If the phone failed to ring and he could think of no one else to call, he might call in Meyer and outline a series of intricate errands to be run, detailing everything short of how many right turns were involved. Yet we somehow managed to consummate a relationship, and it wasn't bad. In fact, it got better as time went on. It might have been on the clinical side, but that was the way with Howard Hughes. It didn't take very long at all for me to fall in love with him.

We were in Vancouver together for a week, and the time was approaching when both of us would have to return to L.A. Howard gave me a kiss on the nose and asked, "How would you like to throw a farewell party for all your special Vancouver friends?" I thought it was a great idea and made out a guest list. Howard added a few names, mostly of local dignitaries, and left all the details up to Johnny. The party site would be one of the larger suites near the top of the Vancouver Hotel. Childishly excited about his brainchild, Howard tried not to show it. He usually dressed in plain trousers, a white shirt, and sometimes a wrinkled linen jacket, but on party night he surprised me by dressing up in a well-tailored navy-blue suit. I had never seen him looking better—and, come to think of it, I never would again.

The party suite was grandly furnished, and Howard looked very much in place as he stood at the door to welcome the guests. There was a small but respectable orchestra playing, a wide variety of canapés, and plenty to drink. I remember June Roper cornering me to tell me how lucky I was to have such a charming and generous friend. It was an evening to remember and a perfect way to end my happiest of all homecomings. I felt like a queen.

In the morning, as I was basking in my recollections of the night before, Howard called. "How would you like to see Las Vegas before reporting back to the studio?"

"Why, I'd love it."

"Are you sure it will be okay with the studio?" he asked. "You'd better make sure." Howard, as always, was viewing things from the establishment point of view. He was a maverick in many ways but had a rigid moral standard when it came to loyalties. During our relationship he would frequently lecture me about being "a good soldier" when it came to studio dictates.

As we cruised southward in his DC-3, Howard spent several hours trying to teach me the basics of flying; for a portion of the trip I was piloting the ship on my own. By the time our relationship had run its course, I had learned how to fly, but never how to take off or land—something of a void in my aeronautical education.

While we were refueling Howard would excuse himself and stride off the tarmac. On one occasion, he had been gone so long I became concerned and went to the operations shack to see if I could find him. As I neared the building I could hear Howard's voice booming through the open door, sounding more intense than I had ever heard. "Is that your answer?" I heard him say angrily. "You just plain don't give a damn, do you? You never cared at all, did you?"

It seemed a bad idea to make my presence known, so I tippy-toed back to the plane. It was another fifteen or twenty minutes before he finally trudged back. When he saw me watching him, he straightened, managed a flickering smile, walked up to where I stood, and grasped my shoulders. "Are you serious about me?" he demanded, giving me a firm shake.

"Why . . . uh, yes . . . yes, I am."

He didn't say, "Swell," or "Hey, that's neat. . . . Hooray!" or anything. He just gave a firm nod and bounded into the cockpit. I had to hurry after him to make sure I wasn't left behind.

Later the puzzle would be solved. The party on the other end of the line had been Ava Gardner, who was giving him the standard Ava Gardner treatment. The time would come when Ava and I would compare notes on some of our lovers, but it was Howard himself who explained the telephone call, as well as other episodes with her. She had once cracked him across the mouth with a statuette, breaking two front teeth, and Howard had had to roust out his dentist in the middle of the night to make the necessary repairs. But these confessions came later. As we continued the flight to Las Vegas, I was simply confused.

Chapter 16

After landing in Las Vegas in the mid-afternoon, we checked into the rambling casino hotel El Rancho Vegas. Howard took his shower; I preferred the leisure of a hot bath. As he toweled himself he gazed at me in the tub, tossed the towel aside, and knelt down to help scrub my back. Everything about Howard was gentle: his lovemaking, his touch. It was obvious that he revered women, and it was also clear that there were certain female attributes that excited him more than others. He looked me over. "Ah, yes," he said, "there's nothing quite so appealing on a woman as a nice set of lavalieres." That was a favorite expression of Howard's, and I'd never heard it used elsewhere. I guess one might make the observation that he was something of a "lavaliere man." What a genteel way of putting it.

We stayed in Las Vegas for several days and it began to dawn on me that for all the going out we did, there was precious little publicity about us in any of the newspapers. In these times Howard was not at all shy about being seen in public, and it was Johnny Meyer who later explained Howard's deals with many members of the press. The top columnists were given expensive gifts: gold watches, French perfume, Dunhill cigarette lighters, and whatever other goodies came to mind, all for silence about his social activities.

One night he asked if I had enough of Las Vegas. If so, he would like to fly me to Pebble Beach for the remainder of our free time. Sounded good to me, so we were off the next morning. We checked into the Del Monte Lodge, where Howard rented adjoining suites, and dined that night in the hotel's long dining room that overlooked the very blue ocean and the very green golf course. What a paradise for young lovers. I learned over dinner that there had been a time when Howard was a regular weekend guest at the establishment. On one of those weekends he brought actress Billy Dove with him, and he chose the occasion to propose marriage. She turned him down, and he had avoided the hotel ever since—until today. I wondered if he was leading up to a proposal to me, but it didn't come. He probably knew I *wouldn't* have turned him down.

It was difficult to come to terms with all the changes that had occurred since leaving Los Angeles just three weeks earlier. To say I had been happy would be a gross understatement. I had gone home to brass bands and flashing cameras, met a loving rich man who gave me a fabulous party, and after two weeks of love and laughter I was very seriously in love. I hadn't won anything playing the Las Vegas slot machines, but I certainly felt like a jackpot winner in just about everything else.

Howard's Los Angeles headquarters was in the Town House Hotel at that time and I visited him there on many occasions. We would have quiet dinners in the hotel dining room, and then go up his rooms to spend long hours talking and making love. It was his frequent habit to work through the night, and the project at this time was his movie *The Outlaw.* He was also planning a publicity campaign, and there were dozens of photographs covering every flat surface in the room. Howard's late-night way of life made it very difficult for me when I was working. It got so I would almost look forward to his out-of-town trips so I could catch up on my rest, and then immediately start looking forward to his return. Some things, in their absence, are more important than sleep.

I don't think I could describe Howard as a passionate lover; he was more of an "expert" lover. What he did was calculated to please, and it was important to him that whatever he did, was done right. He also liked to theorize about sex as we lay next to each other, before and after making love. He would get into the differences between the male and the female orgasm, for example. The female climax, he explained, was an implosion, a reaction to the male *ex*plosion. He went in for extended foreplay while all the yakking was going on, and I thought that was just fine, though all of the verbiage could get boring too. I have a hunch he had done a lot of reading on the subject and enjoyed showing off his knowledge. As for me, I didn't care about explosion and implosion. If it was good, it was good—period.

Something very curious about Howard came to my attention during our period of intimacy. He had long, curling toenails that nearly wrapped themselves around his toes. They struck me as a bit strange, but I shrugged it off, figuring he must have some well-thought reason for them.

What really did bother me about Howard was his tendency to dwell on his past lovers. He must have been particularly taken with Billie Dove, because she came up in conversation at least once a day. He told me how beautiful and young she was, while she would actually have been several years older than I was when Howard and I met. It was in 1931 or 1932 when they made the movie *Cock of the Air* and she would have been in her early thirties then. Their love was long past, but I still felt a little jealous of her; he kept her image so constantly present.

It has taken some time for me evaluate Howard Hughes. At the time I was just doing what I could to keep the man I had fallen for. Now, in retrospect, everything I had missed before suddenly falls into place. I am sure, for instance, that Howard was disappointed that I wasn't a virgin. He was quite Victorian in his thinking, and expected all girls to be virgins until their wedding nights. Unless, I suppose, the girl wanted him to be the first. He relentlessly probed for information, and I finally explained my background in general terms, but then he pursued it even harder, wanting details, right down to dimensions and exact words, until I finally asked him to get off the subject. He fell short of asking me to name names, but I'm sure he thought I had had many more lovers than I admitted to.

Howard enjoyed visiting my home on Valley Spring Lane, but not when it meant sitting on the floor. One day at the Town House he said, "Let's go and buy you some furniture." We went to a very expensive place near his hotel but the furniture had to be ordered, so we stopped at a less elegant store not far from my house. Howard went through the showroom, saying, "That, and that . . . We'd better have one of those. . . . Give us that dining room suite, and this lamp." I saw several pieces I really liked, and I did pick a few things, but it was mostly Howard's taste that furnished my first little home. I especially recall a red-and-white striped couch, a leather bar with matching stools, and a desk with green leather trim. The furniture was delivered the next day, and Marie and I were delighted.

Marie treated Howard the same as she would any other "young man," and he loved the family atmosphere. He would get up to go to the bathroom and say to Marie, "I'm going to use the bathroom but don't worry. . . . I won't use the big towel." If he tracked in mud, Marie would scold him, and like a little boy he would say, "Yes, ma'am. Sorry, ma'am."

In some respects Howard was not unlike some of the less affluent lads I'd been dating. Generous in many ways, he wasn't a big spender. We would always eat in the better restaurants and the prices didn't bother him, but he would spend ages studying the check, item by item. I noticed that he tipped appropriately but never lavishly. He, after all, had nothing to prove.

In addition to the furniture there were other gifts, but never anything extravagant like diamonds or furs. One night he came to the house with a devilish glint in his eye. He told me he had a very special gift for me, and handed me a gift-wrapped box, beaming as I hurriedly unwrapped it. It was the size of a watch box, and with that in mind, I was already rehearsing a wristwatch "Thank you!" I finally opened the box and there was a tiny watch with a black ribbon strap, a watch that one could find for ten dollars at any corner drugstore. "Oh, thanks!" I cried, giving him a hug and a kiss. "It's beautiful—a watch. Just what I wanted!"

While all this is playing, Howard is grinning and reaching into his pocket. "If you like that one so much," he said. "Let's see how you like this." He pulled an unwrapped watch out of his pocket, gold and delicate, obviously a very expensive piece of jewelry. Here was Howard's slightly perverse sense of humor.

His generosity came across another time when Marie got into a little difficulty over one of her lovers. The man's wife named Marie as corespondent in a divorce case. Marie was frightened to death, of course, so Howard hired a lawyer who easily got her off the hook.

One of Howard Hughes's most notable qualities was his single-minded determination. He knew exactly what he wanted, always, and no man could change his mind. As a lavaliere man, Howard knew something special had to be done to make Jane Russell's show themselves to their best advantage in *The Outlaw.* When he couldn't buy the perfect bra for the job, he designed one. Whether it was the tail assembly of a fighter plane or the uplifting properties of a woman's bra, Howard knew what he wanted—and went for it.

When Howard and I were in San Francisco, we went shopping to buy a dress for me. We went to the most elegant shops, and I spent hours trying things on. There were several that caught my fancy, but I could tell Howard didn't share my enthusiasm so I restrained my own reactions until I could see a glimmer of approval in his eye. The glimmer didn't come.

This went on for several hours until Howard sat down at a small glass-topped table in a very chic fashion salon. He pulled out a pencil and piece of paper and started sketching. The clerk and I looked at each other with questioning shrugs as Howard doodled away. Finally, he handed the paper to the girl and asked, "Can you make one up like this?" The girl studied the paper for a moment and then excused herself to consult with her boss. In a few minutes she was back with news that the dress could be made.

The dress was ready in two weeks, and to be very frank about it, Howard's design would have been better for an airship. It had shoulders that looked like the wings of a plane, the waist was tucked in, and the jacket fell below my hips. It was dark brown with a cream-colored trim and Howard loved it. I pretended to. I wore it on several consecutive dates and then retired it to the back of my closet. He subsequently designed two evening gowns for me, but then haute couture began to bore him and he went back to designing airplanes.

In the dress shop that day, I learned how single-minded Howard could be when he wanted something. I also learned that he didn't mind spending any amount of money to get what he regarded as a quality product. He didn't even ask the sales clerk how much the dress would cost, and I'm sure it was plenty. Of course, he could have had Johnny Meyer call them back to do some haggling for him, and you know, now that I think about it, I bet he did.

Johnny Meyer's job was handling Howard's dirty work, and Howard thought nothing of waking Johnny at three A.M. to go to an all-night market for yogurt or a banana or whatever, and he would frequently stick him with dinner checks. Once, following an afternoon-long cab ride in San Diego, Howard told Meyer, "Pay the man, Johnny."

"Hey, wait a minute, Howard," Johnny said. "You can't stick me with a fifty-dollar fare." This was Howard's idea of a practical joke, and eventually Johnny was reimbursed. Howard's humor appealed to me; however, on the serious side of the money question I observed several times that he would not forgive anyone who gouged him—even for a small amount.

Other than those long uncut curling toenails, Howard was no more idiosyncratic than most people. I think much of his curious behavior emerged after his near-fatal plane crash. I can't recall seeing him wear dirty tennis shoes, for instance. What I remember are plain black oxfords—not too stylish I admit, but regular shoes. As for his wearing a hearing aid? No—I'm sure not. He would have been far too vain for that when I knew him. He was hard of hearing, but it wasn't at all an extreme condition. Another rumor circulated about his so-called germ phobia. He was said to wear gloves and wash his hands continually, but I recall no such behavior. He was a very clean man, thank God, but not to the point of obsession.

I do recall one incident where I suspected he had gone over the edge. Howard had given me a key to his apartment. When I arrived at his apartment, I could hear the shower, so I waited. After twenty minutes or so, I went into the bedroom and called, "Hi, Howard, I'm here." Then I heard, "There shall be no cancellations! There shall be no cancellations! He repeated these same words over and over again for at least fifteen more minutes. Howard was to hold a management meeting at Hughes Tool Company in a few days, I knew, and I finally deduced that he was rehearsing his speech. We must also consider that the man was under the impression he was alone and that the rushing water would drown out his voice.

Howard had plenty of traits that could be frustrating. He would never acknowledge a birthday, for instance, and he refused to have anything to do with Christmas activities. He saw Christmas as a commercial mess and would probably have thrown stones at carolers. Howard made it a point to lay low during that time of the year possibly because years earlier he had broken up with Ginger Rogers on that date. I hated his attitude toward Christmas, not because I didn't get a gift—he gave me plenty of those on other occasions—but because I have always loved to share Christmas with loved ones.

In the beginning I had the childish notion I could change some of Howard's ingrained ways. I placed a pretty high value on my own sexuality, and I guess I expected that would buy some concessions. How wrong I was. There was no force on earth that could change Howard Hughes's thinking. I wanted to hear wedding bells but Howard never even publicly acknowledged that we were dating. The fact that he'd never broached the subject of marriage should have told me something, but I was in love, and blind.

Chapter 17

Fortunately, I was becoming more active at the studio, which left me less time to agonize over my unpredictable multimillionaire. The work came about as a result of a meeting set up by my agent, Paul Kohner. We had lunch at the Vendôme restaurant, where we met Paul's friend of many years, Walter Reisch. He was from Vienna and had written several screenplays for MGM, including *Ninotchka* and *Gaslight.*

He seemed very charming in the old-world way, and I started to wonder if it was a European custom to stare openly at the person across the dining table. "Is something the matter?" I finally asked.

"Oh, no . . . forgive me. It's your eyes. Now they're gray. I thought earlier they were blue."

"I can never depend on them, Mr. Reisch," I said, laughing. "They change on me without notice."

Then we eased into business talk. Reisch had come to check me out for the possible lead in a screenplay that depicted the life of the Russian composer Rimsky-Korsakoff. He had been offered Maria Montez or Yvonne De Carlo, and he first turned to his close friend Billy Wilder for advice. Billy, friend that he was, told Reisch that I could sing, dance —do everything.

I was set for the role of Cara de Talavera a couple of weeks later in the film they called *Song of Scheherazade.* Curiously enough, I would play opposite Maria Montez's husband, Jean-Pierre Aumont, an interesting bit of casting. Walter Reisch was unhappy that while everybody else would be working with an American accent Aumont would be playing a Slav with a heavy French accent, but his objections to the casting were overruled.

There were three dancing solos for me in the picture and Tilly Losch, the Austrian ballerina, was brought in to coach me. She talked to me as though I hadn't taken a ballet lesson in my life and gave me unflattering body movements, and when I tried to tactfully reason with her, she refused to listen. I had grown very fond of Walter Reisch and Tilly Losch was his friend, so I had to bite my tongue throughout the filming.

Walter mentioned that he and his wife, Lisl, held open house every Sunday, and asked if I would care to join them for strudel and coffee. I did so the following week, and was introduced into a social circle that I would never have otherwise known. And what a delightful and lively group it was. Intimate friends of the Reischs included Marlene Dietrich, Otto Preminger, William Wyler, Billy Wilder, Paul and Lupita Kohner, composer Franz Waxman, Mike Romanoff, and Ernst Lubitsch, who lived just a few houses away.

In Ernst Lubitsch, I found a kindred spirit. I think we must have existed together in a previous life. I would complain about Howard Hughes and he would commiserate, complaining about the behavior of Sania, his estranged wife. He spoke also of his failing health, and his recently started contract to direct a picture at Twentieth. He hoped he would be able to fulfill his obligation after a recent heart attack. He was a frail man in his mid-fifties who often needed a wheelchair to get around and brought a nurse with him to parties and restauránts.

Ernst had a warm and wonderful sense of humor despite his ill health, and I adored being around him. I would drop by his home and spend hours asking endless questions about his filmmaking. When Ernst was lonely, he might call and ask me to go to a party with him. We would go to visit George Cukor, perhaps, or Paul Kohner, or maybe to a gathering at Buzz Meredith and Paulette Goddard's place. We always had a good time.

When I learned I wouldn't see Howard on New Year's Eve—he was still hiding out from Christmas—Ernst invited me to an intimate gathering, and he continued to play an integral role in my life for the next two years—just being there. I was in Paris when he died in November of 1947. Paul Kohner cabled me the news, which upset me terribly. Ernst died while directing Betty Grable and Douglas Fairbanks Jr. in *That Lady in Ermine.* His friend Otto Preminger stepped in to complete the film.

I never worked with Otto Preminger, but as a friend he was as nice as anyone I had ever met. Sensing my loneliness, he would often be the one to cheer me up. On one occasion I was terribly upset, and it wasn't because of Howard. I had been to a doctor who told me I might never have children because I had developed an ovarian cyst. Otto was a sympathetic listener. So when I mentioned this to him, he immediately made an appointment for me with a doctor friend who totally refuted what the other had said, so I was back to reasonable happiness once more. Now, all I had to worry about was Howard.

The following Sunday I was seated on a window seat in the Reisch home visiting with Otto when the doorbell sounded. People were always coming and going during the brunch activities so little notice was paid to new arrivals. Notice was paid to *this* new arrival. All conversation hushed after the door had been opened. Then I saw why. In the doorway was a tall, skinny, and awkward man, nervously fingering a gray felt hat. At a glance, everyone in the house knew it was Howard Hughes. He introduced himself to the Reischs, and they cheerfully introduced him to any of the guests he didn't know. I was stunned. I had mentioned these special Sundays frequently to Howard, but wasn't sure he even heard what I said. Now, he was here.

Maybe it was the element of unpredictability that made Howard so consistently interesting. I've never know anyone more difficult to second-guess. I would sooner have expected to see King Farouk at the door with a string of camels. I was pleased, of course, but quite tense for a while. I wasn't sure how he would mix with the others.

Lisl had been getting ready to serve her famous poppyseed cake when Howard appeared. She started passing out plates of it and when she reached Howard he said, "Thanks, but desserts aren't in my diet." All the rest of us started to eat, and as usual we all waxed ecstatic over the near miracle of her baking. Howard took all of this in and said, "Well, maybe I will have just a small piece."

Lisl gave it to him and asked, "Coffee or tea?"

"Just some tomato juice, please," said Howard.

Tomato juice with coffee cake? But nobody questioned it. By the time Lisl brought him the juice, Howard was at the table sawing off another piece of cake. The second piece seemed to break the barriers, because he then joined in with everybody in laughter and casual conversation. Everyone had a good time, Howard included. He would drop in more or less regularly over the following months—always unannounced and unexpected.

Several weeks passed, when on a Monday morning I received an unusual call from Walter Reisch. "Yvonne," he said, "I had a phone call last night about midnight. It was Howard Hughes."

I asked Walter what in the world Howard wanted, and he gave me this verbatim account:

"What can I do for you, Mr. Hughes?"

"Is Yvonne there?"

"No, she isn't here."

"She must be there . . . she's not home."

"But I assure you she isn't here, Mr. Hughes. She left about seven o'clock. None of the guests are here now."

"Look under the piano . . . she might be asleep there."

"I know she isn't there."

"Will you go and look, please?"

Walter did as he was asked and returned to the phone. "She isn't there, Mr. Hughes."

"I see." He then hung up.

I didn't see Howard for several days after that because I was busy at the studio, but he never mentioned the phone call nor did he ask where I had been that Sunday night. Where I actually went was to a movie with Marie, but the issue was never raised.

Maria Montez came on the set after we had been shooting a few days. I saw her go to her husband and kiss him, and then, to my astonishment, she turned toward me. Oh, boy, this was it—the big shootout at the old corral. As she neared, she let out a warm smile, and I uncocked my imaginary six-gun. She introduced herself cordially, and after a brief bit of weather talk, she said in parting, "Mek them geev you more loff scenes with Jean-Pierre. You should both haf close-ups."

She couldn't have been more pleasant. She even invited me to her home to see their baby, Maria Christina, which I did a few days later. We became very friendly, and I learned that Maria Montez was not to be judged by ordinary standards. She inhabited a self-designed world in which she was royalty, and this was something she sincerely believed. She told me she had lived as royalty in the Mayan period of history and showed me a scarf that she said came from that life. Who was I to argue? I listened, nodded, and silently marveled at the quality of cloth that could survive so many centuries. A little while later I kissed her ring, curtsied, and backed out of the room. I didn't, actually, but I think that was what she hoped I would do.

It was Maria, incidentally, who was among the first to discourage me about my romance with Howard. I had lunch with her and her man-about-town agent, Pat di Cicco, at the Brown Derby, and Maria started in. "Thees Howard Hughes. He ees not for you."

"You must be wearing blinders," di Cicco said. "Don't you know about all the other girls in his life?"

I could recite a pretty good list by this time, but my names were from his past.

"And don't overlook Linda Darnell," said di Cicco, with him and Maria exchanging knowing glances.

I couldn't say anything. I felt sick inside.

"When eet comes to women," said Maria, "he ees a habitual liar."

"Maria's right," said di Cicco. "He always has a stable of chicks stashed around."

I had heard it all before, but this time it struck home—these two people were trying to help me. In spite of the fact that I hated what they were saying, an inner bell started to toll very softly—a death knell for my great love.

The early part of 1946 was a busy time for Howard and, fortunately, also for me. On February 18, Howard made the first nonstop transcontinental flight from Los Angeles to New York in his new airliner, the Constellation, and by this time just about everyone knew who Howard Hughes was. I was proud to play a role in his life, but when you love somebody, you like to show him off: "Hey, folks, he's mine." Howard never allowed me this luxury.

By the time summer breezes fanned my flames of love, I summoned the courage to lay it on the line with my peripatetic lover. "Howard," I said, clinging to him, "will we ever be married?"

"No," he replied.

I could never accuse him of being wishy-washy. I went home and cried for hours, then cried periodically over the next several days. Finally, the tears dried, and I accepted my fate. The cooling off had begun.

A week or so later I was paying my usual Sunday visit to the Reischs, and was in the pool helping their daughter swim when without warning a shuddering sensation tore through my body. Having never experienced anything like it before, I was frightened. I lifted the little girl out of the water, and said to Walter, "I feel strange."

"What is it?"

"I don't know, but something's wrong."

I lay down for a while, and when I felt a little better I joined the others in the living room, where it was the Sunday-evening custom to listen to the radio broadcasts of Walter Winchell and Louella Parsons. As Winchell's broadcast ended he exclaimed, "An important newsflash is just coming in. Be sure to stay tuned for Louella Parsons, who will have all the details."

Louella got right into the story: "News has just come in that Howard Hughes in his private plane has just had a possibly fatal crash in Beverly Hills on Whittier Drive. His plane crashed into a private residence, and Howard is now undergoing surgery at the Good Samaritan Hospital in Los Angeles. There are no further details available on his condition."

I turned white. Later, after I had better control of myself, Walter Reisch asked, "You sensed that, didn't you, Yvonne?"

"I knew something terrible had happened," I said, "but I didn't know what it was."

The next edition of the newspapers carried all the details. Howard had crashed his experimental XF-11 into a house not more than a mile from the Reisch home. A passing Marine had dragged Howard out of the flaming wreckage, or he would surely have been killed. His injuries included a crushed chest, nine broken ribs, a collapsed lung, and severe skull lacerations. Howard was not expected to live, but not only did he survive, he recovered with remarkable swiftness. It was said that he told the medical people exactly what he wanted done and how to do it.

A list of celebrities paraded through the Good Samaritan corridors from the time he went into surgery until the day he left the hospital. Lana Turner and Linda Darnell were among the daily visitors. I wanted to visit Howard, but not under those circumstances. Since my relationship with him was unknown, the press would surely suspect I was just a Hollywood actress trying to get publicity out of another's misfortune.

After Howard's recovery, he became deeply enmeshed in the Congressional hearings about his questionable dealings with the government. With the passage of time the romance died, but our friendship lived on. He told me to let him know if I ever needed anything, and that complimentary TWA flights would be arranged whenever I needed to travel. I took him up on that several times.

I saw Howard again about three years later, just after he had taken over RKO Studios. His office called to say he would be coming to my house that evening at eight, and he arrived on time with a script under his arm. We had a long visit, mostly small talk about family and mutual friends. But throughout the conversation he kept asking questions like "Do I look different to you?" and "Have I changed much?"

"Why, you look fine, Howard. You haven't changed a bit."

I lied. He looked dreadful—like a caricature of his former self. His face seemed drawn, there was a pronounced stoop to one of his shoulders, and he walked with a slight limp. He had aged at least twenty years and become a shell of the man I had known and loved. He must have been deeply concerned about his appearance, because I had never known him to seek reassurance before.

He finally got around to the script, saying it had two excellent female roles, one for Ava, the other for me. I read it, but the part he had in mind for me was all wrong. I had a hunch that Howard knew this, but that the script gave him an excuse to drop by.

That was the last time I came face to face with Howard Hughes. His furniture lasted a long time, and the watch would probably have lasted forever, but it was stolen with most of my other jewelry a few years later. After that, the only legacy I had of our relationship was the memories, and those were pretty good. Howard Hughes was one of the most important loves of my life.

Chapter 18

As a newcomer to the ranks of Hollywood stars, I may have been less reverent than some toward the sacred traditions. I did not eat, drink, and breathe movies twenty-four hours a day. Nor was I interested in emulating the Joan Crawfords: when the day's work was done I wanted to go home and get on with my real life. The studio, of course, had a different point of view.

They drummed up all kinds of extracurricular activities to keep my name in print. When I wasn't on a junket of some kind, I was expected to make appearances with male stars of their choosing, most of whom I didn't like. When I was going with Howard Hughes I didn't want to date other men, but of course I couldn't tell the studio about Howard. Afterwards I wanted to go out more often, but not with a member of the Universal stable and certainly not with a Rory Calhoun. But there was a young actor-about-town with whom I had felt an affinity earlier, a handsome young star, recently out of the service, Robert Stack.

Bob came as close as any boy friend I ever had to fitting my blond, blue-eyed, muscular ideal. Everything was there, even the blond hair. He could be my perfect reason to get over Howard—bright, likable, with an infectious laugh and a great sense of humor and consistently upbeat despite problems of his own. His big problem at the time was that after spending the war years in the Navy he was remembered only for having given Deanna Durbin her first screen kiss. But he weathered

Baby Peggy
in Vancouver
at two years old.

My mother, Marie, and I in the 1920s.

My first pinup was
for the birds.

Cousin Ken and I
outside St. Paul's
Anglican Church. Ken
was the cross-bearer.
I sang in the choir.

Hawaiian beauty third from left in "Waikiki Revue," Orpheum Theatre, 1939.

Third prize at the Venice Beauty Contest
in 1940.

My first nightclub act, age fifteen.

Sterling Hayden,
my first unrequited
"love."

Little King and I
—during my rodeo days.

YDC-P144

Salome, Where She Danced—doing my "torrid" Salome dance.

One of Howard Hughes's favorite photos of himself (he didn't have many)
directing on the set of *The Outlaws*.

The De Carlo women
gather at Valley
Spring Lane,
my first house.
(Clockwise) My grandma,
my Aunt Connie,
me, and *(far right)* Marie.

Hedda Hopper and I
on our first interview
at the Brown Derby
in Hollywood.

Hollywood nightlife:
(clockwise) Bob
Stack's arm, me, my
friend Pat, and Rod
Cameron.

Robert Siodmak directing Burt
Lancaster and me in a scene from
Criss Cross, (1949).

Cousin Ken took this shot of Jocko
Mahoney and I strolling in Palm
Springs.

With Peter Ustinov and David Tomlinson on the set of *Hotel Sahara*.

Carlos Thompson and a bejeweled me at the Mocambo in Hollywood.

Opera days. *(Left to right)* Aunt Connie, Jerome Hines, a coy senorita, and maestro Gennaro Curci.

A special photo session at the Pyramids arranged by my escort Captain Salah Sayed Ahmed of the Cairo police. Ken was our photographer.

Vittorio Gassman and me in the film *Sombrero*. This scene
inspired Cecil B. De Mille to cast me as Sephora in *The
Ten Commandments*.

A pleasant conversation with Cecil B. De
Mille; me garbed as Sephora.

The proposal scene with Charlton
Heston as Moses.

With HRH Prince Abdorezza Pahlavi of Iran. Photograph taken at my home in California.

Mario Cabre and me in a restaurant high above the Grand Corniche on the French Riviera.

Happy memories at the Compleat Angler in Henley-on-Thames with my fiancé, Cornel Lucas.

Our first encounter: dancing with Prince Aly Khan at his villa in Cannes.

Denis Lord
Lanesborough, earl of
Leicester, and I at a
royal hunt ball.

"Smile! You've done it
at last." Reno, Nevada,
November 1955 with
Bob Morgan.

With Bob Morgan (my
new husband) in a scene
from *Death of a
Scoundrel* (1956).

With Bob Morgan and
Clark Gable in *Band of
Angels* (1957).

My personal Munster Jaguar: solid brass wolf on the hood, spiderweb hubcaps, gilded coffin rails on baggage rack, Dracula insignia on door.

The geniuses and performers of *Follies. (Back row)* James Goldman, John McMartin, Michael Bennett, Gene Nelson, Hal Prince, Dorothy Collins, Boris Aronson, Jonathan Tunick. *(Front row)* Stephen Sondheim, Alexis Smith, me, and a showgirl.

Yvonne De Carlo today.

these difficult times gracefully and never burdened anyone else with his complaints. It helped, I suppose, that he didn't have to worry about starvation while he maneuvered his career into a better direction. He lived on a beautiful estate in Bel Air with his widowed mother and his brother Jim, who lived in the main house while Bob enjoyed separate quarters in a snug rear bungalow just beyond the swimming pool. Whenever we wanted privacy, and it was not infrequently, we would slip into Bob's little house and would never be disturbed.

Bob was a natural athlete, and he and Jim were champion skeet shooters. My own interest in guns probably enhanced our relationship. He once made me a gift of a fine .22-caliber rifle. There were frequent poolside parties attended by the cream of Hollywood society. One of the more frequent guests was a fun-loving young man named Ronnie Reagan, who would show up with or without his wife, Jane Wyman, and was to be elected president of the Screen Actors Guild in about a year.

For some reason I remember going to a very pleasant restaurant with Bob on Melrose Avenue called Romeo's Chianti. I happened to catch a glimpse of the dinner check, which came to eleven dollars, and thought to myself, "Ohhh, what an expensive meal." The Chianti still exists, and I doubt if a shrimp cocktail could now be had for what Bob paid for our entire dinner. I also recall a weird dream in which I was being sent to the electric chair and Bob Stack rescued me in the nick of time. I must have been determined that Bob would be my knight in shining armor, but as I consider it now, I wonder what kind of guilt trip I was on to warrant electrocution as punishment. Are you there, Sigmund Freud?

Also out of the ether comes the recollection of Bob saying to me, "Yvonne, you can look the best of any girl I've ever known . . . and the worst." The context is lost but the naked words remain.

It was at about this time—my post-Howard Hughes era—that I concluded I was not the world's finest actress. At least it was then that I took on some special coaching. The Universal test director, Elsa Shdanoff, recommended her husband, George, for the job—Yura, as he was known to his friends. I signed up and began to learn something about the art of acting.

Later I was so pleased with the results, I suggested that Bob avail himself of Shdanoff's services. Bob was afraid he'd be asked to crawl around as a worm, in the "method" tradition, but I assured him it would be nothing like that and finally persuaded him to join me in a session. We were shown techniques for inner motivation, body movement, and vocal ease among other exercises, and Bob was impressed enough to come aboard. This led to years of work together, and Yura became very proud of Bob as an actor.

Part of my own motivation for seeking help started with Mike Todd. He always liked to take out young, good-looking actresses, and I was flattered to be asked out to lunch. Everything was delightful, he was very complimentary about my looks, and I was feeling very pleased with myself. Then he said, "Oh, by the way, Yvonne. I've seen your test."

"Oh, really?" I said, fully expecting more flattery.

"Yeah, and I wanta tell you it was the worst fucking thing I've ever seen in my life."

That was our first and last date but I didn't forget his remark. (God, who could?) After a few months of training with Yura, I started feeling much better about myself, and as my confidence increased I started daydreaming about meaty, dramatic parts that would show the world what I could do.

At this time, word was circulating that Garson Kanin and his wife, Ruth Gordon, had written a terrific script that would be produced by Universal. It would star Ronald Colman, and contained a young wait-ress's part that was supposed to be outstanding. The story revolved around a Shakespearian actor who gets his real life confused with his stage roles. He ends up killing the waitress because he thinks he is Othello doing away with Desdemona. This sounded like the kind of role I'd been looking for—real drama, real grit.

I made an appointment to see Nate Blumberg, the studio's top executive. We went through the usual platitudes, and he brought up *Song of Norway,* which he said would be perfect for me. But that wasn't what I had come to talk about, was it? I finally broached the matter of *A Double Life.* "I hear the role of the waitress is a really good part," I said, "and I'd like very much to be considered for it."

"It isn't a starring part, you know."

"I know. But I'd really like to play it."

He frowned, and rearranged all the papers on his desk. "There is something about this business you should understand, Yvonne," he finally said. "You are something we consider as rock candy—it sells and sells. Now, there are dipped chocolates too, but they don't sell in great quantity. We want to make sure you keep on selling for a long, long time. Do you understand?"

"I guess so," I told him.

That was something I would have to think over for a long time. Rock candy? Dipped chocolates? The only thing I knew was that I loved dipped chocolates and hated rock candy, but we weren't running a candy store. As I left his office, I was really seeing myself as chopped liver—and we weren't running a delicatessen either.

It was Shelley Winters who played the waitress role, and it made her a star. I had heard Winters was quite temperamental. This was later confirmed when, in a tantrum, she flung herself into the flower bed outside the studio commissary and stomped all the flowers into pulp. Then there was the day my hairdresser was late on the set, telling me it was because she had had to go and pray.

"Why were you praying?" I asked.

"I was praying that I'd never have to work with Shelley Winters again."

I only knew Shelley casually, which made me wonder why in her autobiography she said something about my trying to fix her up with Clark Gable and Errol Flynn, suggesting I was something of a female pimp. For the record, I never had any contact whatever with Flynn and didn't meet Gable until I played opposite him in *Band of Angels,* which would have been several years after the alleged incident.

While Shelley was throwing her tantrums and playing the meaty role in *A Double Life,* little Miss Rock Candy was back in her filmy pantaloons for *Slave Girl,* in which George Brent was the male lead. He was well into middle age, and made no pretense otherwise. His favorite phrase throughout the movie was, "I'm getting too old for this," which was true.

At this time the studio was undergoing a corporate change. The low-budget programmers were to give way to quality features with the J. Arthur Rank Organization. William Goetz and Leo Spitz would supplant the people who hired me. I didn't know what effect this would have on my contract, but I could see the consequences for the movie. First *Slave Girl* was temporarily shelved. Then it went back into re-editing and some additional shooting, incorporating a new actor, "Humpy, the Talking Camel," which changed the movie into a comedy-spoof. Many scenes were cut, along with several of my dances.

The studio was now known as Universal-International and its new production unit was headed by ex-newspaperman Mark Hellinger. His company was now enjoying tremendous success with the recently released *The Killers,* which was the first film to star Burt Lancaster and made a star of Ava Gardner.

When I first met Ava at Universal, she invited me to come and visit her at her San Fernando Valley home. We knew about each other mostly because of our mutual tastes in men—namely Artie Shaw and Howard Hughes. Later we would have other lovers in common—and tear them *all* apart—but at this time Ava was very concerned about Artie Shaw, and wondered how she might save their marriage. I only knew Artie as a friend, but I could sense the kind of hell he was capable of dishing out. I was sympathetic, but I was also wondering if her connection with Howard had something to do with her marital problems.

Ava had lost much weight during her depression as I had done in my breakup with Howard. (It has often occurred to me that the best diet in the world is a catastrophic love affair.) Ava and I also shared a tendency to thrive on the emotion of our affairs, both of us stimulated by conflict. When a man gives me trouble, I stay in love with him. If he's Mr. Nice-guy, I forget his name. I wish it had been otherwise, but it wasn't—and isn't.

If *The Killers* had done wonders for Ava's career, it might have done even more for Burt. He was in great demand. Hellinger had an agreement with Burt to do *Brute Force,* a prison picture with four flashbacks requiring four different actresses. I was one of them. The part I played was the Italian girl named Gina.

Hellinger and I had met earlier through Walter Wanger, and I was anxious to play the sympathetic Italian role—anything to get away from sand and sandals. At the preproduction conference, Hellinger introduced me to Burt Lancaster. I had no doubts that Burt knew exactly what he wanted, and at the moment it was me. He had tremendous intensity, and was the kind of macho man who says nothing but takes the girl by the hand and leads her off to his lair. When he asked me out to a cocktail party and dinner afterward, I was already imagining how the ultimate love scene would play. After dinner, though it was still early, we returned to my home. While the house was four or five times bigger than the little court apartments of the earlier days, it still wasn't *that* big. "Look," I said to him, "my mother is inside."

Here was a far different leading man from others I had known. Nothing was taken lightly by this powerful man; there was his New York street background, the years as a circus acrobat . . . He was brash and tough, and ready for action. It would be no "Goodnight, Sweetheart" à la Jimmy Stewart with him—and we both knew it.

"Let's go around to the back," I said, taking his hand. I led him into the back yard, already slipping out of my mink coat. I handed it to him and he laid it at the base of an oleander bush. He touched me and we went down together in an embrace that would rival his future beach scene with Deborah Kerr in *From Here to Eternity.* It was so spontaneous and so explosive, I thought I was playing a scene from a blazing romantic novel. Talk about being swept away!

The next day, I kept repeating to myself, "I can't believe I really did that." It was a first, that was for certain, and while I enjoyed the mental replay there were also deep misgivings. I was always robbed of the full pleasure of sex by my compelling fear of pregnancy. I also knew that Burt had very strong convictions regarding abortion. So what if . . . ? I was terrified to even think of it. When I saw him next, I expressed my fear. His response? "You worry too much, kid."

The following week he left for New York on a promotion tour. While he was away, I experienced that most wonderful of all periodic occurrences—at least under these circumstances. I had lunch the next day with Mark Hellinger. "I'll be going to New York at the end of the week," he said to me. "Is there any message you'd like to send Burt?"

"Yes," I said, hastily. "Tell him everything is all right."

Mark looked up from his plate, his expression enigmatic. "That's the message?"

"Mm-hmm. That's it."

It was only then that I realized I couldn't have been more obvious if I had drawn a diagram. I felt my cheeks burn in embarrassment and realized that my one-night affair with Burt Lancaster was a secret no more.

Chapter 19

The Burt Lancaster episode could hardly have been called a romance, or even an affair. A better term for it would probably be a mutual fling, brief but memorable. It wasn't long after this time that Burt met and married Norma Anderson, so that took care of him. But there was yet another brute force that would sweep me away during the shooting of *Brute Force.* This second man of distinction was another of Mark Hellinger's discoveries, Howard Duff. He was recruited for movies from radio ranks, where he starred as the tough-talking detective Sam Spade.

With his deep and resonant voice Howard was a natural for radio, but Hellinger gave him an opportunity to expand his acting horizons. This was Howard's first picture, and his virile good looks made him a prime prospect for movie stardom.

Howard's amiable sense of humor made him appear easygoing, but beneath the facade dwelled a serious and stubborn individual whose likes and dislikes were both firm and varied. It was thumbs down on classical music—which I loved. The out-of-doors was a bore to him, and horses were regarded as mortal enemies. He wasn't very crazy about movie acting and generally despised the people in the business. In fact, his interests could be narrowed down to the sport of drinking and the good times that came with it. At this stage of his life he handled alcohol pretty well, but there were the inevitable times when the inner demons would erupt in violent anger. Once, angry at having left his keys inside his apartment, he bashed in the door with his bare fists. Hard on the door, worse on the fists. Howard Duff and I had almost nothing in common, but . . . well, I fell for him. The fact that he was at our studio brought an automatic stamp of approval from the ruling powers, and that, I suppose, also encouraged my interest. We were in the same picture as well, which made it even better from a publicity point of view.

Practically all of my previous loves evaded thoughts of serious commitment and started sprinting at the mention of marriage. Howard, conversely, was not one to dabble in affairs of the heart. This, of course, frightened me. I was happiest when I was doing the chasing and didn't like it when somebody started calling my bluff. All my life I basked in the dream of storybook romance, happy marriage, homes with picket fences, and kiddies with blond hair and blue eyes. Now, I was dealing with someone who might actually make it come true. Once, as we were driving home from dinner, Howard asked, "Do you love me more than life itself?"

How was this for an after-dinner quiz? I pondered a moment and said, "No—not more than life."

He sulked for the rest of the evening.

We socialized with Howard's friends, who included John McIntire and his wife, June Havoc and her husband, and assorted male cronies. The heavy drinking made me nervous but since I was totally enamored I put up with it. When the movie was completed at the end of April, Howard and I became engaged. There were the rounds of congratulatory parties, with special good wishes from Ava, Edmond O'Brien, and, yes, even Burt Lancaster. All was well, except that with the little diamond ring on the third finger I began to get that old trapped feeling. When the press pressured me about the marriage date, I hedged as best I could. "We plan to wait a while—maybe six months or more. We intend to get to know each other really well before we take the plunge." My brain was cautious if not my heart.

Howard soon went to New York to work on *The Naked City,* and I took advantage of the other Howard's free transportation promise. I flew via TWA Constellation to New York to spend a weekend with my fiancé and we had a wonderfully romantic reunion, closing ourselves off behind bedroom doors for most of the time. Then our bliss was shattered at three A.M. Sunday morning by the ringing of the telephone.

"Oh, uh . . . no . . . can't. Not now. Uh . . . let me call you in the morning. . . . Yeah . . . okay, 'bye." That was Howard whispering into the phone, assuming I was asleep. I would never learn who the call had been from, but I was pretty sure it wasn't his stockbroker. The seeds of doubt were sown.

A few weeks later Howard was back in Hollywood, and we went to a small party at Ava Gardner's apartment. By two A.M. I had done all the drinking I wanted to and asked Howard if we could go home. "Not yet" was his reply.

I couldn't stay up any longer so I drove myself home, angry at Howard but more tired than anything else. It seemed as though I had been in bed only minutes when I was wakened by the telephone. It was almost dawn, and the call was from Ava. "Come and get this boy friend of yours, Yvonne."

"Not a chance, Ava," I said. "Pour him into a cab and aim it at his apartment."

"But he's all over me."

"You can deal with it, Ava."

"Okay," she said, "if that's the way you want it."

A few evenings later Howard and I attended a studio screening of his movie. He brought along half a dozen cronies and expected to do some partying afterward, but I had an early call the next morning and asked Howard if he couldn't come on home alone with me, just this once. He agreed and sent his pals off on their own. At the house, he fixed a stiff drink and unleashed his anger, calling me a shrew and saying I had embarrassed him in front of his friends. "Perhaps," he finally said, "we should just call it quits."

"Perhaps we should," I replied. And we did.

After we parted company, Howard took up with Ava Gardner in a relationship that lasted for several months. I doubt if she was especially taken with him, but he seemed to fill a void of the moment. Ava finally shut the door on him when she learned he had been discussing every detail of their hectic love life with many of their mutual friends. She was quoted as saying, "What's Howard trying to do—get elected?"

The next picture for "Miss Rock Candy of 1947" was *Black Bart*, in which I played Lola Montez, a lusty dancer and singer in the days of the Old West. I played opposite Dan Duryea, who was nervous about his first role as a screen lover, as opposed to a straight heavy. When this one wrapped, it was around the bend for Dan and me again in *River Lady*. This one had Rod Cameron in it as well. The work was physically taxing but not creatively inspiring. I was trying, however. For both pictures, I was working on all the big scenes with Yura to make sure that I gave it my best.

To help promote the release of *Song of Scheherazade,* I was sent on a tour of the Pacific Northwest, and then to Indianapolis. There I headlined a stage bill at the Oriental Theatre in which I had to dance and sing in five shows a day. As it turned out, I was competing against another movie of mine just down the street.

Tony Martin, the nightclub singer, was back in circulation after serving in the Air Force, and trying to make up for lost time in the woman department. He and I met at a party, and since the conversation was stimulating I accepted his invitation for a date. I found Tony as charming as anyone I had ever known, and he was certainly good-looking enough, but the chemistry wasn't strong enough to take it beyond friendship.

I had a hunch Tony was plotting a conquest when he asked me out on another occasion, so I prepared for it. I had Cousin Kenny, who was now in Hollywood, drive me to Tony's hotel, the Bel Air, and asked that he go back home and await my call—just in case. Tony and I had dinner at the Mocambo, and sure enough afterwards we made a beeline to his place. What he didn't know was that on a trip to the Mocambo powder room I had placed my conspiratorial call to Kenny. He showed up at Tony's bungalow just as our wrestling match had reached two-and-a-half falls. I thanked Tony for a delightful dinner and dancing, and hoped he had enough phone numbers to accommodate his pressing needs.

Within a few months I learned that I would be working with Tony on a musical version of *Algiers,* which was fine with me, except for one detail. I was being cast in the role of Inez, the gypsy, and the leading role was going to the Swedish newcomer Marta Toren. I hadn't been cast as the waitress in *A Double Life* because it wasn't the lead but now they were casting me in a really subordinate role. I was not happy. I argued the point with William Goetz in the executive office, but he wasn't the one with whom I had had the previous conference. For the first time in my career I demanded to be taken out of a film. Goetz made a demand of me: "Play the role, or else." I played the role.

Tony was very nervous before his scenes and had to do countless retakes. He would confide in me, "I'm just not used to this. Singing in clubs is my bag—not this." The joke around the set was "Tony Martin does his own singing, but they dub in his acting." Marta Toren was being constantly ushered off the stage for press interviews or publicity stills while the rest of us waited. It was bedlam throughout the filming, and I breathed a giant sigh of relief when it ended.

I went again to Mr. Goetz's office after seeing the rough cut. I didn't like my performance in the movie and thought the music was the movie's only saving factor. "This will hurt my career," I said to him. "I was miscast."

He shrugged. "What the hell do you want me to do—eat the film?"

"Good idea," I said as I made a haughty exit. Just outside the door I added, "And I hope you choke on it!" You'll notice that I said *outside* the door. I was too cowardly to tell off a studio head.

Pat Starling and I were still as close as ever, and it was she who invited me to a party being given by the A&P food store heir Huntington Hartford. I had heard a lot about this dabbler in the arts and man about town, and said I would go to the party with her. It wasn't that I was interested in wealth, but I have always been fascinated by the men who have it. I found him intelligent and cultured, and quite attractive. He was probably in his early thirties at the time. By this time I had accepted the fact that certain men liked being seen with pretty and famous women. On occasion I would accept dates knowing this motivation full well. I believed this to be the case with Hartford. We went out a few times, and I enjoyed his company. He would talk a great deal about his hope to build an art center in New York and his plans to produce plays; eventually he succeeded in both endeavors.

Hunt also picked my brain about the inside machinations of the movie industry, a subject that seemed to fascinate him. We were discussing the industry one evening when without preamble he asked if I'd come with him to Yosemite. The invitation came as a surprise but I liked the idea and told him I'd be glad to come if I could bring my aunt Connie. She had been in Southern California only a short time and it would give her a chance to see some of the scenery. He agreed.

The long ride through the mountains was lovely, and we arrived at the park during late evening. When Hunt checked us into the lodge, I noticed that he told the bellboy to take Connie's bags to 214 and mine to 212. I spoke up. "That must be a mistake," I said. "Those bags are mine—they go to two fourteen."

Hunt glared at me but said nothing. When we reached our rooms he went into 212 and slammed the door. Connie and I unpacked and got ready for dinner, assuming that our host would eventually emerge from his peevishness. When no call came by a reasonable hour, Connie and I went down to the dining room and had dinner without him. In the morning after breakfast, I spotted Hunt sprawled on a lounge chair on the back lawn of the hotel. I went over and said good morning but he continued to pout.

"I have one question," he said. "Did you come here to be with your aunt or with me?"

"Well, both, I guess. Don't you think you're behaving rather child-ishly?"

He got up and started back toward the hotel.

"Wait a minute, Hunt," I called after him. "Isn't there some way we can resolve our differences?"

"Yes," he said, turning to me. "I'm returning to Los Angeles by train. You and your aunt can bring the car back whenever you're ready."

It sounded fair enough to me. "As you wish, Hunt," I replied. He left the keys at the front desk, and Connie and I stayed at Yosemite for the remainder of the weekend. We had a great time on our leisurely drive home. I was sure that with the return of his car the chapter would be closed on Huntington Hartford forever—but not quite.

After several weeks, I received another call. "I'm having a dinner party," Hunt told me, "and I'd like you to come."

"What's the occasion?"

"The Prince of Iran is visiting Beverly Hills. There are certain movie stars he asked to meet—and you're one of them."

It was a kind of lefthanded invitation, but I accepted. I had never met royalty, and this was my chance. I dressed in my formal finery for the occasion and felt beautiful as I stood in the receiving line to be intro-duced to: "His Royal Highness Prince Abdorezza Pahlavi of Iran."

"Miss De Carlo," he said, with a jaunty bow and light handclasp. He was young and quite attractive, I thought, but there was certainly no electricity. After cocktails I was placed next to the prince at the dinner table, and he turned out to be a confident and sophisticated conversa-tionalist. As I started to look more deeply into his velvet-brown eyes, I allowed a fantasy to play: the Western commoner, swept off her feet by a handsome Middle Eastern prince.

Later several of us went to Mocambo for some dancing, and the prince and I were closed into a bodily embrace—on the dance floor, of course—and the electricity now came surging through. By the end of the evening I was calling him Dorez at his insistence, and his name for me was "Djounam." I didn't know what the name meant; he wouldn't tell me.

He told me he regretted that there would be no free time before his trip a few days hence to New York. To make sure nothing would change the subject, I quickly interjected, "How coincidental. You mention New York, and I expect to be there next week myself. I have a doctor's appointment, among other things, and will be there about a week." This spur-of-the-moment declaration surprised me later when I thought it over, agonizing over how to get there. Pleased at learning

I would be in New York, Dorez promised I would discover the meaning of "djounam" the very next time we were together.

I had no idea what might develop in New York; I only knew I had to give it a chance. I was still young and naive enough to believe in fairy tales and could see nothing to keep my prince and me from riding off into the sunset as man and wife. The fact that he had coal-black hair instead of blond and that his eyes were dark brown instead of pale blue, somehow didn't matter—wasn't he Prince Charming?

Chapter 20

I checked into the Sherry Netherland Hotel and called Dorez at the Pierre. We got together the same evening and did the town royally, and that's not just a figure of speech. Superb restaurants, hit Broadway shows, and shopping sprees made up the menu for the entire week.

At an exclusive sporting-goods shop, Dorez bought great masses of hunting paraphernalia, safari clothes, tents, cook stoves, firearms. It would seem he was outfitting a small army. Then he bought a riding crop with a concealed dagger. When he saw my interest in the illegal weapon, he bought not one but two of them for me, one of which I would later give to Robert Taylor.

As for Dorez and me, our passions carried us into a sudden and very compelling affair. I was madly in love, of course, and was certain we would conquer the world together on his steed, buddy style. For the moment, however, we could only reach stage one of our ascent because I had to get back to report for work on *Casbah*. Dorez sailed for England and we pledged to meet soon in Paris. By now I had learned that "djounam" means *darling*.

A few days later I was on a Universal backlot that had been transformed into the Casbah. In the middle of a scene with Tony Martin and Peter Lorre we broke for a new camera angle, and I was told that an important telephone call awaited me. It was a ship-to-shore call from somewhere in the middle of the Atlantic.

Dorez said he couldn't wait to see me in Paris and just had to hear the sound of my voice. Everyone on the set must have heard all my "I love yous" as I shouted to Dorez across the high seas, and when the call was completed, the people on the set broke into applause. Was I embarrassed? Nope. I was in love.

Dorez's half brother was the Shah of Iran, the one who died in exile and was succeeded by the Ayatollah Khomeini. Then single, the Shah had rather hedonistic tastes, but everything had to be done with the utmost decorum, and the same rules applied to Dorez. He could do nothing that might discredit his homeland. Nor was I totally free, because of the morals clause in every film contract. In those days bad press could badly damage a career—look at Ingrid Bergman. So discretion was the key word.

Cousin Kenny was back in Vancouver at this time, and I conspired with him to help keep my trip to Paris a secret. I told the studio I was going to Vancouver for the Christmas holidays, but there would be no way to contact me by telephone. I would keep in touch with them by the mails and through Western Union. Ken then sent the studio daily bulletins of my activities, including imaginary men I was supposed to be going out with. With this in the works, it was off to Paris.

Dorez had instructed me about the requirements for the trip, but since I had to work up to the day of departure I saved my smallpox and plague inoculations for my stopover in New York. That was a mistake. On the trip over the Atlantic I was feeling woozy, and by the time we reached Paris I was sick. I struggled through our first night in a feverish sleep and in the morning asked Dorez to find me a doctor. After looking me over, the doctor ordered me to bed for at least two days and nights. That was hardly the way to start a lovers' tryst, but it worked out all right.

This was my first trip to Europe, and being in love made all the good things even better. Dorez was well known in Paris, so special treatment was par for the course. Dorez introduced me to his brother Mahmud and to his sister Shams and her husband. They were all movie fans and a bit star-struck, so I was given deferential treatment—by royalty.

Before our Christmas trip to Switzerland, Dorez took me to Jacques Fath, the famous couturier, because he wanted me to have something chic in my wardrobe. I selected an ice-blue satin evening gown with pearls embroidered on the bodice and also what I called my Rita Hayworth dress. It was, I learned later, an exact duplicate of the gown she wore at her wedding with Aly Khan. Hers was blue and in heavy silk; mine was champagne satin. The dresses were to be shipped to St. Moritz in time for New Year's Eve.

We went by car to Switzerland with Dorez's aide, Emad, behind the wheel. As we traveled through France, Dorez casually asked me if my papers were in order. Papers? It turned out that I had no visa for Switzerland. Hadn't Dorez told the officials that I was coming? This dumb question threw off Emad's concentration enough for him to spin the car out of control. We spun around on the icy pavement and plunged off the roadway into a snowbank, where we spent the rest of the blustery night shivering and counting the hours until daylight, neither man speaking to me. After dawn, a farmer dug us out of the snow, and we managed to enter Switzerland without much trouble thanks to Dorez's diplomatic passport.

Switzerland was beautiful over the holidays, but the festivities can't compare with the Christmas season back home. All went well, however, until New Year's Eve approached and my dresses hadn't arrived from Paris. We were scheduled for a very posh affair and I had to find something to wear. In a boutique, I found a Victorian lace blouse and a long black skirt. I liked it, but Dorez didn't. "You look like Whistler's Mother," he said. "Only the lace cap is missing."

You can image how this made me feel. Dorez could become insufferable when he was on his high Persian horse, but I knew he loved me. I had only to look at the exquisite wristwatch he had given me for Christmas to realize it. It was inscribed, "All My Love, Dorez—1948."

The next stop was Venice, and from there we went on to Rome and then to Naples, with a side trip to Pompeii. What a joyful time we had. I tried to keep my spirits up on the drive back to Rome, but we both faced separation. On our last night together no time was wasted on sleep; we clung to each other until dawn. I can still see it now—that parting. It was six A.M. on a dreary Roman morning. All the dreamlike days and hours had been spent. It was back to Hollywood for me, and for my *djounam* it was back to his fairytale land. (That was how I thought of Persia at the time.)

Two sad events took place while I was in Europe. Paul Kohner had wired me about the death of Ernst Lubitsch in November, but I wouldn't learn of Mark Hellinger's death on December 21 until my return. I had to face the New Year of 1948 with the loss of two good friends.

As for the ploy with the studio, Ken's bulletins fooled them, but they weren't giggling over their inability to reach me by phone. The chief casting director gave me hell and swore that the next such shenanigans would result in my suspension. He even threatened to put me into B pictures.

Promising to be a good little girl from then on, I immediately began to plot my next subterfuge. I would be attending the Cannes Film Festival the following spring, and I hoped Dorez and I could meet there.

Dorez's letters were filled with serious talk about his expanding role in politics. His brother, the Shah, was trying to lift their country into the twentieth century, and the entire family was committed to the task. In July the Shah visited the United States, and Dorez was delegated to handle affairs back home. I did go to the Cannes festival, but there was no Dorez.

Almost a year passed before, on a break from the studio, I was able to meet Dorez at Boca Raton, Florida. The weather was great and we were hungry to be with each other, but the reunion wasn't perfect. Not only was I sick for part of the time, but hotel heir David Schine paid more attention to me than Dorez thought he should and I saw Dorez in all-out anger for the first time. His jealousy proved that Dorez cared for me, but I wondered what would become of us. Dorez was caught up in his duty to his homeland and family, but there was also a compulsion in him to be free to live and love as he pleased. I'm certain he hoped for something more to come from our romance, but he knew better than I how impossible it would be. I was still living a daydream.

By the time Dorez got back to Iran, the country was under martial law. An assassination attempt against the Shah had almost succeeded, and Dorez was guilt-ridden for having been abroad at such a time. The crisis soon ended, however, and our correspondence continued, arranging our next rendezvous in Teheran. Dorez asked me to try to bring someone for his brother, the divorced and lonely Shah. Dorez had met Pat Starling briefly at Hunt Hartford's party and felt she was his brother's type. I loved the idea of a pal to travel with.

After having known the Shah for less than an hour, Pat asked him about the attempt on his life. The Shah (whose full name, by the way, was Mohammed Reza Pahlavi) made light of it but showed us the bullet hole in the cap he had been wearing. It was not his destiny to die that day, he told us. He believed it was preordained that he would carry out his master plan for his people before death took him away.

In a private talk I had with Reza I learned something of the inner feelings of those who rule. He said he had an "impossible dream" which was so simple it was poignant. His dream was "an island," a place where he could escape all the problems of his world, a place of peace and serenity. On this island, he could walk through the streets wearing old clothes—even shorts if he wished. He could get roaring drunk if he so desired, could laugh loudly and make passes at all the pretty girls. In this make-believe land he could blend in with everyone else and just be human, common, and free. For most of us, the Shah's daydream is too familiar to be worth imagining, for him it was more than he could expect.

In Iran, we were never really alone until the bedroom doors were locked at night. Guards were everywhere. One day we had a picnic on the grounds of the summer palace. The four of us were chauffered by limousine and followed by servants and soldiers. When we arrived the servants scurried about setting up our lace tablecloth, covered by price-less silver. There were gorgeous pillows for us to sit upon, and oh yes, French champagne. The food consisted of Persian caviar, Strasbourg paté, and cold partridge. After lunch we lay on our backs, told jokes, and giggled like kids. Reza suggested some target practice. That idea pleased me no end, but each time the Shah changed the target to a fresh one he would turn his back to us and I found myself thinking how easy it would be to pick him off. Click, bang! No more monarch. Then I remembered all the soldiers and imagined them dragging me away to prison until my execution. Such drama! As you can see, it was easy for Pat and me to forget the lofty status of our hosts. We were simply four friends having fun together.

Pat and I had plenty of time to wander around the palaces. There were four in all, facing each other in the center of Teheran. I took my 16 mm movie camera wherever I went. I had gotten some particularly good shots of Reza on his favorite steed throwing me kisses, and when I returned to California I was eager to see how they had come out. Boy, was I surprised. That whole reel was blank. I found out later that Abdorezza had secretly exposed my film so that there would be no record of the king acting so silly. I was terribly upset at the sneakiness of this treachery.

Something struck me as curious while I was there. For all their wealth, they put up with so many outmoded living conditions: The royal kitchen is a good example. We dined every night in His Majesty's palace, regal and resplendent—yet the food was always cold when it was served because the servants had to carry the trays of food from one palace to another. One night I suggested that they install a modern kitchen adjacent to the main dining room. I glanced at Dorez, only to see his mouth drop open in disbelief. The Shah listened, though I could tell by his expression that he was shocked by my audacity and merely being tolerant of a silly little American girl who knew nothing of tradition. Okay, so it's tradition, but is it irreligious or something to put in a steam table or two?

After dinner, when the Shah and Dorez excused themselves to attend to matters of state, Pat and I would get together to compare notes. My bedroom had furniture of delicately inlaid wood, Persian carpets, and priceless paintings interspersed with magnificent tapestries on the walls. The walls were a couple of feet thick, and deep fireplaces were sculptured out of them. My bed had a golden crown on its headboard. Pat and I were both enjoying our taste of royal living, and despite my warning Pat was beginning to entertain serious thoughts about the Shah.

During the day Pat and I were given free rein of the palace and the grounds and had a chauffeured limousine at our disposal. We brought our own mad money and shopped the bazaars until we ran out of mials. Handcrafted silver was our favorite: jars, plates, cigarette cases with dirty illustrations inside, FILTHY—oh, what fun! We lunched on typical Persian menus of *chelakebab,* rice, pomegranates, lamb. The Persian rugs were magnificent, but we left that shopping for His Majesty and His Highness, and Dorez did send me three rugs and two carpets which I cherish to this day.

When we did return home, it was with no definite date set for a future meeting. As it turned out, I would return to Iran once more alone, in March of 1950, some years later. I had had plenty of time to evaluate my relationship with Dorez by then. I couldn't help but project myself into my own "impossible dream" of becoming Dorez's wife. But suppose I did achieve this ultimate goal? Would I be willing to give up my career, to live far away from family and friends? I wasn't sure, but a first step was seeing if marriage was part of the plan.

It was a hunting trip into the country that clarified matters. We drove for many miles, then mounted the magnificent Arabian horses awaiting us. According to protocol, the Shah and I headed the procession and Dorez brought up the rear. As we reached the rolling hills, in search of curly-horned mountain goats, I saw one shadowy figure, then another, and then they seemed to be everywhere. Behind every rock, bush, and tree, some mounted and some on foot, were heavily armed soldiers. It gave me a clear picture of what royal life in Iran was all about. The Shah and Dorez seemed oblivious to the soldiers' presence. I wasn't. This, too, was my first experience of hunting, and though I had always loved guns I could now see that hunting would never be for me, though I didn't complain to the others.

While I was sitting on the steps of an ancient country palace one afternoon during that second visit to Iran, I began to see things clearly.

My relationship with Dorez had lasted nearly five years, and now there was no future in sight for it. It came to me that this phase of my life was at an end, but somehow I couldn't bring myself to tell Dorez then. I chose the coward's way out by writing him a "Dear John" letter on my return flight to New York. The fairy tale was over, but I had no regrets. How many gals can say they were really involved with a true-life Prince Charming?

Chapter 21

I had just returned from an extended publicity tour in the spring of 1948 when a family disaster struck. Cousin Ken had a terrible auto crash in San Luis Obispo and was left in grave physical condition. It seems that I was *it:* the one elected to arrange Ken's medical treatment, handle the legal details, and last but not least, pay for it.

The accident was widely publicized, and help was offered from far afield. The most generous gesture came from Howard Hughes, who summoned the best possible medical specialists and then hired a private ambulance to transport Ken from San Luis Obispo two hundred miles south to the Good Samaritan Hospital in Los Angeles, which by now Howard had come to call *his* hospital. Ken slowly recovered, and once again I could thank Howard for remaining my good friend—a good friend indeed.

Before his death, Mark Hellinger had promised me the role of Anna in a hard-hitting crime story, *Criss Cross.* It was a good dramatic role and out of the "rock candy" category, so I assumed that without Mark I wouldn't stand a chance. Burt Lancaster was set for the lead, with Dan Duryea supporting him. As I went about my studio routines I heard that it would be either Ava or Shelley Winters for female lead. There was some doubt that the project would go at all without Mark but suddenly it was all systems go, and surprise of surprises, I got the role of Anna.

I was told that producer Michael Kraike and director Robert Siodmak had done battle with the high brass to see that they honored Hellinger's promise to me.

With the exception of my cameo role in *Brute Force,* I had never played a real down-to-earth character nor had I been allowed to speak like one. Everything had been theatrical, with me as the princess or slave girl. This was a solid characterization of a scheming two-timer whose greed takes its toll on her lovers. I worked very hard with Yura to make certain my development of the role would be realistic.

With so much energy surging through the set, there were moments of tension. One day Siodmak shouted down at me from his position high on the camera boom. He did it again and again, until my shattered nerves finally broke. "You will apologize to me, Mr. Siodmak," I yelled up at him, "or you'll be setting up your artistic scene with an invisible actress."

The tension was almost palpable for a few moments, then "Pliss, Yvonne, dear," he said in a voice soft and mellifluous, "vould you giff me ze emotion I need for dis scene—eeffen though it iss only a rehearsal. Danke schön, Yvonne."

That broke the tension, and everybody on the set began laughing. Siodmak never demeaned me again in front of the cast and crew, or at any other time. I proceeded in the film with a sense of confidence as I piled up three Yvonne De Carlo firsts: I smoked my first cigarette on camera, did my first crying scene, and played my first death scene.

A new Universal contract player was given his first part in *Criss Cross* —a bit, actually. His name was Bernie Schwartz, and since he was so cute and likable I went out with him a couple of times. I don't think he was much younger than I, but his exuberance and cockiness made him seem like a kid. Though we were friends rather than lovers, Bernie loved to share his bedroom experiences with anyone who would listen. He told me about one escapade with a young Spanish-dancer type being groomed at Universal. He said he got her to lovers' lane on Mulholland Drive easily enough, but as he began to turn on his afterburner she started to protest. "No, no, please don't, please," she said, pushing him away. "I should have a duenna."

"Okay, sweetie," he told her. "We'll just run down to the drugstore and get one."

Bernie caught on readily to the ways of most other girls in Hollywood and of Hollywood itself. He also caught on as an actor—under the name Tony Curtis.

Several months later, I was sent to Europe to help promote *Criss Cross* and Cousin Ken, who had recovered from his injuries, made the trip with me. He or Aunt Connie would often travel with me. Marie simply didn't care for long trips, and wasn't at all slighted when someone else was asked.

I attended a special screening in Antwerp at which I met the Mayor and did the same in Brussels. I was astonished at the warm reception I received from European fans. Thousands of them lined the streets shouting, "Yvonne, Yvonne!" My reaction to such adulation was almost a denial: Can they really be cheering *me?* I thought. Is this for real? I was always pleased—and also embarrassed.

In Paris I gave a speech in French and held a press conference. Most of the questions were about my love life, since I was known there for having dated Prince Abdorezza, but whenever his name came up I would refuse to reply, knowing that almost anything could be misquoted.

In London, in addition to the promotional chores Ken and I did some sightseeing. We made a pilgrimage to Stratford-on-Avon for a taste of Shakespeare and were fortunate to see a production of *Henry IV, Part II,* with Laurence Harvey and Margaret Leighton as well as the brilliant young Richard Burton. Ken and I enjoyed staying at tiny hotels like the Crooked Dog and the Beef 'n Ale. I loved England and could have stayed weeks longer, but finally it was back to Hollywood. This assignment would find me playing opposite my old flame Howard Duff in *Calamity Jane and Sam Bass.* We would be working on location at Kanab, Utah, which was just fine with me because I could get my fill of horseback riding.

When this film was in the can, I found out my next assignment was *The Gal Who Took the West.* I was disappointed with the prospects of yet another "gal" picture, but this one offered more promise than some as it was to be made in color, and would allow me to try my hand at comedy. I played Lillian Marlowe, a back-East woman who comes out West to perform in a frontier opera house owned by oldtimer Charles Coburn and stays on to flirt with Coburn's sons, John Russell and Scott Brady. The script called for me to sing and dance concert-hall style.

The story was done in flashback. In the present-day scenes I was made up to look very old, which meant having to report for work two hours earlier than usual for Bud Westmore to apply the rubber-skin mask and special makeup. The time it took to put on all the makeup would age anyone.

One scene called for Russell and Brady to have a battle royal in their own living room with Coburn and me watching. The fight had to be of epic proportions, so a pair of stuntmen were called in to choreograph and double for the rough stuff. One of them was tall, well-built, blue-eyed Jacques O'Mahoney (Jocko Mahoney, as he would later be called) and if you think my bells weren't ringing—you're wrong.

I asked my stand-in, Marie Bodie, to find out whatever she could about this Adonis. She returned a while later with practically a full-length biography. He had come to Hollywood from Iowa, had been a swimming instructor, a pilot, and a U.S. Marine. After the war he raised horses in the San Fernando Valley and got involved in movie stunt work. He had two small children from a dissolved marriage and his pals called him Jocko.

We made contact on the set, and soon he was saying nice things about my eyes and asking me out to dinner. There was no mistaking the mutual attraction but we had several dates before anything serious happened. I think he was something of a romantic, and so was I. We went to the Circle J Ranch on a date one day, and on the way home, he pulled off to the side of the road, put his arm around me, and gave me a kiss. What a rush of passion. We were silent on the way back to town, but we *knew* that the very next time we met that passion would have to be satisfied. It was exciting to wait for that to happen. Could Jocko be the answer to all my lifelong dreams? He had all the attributes, and then some.

I was warned by all my knowing friends that when an established star hooked up with a screen aspirant it almost never worked. I tried very hard to help Jocko in the industry since he wanted to become a star so badly. One day, as a total surprise, Jocko slipped a sweet but simple diamond ring on my third finger left hand. At the time we were in a country-type bar in the Sierras, and the simplicity of the surroundings played like a good omen to me. I had the feeling this marked the beginning of the romance I'd longed for.

Jocko started drawing location assignments while I was busy on the Universal backlot. I tried to get away to join him for a weekend visit, but I hadn't been feeling well. I had no idea what was wrong, but finally I made the five-hour drive to Lone Pine. Jocko was waiting for me outside the motel and we rushed into each other's arms. He carried me inside, where we caught up on everything and I do mean everything.

Later, we started thinking about food. The town had one nice restaurant and I had anticipated a wonderful meal with Jocko, but from the start there were long uncomfortable periods of silence. I found myself looking at the knives and forks, thinking, "What if we ended up this way, an aging couple digesting their food with nothing to say?" My depressing thoughts ended, thank goodness, after we returned to the motel. Conversation then was unnecessary.

We had made plans for Jocko's day off, a climb in the mountains. I gamely went off with him, hoping to enjoy the hike, but after a few hundred yards uphill I began to fail. Jocko couldn't understand what was wrong with me and neither could I. After I got home I wasted no time in seeing the doctor. After examining me, he asked, "How long have you been pregnant, Yvonne?" "Pregnant . . . why do you say that?" I found his diagnosis incredible. "I think that's what your problem is," he said, "but let's run a test." His hunch was right, but that wasn't all. He also discovered that I had a large tumor—an ovarian cyst, which had to be removed. I couldn't believe my ears—I was shocked and upset. By now Jocko was back in town, and I told him the news. He was very supportive and understanding, and didn't mind that we had conceived a baby, but I didn't mention the other complications; I simply couldn't.

Marie was living in the East at that time and Connie was in Vancouver, so I was all alone facing a crisis situation. I was at home one evening, trying to keep calm, when the doorbell sounded. I opened the door to find Jocko's mother, come to offer me comfort and show me God's way. Well-meaning as she was, his mother did little but further depress me. She was something of a religious zealot, and spoke in Biblical quotes and looked heavenward in making her points. I was greatly relieved when she finally got up to leave. At the door, she turned back and said, "Grit your loins . . . grit your loins." I stared after her, not knowing what she was talking about. I think she meant to say "Gird your loins," but at the time I didn't know what that meant either. I did know that I resented her interference.

My next problem was to get out of the movie I'd just started. The rigorous dance rehearsals were scheduled to begin immediately. What to do? Jocko recommended a physician who had been his family doctor for years. Thinking that he would keep it all a big secret, I went to him for a checkup. Well, not only did the doctor snitch on me to Jocko's mother (thus her visit), but he also told the heads of Universal that I was pregnant. They promptly took me off the film, which was fine with me, but I wish that I had been the one to tell them.

When the day for my surgery arrived, I remember lying on a hospital bed with waves of pain going through my body. It made me angry. After days of enduring this pain, I said aloud, "Goddamn you—you lousy stinking pain. Get the hell out—back off!" Lo and behold, I felt the pain diminish. Oh how wondrous if we could rediscover the abilities of our minds' powers that lie hidden and that surface only with extreme emotion.

I was soon wheeled into surgery and when I awoke, the cyst was gone, and unfortunately, so was the baby. I cried and cried and when there were no more tears I fell into a deep depression. I felt then that it was probably as close as I would ever come to bearing the blond-haired, blue-eyed baby I so often dreamed of.

As Paul Kohner drove me home from the hospital, I was given some good agently advice. "Now that this is all behind you, Yvonne," he said, "I think you should think things over carefully. I don't think Mahoney is the right man for you."

My protests weren't quite as strong as they would have been a few weeks earlier. I just listened, promising myself I would indeed take stock of the situation, and things were never quite the same between Jocko and me from then on. I think our greatest problems had to do with career. He may have resented my success and his own lack of it, and while he said he appreciated my help in trying to get him jobs, he probably resented that as well. He was a big man, with an ego to match.

I had lost so much weight that Maureen O'Hara was given my role in *Bagdad*. With nothing to keep me in Hollywood, I decided to give myself a vacation, where I could think things out. I chose Europe, and took Cousin Kenny with me. We were in Venice for the spring film festival, and one day we went swimming. I picked a secluded spot, since I was rather self-conscious about my thin body, but the paparazzi found us anyway, wading into the water with their pants rolled up. We were in the short subjects of the next night's film screening, Kenny and I in the water, and me with skinny body and bony shoulders. The newsreel footage showed all the photographers snapping us. As we watched, a woman seated in front of us leaned over to her companion and loudly whispered, "Brutta—brutta!" (Ugly—ugly!) I'll admit I didn't look very glamorous—but ugly? I guess that by Italian standards I was just too thin.

We had shipped my MG roadster from the States and it sagged under the weight of two passengers and fourteen suitcases. We picnicked beside Lakes Lugano and Como in the Swiss Alps, took movies of the spectacular scenery, and had a great time. We made our way to Milano, and as we approached the Principe di Savoia Hotel we were confronted by paparazzi as thick as ants and angry because we were later than planned. Nor were they pleased with pigtails and pedal pushers in a roadster instead of furs and jewels in a limousine. They snapped us checking in, making sure they got a glimpse of my passport to learn my age. The next morning our picture appeared with the caption: THE MOST BEAUTIFUL GIRL IN THE WORLD TRAVELS LIKE THIS???!!!

Next stop, Vienna. We passed through the Austrian and American sectors without event and were prepared to deal with the Russians when the time came, finally spotting something that suggested it could be a barrier. But the rail was up and we saw no one, so we buzzed on through. As Ken reached the hilltop, I looked behind to see a uniformed guard rise up from a table where he had been napping. Around his shoulder was strapped an ugly Sten gun. We thought about it for a moment, and then dismissed it.

We saw pictures of Stalin on the barns that we passed, and assumed the Russian sector lay ahead. But nothing slowed us down until we reached Vienna a few hours later, where we learned from an American general that we had indeed passed the Russian guard post. It was a wonder, he told us, that we weren't fired upon.

I started to gain weight, thanks to the fabulous Viennese pastries, and by the time I returned to Hollywood I had improved not only physically but emotionally. My waiting assignment was *Buccaneer's Girl,* which was probably the same as all the others, except that this time I was a "girl" instead of a "gal."

The camera director was Russ Metty, with whom I had worked before. One day I heard him shout over to his lighting chief, "Okay now, make it one R.C.H. down." Then later, "Give it just one R.C.H. to the left."

I had heard this reference many times but somehow never questioned what it meant. Now it was beginning to bug me. "Hey, Russ," I said the next time I heard it. "Exactly what do the letters stand for?"

I thought I saw a grin, but he was suddenly too busy to reply. The sound man was no more helpful than Russ. During a lull in the shooting a day or so later, the crew kind of gathered around. "You asked the other day about the meaning of R.C.H.," said the lighting man. "Well, it's a term we use for a fine hairsbreadth measurement."

"Oh," I said, perfectly content to leave it at that.

Russ Metty couldn't let it just dangle. "You see, Yvonne," he said, "there are three such measurements: Y.C.H., B.C.H., and R.C.H. . . . Got it?"

"I got it," I said. I wouldn't ask what those letters stood for now for a million dollars.

"You see," said Metty, "the first letter stands for the color of hair: yellow, black, and red. The finest hair of all is red. That's why we ask for an R.C.H.—a red . . . hair. Get it now?"

I got it.

Chapter 22

At this time I was trying hard to improve my singing voice, and was fortunate to have been referred to the highly respected Gennaro Curci, teacher of opera singers. I went to the maestro's Hollywood home to audition for him, and he was pleased. He said I was a natural lyric soprano but should train to correct the break in my voice when I changed octaves. We started working together, and that is the right word for it: there were no easy days with Gennaro Curci. But at least I was beginning to feel like a professional singer. Among the maestro's students was the young six-foot-six Metropolitan opera star Jerome Hines. I'd heard he was a student of Curci's and had seen his photo in the Curci living room. I decided I *had* to meet him and eventually I did. He was a striking man and *sooo* tall I couldn't help wondering what it would be like to be embraced by a man of his height. Was it Gertrude Stein who said, "A man is a man is a man"? No, I think I'm the one who said that.

Jerry and I teamed up on several occasions for radio and TV shows and we even sang a duet for our supper once at an Italian restaurant in New York. The teaming up of an opera basso with a lyric soprano movie actress gave us considerable publicity and although we enjoyed our time together, there was nothing lasting between us.

Through Jerry, I met Ezio Pinza backstage at the Met, but my greatest thrill was when Jerry introduced me to Cesare Siepi. He was a dark-eyed, personable Italian from Milan, I was a hybrid Sicilian and if that didn't combine for a potent mixture nothing else could. Cesare had been a prizefighter before starting his singing career at La Scala. He was six-foot-six and one of the handsomest of all opera singers.

Our common language was French and after we'd known each other for a while he would say, "Oh, if only you knew Italian—I could tell you off but good!" Cesare was a walking time bomb whose temper could erupt without notice, sometimes surprising even himself. Once in his fury he very nearly backed out of the open window of my fifth-floor hotel room. He would have if I hadn't made a grab for him.

One of his favorite peeves was: "I wish you were a virgin. . . . Why can't you be a virgin?" He was saying that he'd marry me if I were a virgin. His cuts didn't make me bleed, strangely enough. He was so bombastic, and so absurd, that I took his outbursts in stride.

At other times, we'd be trudging through the streets of Manhattan hand in hand like teenage lovers, caring nothing for anyone else. When my work took me to London, I received lovely letters written in lyrical French. The cables back and forth were never-ending. Could we meet somewhere—we must. Or, when I was in Los Angeles and he was in Mexico, could he stop off and see me on the way to New York? Of course he could—and did.

Cesare was ill-equipped emotionally to put up with someone who was a free spirit like me. He would read gossip items—some of them true—in which I'd be linked with other men. Immediately there would be a telegram or a phone call (in French of course): "How could you?" "Don't you care at all?" "Why do you torment me?"

Once, back in New York, Jerome Hines dropped by my hotel room for a visit. While he was there I got a phone call from Cesare to confirm our later dinner date. After speaking with him for a moment, I said, "Oh, by the way, there's an old friend of yours here. He wants to say hello."

I gave Jerry the phone, and he carried on a seemingly cordial conversation with Cesare. He gave me back the phone, and I asked Cesare what time I should expect him. "We are not going out tonight," he shouted. "I refuse to take part in the changing of the guard!"

What finally ended my relationship with Cesare was my involvement a bit later with Prince Aly Khan. Cesare's pride was mortally wounded that I would be interested in another man, and especially one so rich and famous. Cesare and I would see each other several months later at a dinner party given by Mr. and Mrs. Curci. At that point I was anxious to discover if I still had strong feelings for him, and seeing him once again was the solution. The evening progressed pleasantly and I didn't notice my pulse rate speeding up in the least. Good! Now, perhaps I could get him off my mind.

In January of 1950 the studio included me in a junket that was scheduled to tour U.S. military bases in Europe. I joined Donald O'Connor, Patricia Medina, Lois Andrews, and my old pal Hal Belfer in the show that was designed to help promote *Francis,* the first of the Talking Mule movies. We broke in our skits at bases in Newfoundland and then went on to Wiesbaden, where we gave our first performance at the Commander Theater. From there we hopscotched to Frankfurt, Berlin, and Fürstenfeldbruch. It was in the latter city that I experienced one of life's most embarrassing moments. The military hosted a banquet for us after the show, and I was seated next to the commanding general. He leaned over and asked if there was a particular song I would like to have played by the band. I did have a favorite among others in those days; it was "The Russian Marching Song." The general shrugged, amused, and passed the request over to the bandleader. Soon I heard the amplified voice of the bandleader telling the guests that "Miss De Carlo wishes to hear 'The Red Russian Marching Song.' " The "Red" part of the title came as a surprise to me. My face went crimson as the band dutifully played the song.

After playing Brussels and Antwerp the tour came to an end. The others returned home, but I remained in Europe. I had a few weeks free and had met a charming American Army officer, who took me sightseeing. Then followed my scheduled trip to Iran, which ended my romance with Prince Abdorezza. With all of that behind, it was nearing time to return to Hollywood to begin work on *The Desert Hawk.* I stopped off for a few days in New York.

Marie was living in New York at that time, blissfully ensconced in a Riverside Drive apartment with a long-term boy friend. When I visited her, I was given some bad news: my grandmother, only seventy-one, had died while I was away. I felt terrible that I had been away at such a tragic time, but her death was sudden and I couldn't have helped. My grandmother's guidance had made me the person I was. Even the time when she invoked the "wrath of God" after my weeping-willow tree kiss, it was out of love for me. She was a kind and simple woman whom I loved dearly, and I wished that I might have seen her one more time to tell her so.

I still hadn't cleared the slate with Jocko Mahoney, but that was because when I was in town he was gone. I thought I would see him during this term in Hollywood, but just about the time he was due in town I was sent on location to the Black Hills of South Dakota to begin work on *Tomahawk.*

The cast and crew were checked into a hotel in Rapid City, a good-sized town with good restaurants and a bit of night life, but I was going into one of my isolation moods. I found a place many miles into the country called the Sylvan Lake Lodge, and with a car kindly furnished by the local car agency, I was relatively happy. It was early May, but the surrounding mountains were still snow-covered. I loved sitting on the steps of my cabin watching the scenery, and I thrived on the moody skies and the thunderstorms which came and went with angry frequency.

On a side trip with Van Heflin we visited the town of Crazy Horse, where a huge statue was being chiseled into solid rock by dynamite blasts to commemorate the great Sioux Indian chief. There was a museum on the site to offset some of the expenses of the sculptor, Korczak Ziolkowski. Inside the museum Van and I were met by a bearded, powerfully built man wearing a Davy Crockett-type leather jacket. I knew at once we were looking at the sculptor himself, the man who had won the prize for the "Hands of Paderewski." We found him to be a very friendly Bostonian. As we spoke, he seemed to be studying my features, and a few years later he asked me to pose, sculpting a bust of me out of Carrera marble.

I had been fond of Van Heflin since the early Florentine Gardens days, and we had fun on location. We did everything together during our off hours, visiting Mount Rushmore and the homesite of Chief Red Cloud. We also attended numerous parties together, which, inevitably, resulted in publicity. Before long Van had a call from his wife, who informed him that she was joining him in Rapid City and was bringing their two children as well. I saw very little of Van after the family arrived—at least not alone.

I did see plenty of Rock Hudson, however, and we became pals. One day Rock asked for a lift from the location and I said sure. I warned him, though, that I wanted to stop on the way back to see a horse I had been thinking of buying. He agreed. We drove slowly along the country road until I spotted this gorgeous black horse; then we pulled over and got out. Marie Bodie was with us, but she preferred to wait in the car. I had left the engine running, thinking we'd be away only a few minutes, but my horsetrading took some time. When we returned to the car we discovered the engine had stopped, and then we learned why. It had run out of gas.

Rock volunteered to hike the five or so miles to a gas station, assuming he would get a ride along the way. The problem was that Rock wasn't a typical hitchhiker. I don't mean because he was a six-foot-three movie actor—he wasn't that recognizable at the time. It was because he was dressed in his movie costume, a Civil War uniform. But he got a ride. He flagged down a car that looked like something out of *The Grapes of Wrath*. A man and woman were up front with a baby in the mother's lap, and about eight kids were wedged into the back seat. The driver studied Rock as though wondering if he were an escaped lunatic and Rock was equally doubtful about the driver. The farmer not only drove Rock to the station, he brought him back as well.

On another occasion, Rock and I invented a scenario which we then played out. He in his blue Yankee soldier uniform performed a solo and I played cameraman, using the 16 mm camera. The fort was our set and I shot Rock through a knothole in the stockade. He was stumbling and clutching his throat in mock death throes. I thought it was a fine performance, and we all had a chuckle over the scene at parties.

By the time I returned to L.A. three months had passed, and this time I found Jocko in town. There was the chance, I thought, that we could give our romance another try, but we had been apart too long. Jocko was with me the day I happened to see a FOR SALE sign in front of a magnificent house on Coldwater Canyon near Mulholland Drive. After examining the place inside and out, I know it was my dream home. There was only one problem: its price tag of sixty-two thousand dollars was way beyond my means.

I was in the process of trying to erase the house from my mind when I got a call from the owner, who said that if I was still interested he would drop the price to fifty thousand. I said, "Sold!" It was still a lot of money, but I couldn't turn down the chance of a lifetime. I learned later that the owner's wife was responsible, threatening divorce proceedings if her husband didn't return her at once to civilization. There had always been snakes on the grounds, but one day she had entered her baby's bedroom to find a rattlesnake coiled beneath the crib. The studio loaned me the down payment, and the house was soon mine— snakes and all.

The rambling eleven-room ranch house was perched on five-and-a-half acres of hilly wooded land at such a steep incline that the rooms were all on different levels, which presented some problems in decorating. I hired an architect to help design an English-style dining room, with paneling and stained-glass windows.

One morning during renovations Jocko and I were having breakfast in the open area beyond the kitchen. A pair of blue jays flew over and perched themselves on his shoulder. It was such an idyllic scene that I was filled with confidence that we could surmount all of our problems and live happily ever after. But the purchase of the house only made things worse. There were more quarrels, which became more violent, and the good times didn't come frequently enough to offset the bad.

Jocko and I had several partings of the ways, and on one of them I went to his house to pick up the rifle given me by Bob Stack and some of my records. Of course, this mission was an excuse to see Jocko, but he wasn't home.

I was greeted at the door by a very precocious and sweet little girl. "Hi," she said cheerfully.

I forced a smile, wondering where she had come from, and finally asked the big question: "Do you know where Jocko is?"

"No, but he should be coming back soon."

"Are you all alone here?"

"No, my mother's in the bedroom," said the little girl.

On that cue, a seemingly embarrassed young woman emerged from the other part of the house. She said she was Peggy Field, a friend of Jocko's. He had been called to the studio, she said, but he had put my things aside to be picked up. I walked away with my rifle and my records, with full knowledge that I was making my final exit.

I learned later that Peggy Field had been seeing Jocko for some time. They would marry within a year. The cute little girl would grow up on our television screens and a couple of decades later would be the Academy Award–winning actress Sally Field.

Small world, isn't it?

Chapter 23

Great numbers of English-accented men and women have graced our movie screens all through the years, but the British unions make it very difficult to use American actors even for clearly American roles. They simply direct their players to do an American accent, usually with poor results.

I, however, made several British movies over the years and it didn't seem to pose any problems at all. The first was *Hotel Sahara,* in which I starred opposite Peter Ustinov. I brought Aunt Connie with me this time, and we made a winter crossing of the Atlantic to arrive in England December 12, 1950.

We were registered into a deluxe apartment at 55 Park Lane, and this time I brought a steamer trunk, eight suitcases, my full-length black mist mink coat, and a morocco case stuffed with thousands of dollars worth of jewelry. They wanted glamour; I'd give them glamour.

The press turned out in amazing numbers, so many, in fact, that they were asked to form a line to talk with me; then, each reporter was limited to five minutes. Here are some of the resulting quotes:

"The world suffers from a serious shortage of bachelors. Do you think I will find the right man in England? He should be tall, not too handsome, and intelligent."

"You can take it from me, I have only three boy friends and all of them are opera singers. But it's nothing serious, you know. I prefer Nordic types."

"I collect jewelry, furniture, and men. It's so hard finding a man earning more money than I do."

The papers ran headlines equivalent to MISS DE CARLO HERE IN SEARCH OF A HUSBAND. I suppose, in a sense, it was true.

What excited me about this project was the letter I had received from producer George Brown. He said he had seen all my films and saw by the sparkle in my eye that I could play comedy. I was really grateful for the comment, as I had been hoping for years that someone in America would see similar potential. The role of Yasmin Vadis did not entirely break my Hollywood stereotype, however. I played a desert girl, wearing familiar harem outfits, but this time it was satire and that made all the difference.

The production couldn't have run more smoothly, and Peter Ustinov was a delight to work with. I learned a great deal from him about playing farce and was continually entertained by him off camera. On one occasion he took me to dinner at Les Ambassadeurs and entertained everyone within hearing range with his remarkable impressions. What a gifted man. That night was special for him as well, as a young and pretty blond-haired actress named Suzanne Cloutier joined our table, meeting Peter for the first time. I learned later that the meeting had been arranged at Peter's request, and they obviously hit it off, because they were married a short time later.

One of my publicity interviews was for the radio program "In Town Tonight," and it was later revealed that one of the listeners was Denis Anthony Brian Butler, Ninth Earl of Lanesborough. He had been in his bath and had liked the sound of my voice. He subsequently contacted me to ask if I would be Guest of Honor for the Annual Hunt Ball to be given at his estate in Leicester. A charity event, it sounded like it could be fun, so I accepted. The press made a huge thing of it that an American movie star would be so honored at an aristocrat's gala.

The Earl came to London to meet me. In his early thirties, mustached, and quite attractive, he also had a wonderful sense of humor and was divorced. He was considered quite a catch, though as I learned more it became quite evident that the title of earl carried more prestige than riches. Estate taxes and the cost of living kept him hopping to make ends meet, but he was always upbeat about it, referring to himself as "the penniless peer."

For the gala, the white and scarlet ballroom had been decorated to resemble London's 400 Club. The Earl's main house was two hundred years old and was situated on three thousand acres of land. Connie and

I were given a gorgeous suite in the sixty-room house. At the ball there was an orchestra from London, and, according to someone's tally, three hundred bottles of champagne were consumed. I wore a Jacques Fath gown.

Any fantasies I may have had about becoming Lady Yvonne something-or-other were quelled the first night in what was named the "Pink Room." I anticipated feeling like a fairy princess in Magicland, but I instead came out feeling like the Snow Queen of the Arctic Circle. The fire in the hearth and the hot-water bottle just didn't do it. I was never so cold in my life. I was glad to return to the cozy warmth of our London apartment, and upon my return discovered I had become the darling of the press. It seems the Earl had let it be known that he held a special fondness for me. A few days later he paid a call with a basket of wildflowers and a box of country-fresh eggs. The press was under the impression something big was happening between the Earl and me, but in truth we hadn't so much as touched fingers.

Laurence Harvey was my date for the premiere of *Pandora and the Flying Dutchman* and the party afterward. The press tried to liven up that relationship too, but, again—nothing there. The stars of the picture were James Mason and Ava Gardner, neither of whom were on hand for the festivities, but I did meet one of Ava's cast-off lovers, Mario Cabre, who played her bullfighter lover in the film and in real life as well. Now he had been abandoned, as Ava was off in another go-round with her ambivalent lover Frank Sinatra.

Mario was the personification of the Continental Casanova: wide shoulders, narrow waist and hips, flashing black eyes, heavy accent, and brooding charm. Impeccably dressed in a black suit, with narrow tie and a dress cape with red velvet lining, he swaggered over to greet us the moment Larry ushered me into the room. I could see at once a charming and proud man whose ambitions went far beyond success in the bullring. One of his first remarks was that he was a poet at heart and could not wait to get back to his hotel room to compose something for me.

I wasn't really impressed by the lad; he was too obvious, but even so I agreed to go out with him. I didn't say I *hated* him, did I? We had dinners in Mayfair, theater dates, dancing. He invited me to visit him in Spain after the picture was completed, saying it was okay for Connie to come along. (Take note, Huntington Hartford.)

I had no intention of accepting the invitation to Spain, but after the weeks of chilling drizzle in London I was ready for some sunshine, so Connie and I got a flight to Madrid, where we were met by Mario— and every reporter in Spain. Mario must have been working round the clock to get the paparazzi rounded up. I then resigned myself to a very public visit to Spain; there was no such thing as privacy with Mario. He was always on, always posing. Whenever we happened onto a mirror in a store or anywhere—or even a nice, clean store window—Mario would stand before his image, primping and preening. I have never seen a *woman* with more vanity.

One of our mandatory stops was an afternoon at the bullfights. I have never liked the blood and gore of the sport, but I must say it was an altogether different experience to be there in the company of one of the stars of the spectacle. The fan adulation was incredible. We took a drive into the countryside to see the bulls in their natural setting and to watch the matadors at training. Mario tried to explain the psychology of the bull, and how important understanding it was for the bullfighter's survival. I listened attentively, interested in discovering the man behind the pomp and pretense.

In Barcelona we strolled alone down the Ramblas one afternoon. I say "alone" because Connie was having a siesta, but I don't mean alone-alone, because that was impossible. The paparazzi were everywhere, a few steps ahead, a step or two behind, overhead, below. "This is beginning to get to me," I told Mario. "Can't we find someplace a little more peaceful?"

He looked stunned. "Yvonne," he said, "choo are not like Ava. Chee loves publicity, and choo hide your face."

Mario gave me an exquisite ring—kissing birds formed out of gold —and in many ways he was quite sweet. I was warmed, and I was certainly publicized, but it was soon time for Connie and me to start back to the States. This time we crossed the Atlantic on the steamship *Independence.*

When I was loaned out for *Hotel Sahara,* my Universal contract had less than a year to run. Both the studio and I asked for different guarantees if the contract were to be renewed. I asked for a wider selection of roles, and the studio wanted to keep me in the "rock candy" moneymakers. We had reached a stalemate by the time I sailed for London, so I left it to Paul Kohner to negotiate my future.

While I was still abroad Paul wrote that the studio and I were coming to a parting of the ways. This didn't displease me because I knew there was more money to be made as a free-lancer, even though television had created hysteria within the industry. After nearly six years I was ready to go out on my own—sink or swim.

I returned to Hollywood two days before I was to begin work on *Silver City* with Edmond O'Brien. My salary was up to fifty thousand dollars a picture, which was not bad in those days, but I was counting on the release of *Hotel Sahara* to open the way for more interesting roles.

Meanwhile, with my new feeling of independence, I accepted a chance-of-a-lifetime offer. I would open the thirtieth season of the Hollywood Bowl in a performance of *Die Fledermaus,* conducted by Franz Waxman. It would be difficult singing a mezzo-soprano role with a lyric-soprano voice, but this was a challenge I just had to accept. We started rehearsal, with Miliza Korjus and Hugh Herbert as guest stars, and the rehearsals were long and hard. We all knew that the 20,000 seats would be filled with people who wondered if Yvonne De Carlo could carry a tune—let alone carry the leading role in an opera.

Opening night finally arrived and I stood in the wings awaiting my cue. I wore the smart military uniform of a Russian prince, my hair completely hidden beneath the cap and my monocle poised. I was so into my role of a male that I had to think twice about which restroom to use. My heart pounded as I gripped the leashes of the two trained wolfhounds. "Well, guys, here we go," I said when I heard the cue. "We're in this thing together." The week passed swiftly, and I wasn't nervous after the opening performance, instead feeling a wave of depression when we came down to our final performances, closing on July 14. It had been a rewarding experience, the aesthetic highlight of my life. Shortly before the opera closed, I felt devilish, and when the leading lady paused after making one of her speeches to Prince Orlofsky (me), I gave her a resounding whack on her ample bottom. The audience loved it. The star was astounded but she played it up beautifully. After the show, however, Franz came backstage and gave me a good bawling out. "No improvisation, please, Yvonne. Laughs or no laughs. Do not exit from the operetta. Stay within the story!"

A week later I returned to England to promote the release of *Hotel Sahara.* I was in London only a week before striking out on a one-woman concert tour in Israel. Kenny made the trip with me this time.

As a result of an almost catastrophic mix-up, all my music was lost en route to Tel Aviv. It seemed the concert would have to be canceled, but first I agreed to consult with their musical director to see if anything could be improvised. The conductor was as good as I had been told. Within three hours, we had six songs down on paper. He and four other musicians stayed up until dawn to orchestrate the entire concert. Among the songs were: "Come ona My House," "Frankie and Johnny," "Babalu," and "For Every Man There's a Woman." An hour before showtime, my suitcases arrived at the theatre. Not only was the music there, but also my shoes and underwear.

We played to consistently packed houses in Tel Aviv, Haifa, Jerusalem, and Jaffa. I even learned some Hebrew, which I wove into the show to the delight of the audiences. Thanks to Ken the news was kept from me that a terrorist group were said to be plotting to kidnap me for ransom and publicity. The efficient Israeli police kept me out of harm's way. I was grateful afterward that I hadn't known about the situation, especially when, so often, I had to claw through huge crowds of people to get from transportation to hotel, then to auditorium and back.

Hotel Sahara had opened everywhere by the time I returned home. The reviews in America were favorable, but in London they were raves. "The laughs come freely chiefly as a result of Miss De Carlo's hitherto hidden talents as a comedienne.... Miss De Carlo scores a victory. Her weapons: the De Carlo figure, the attractive De Carlo voice, and a bright sense of fun." That was from the *Sunday Graphic.* The *Daily Mail* said: "Miss De Carlo has a whale of a time and gives quite the best performance in the picture."

I went to work for Warners in *The San Francisco Story* with Joel McCrea, and when that was finished it was back to Universal to do *Scarlet Angel* with none other than Rock Hudson playing opposite me. He was doing leads now, and had come a long way since *Tomahawk.* He was no longer awkward before the camera, and I was sure now— a bit late—that Rock was on his way to movie stardom. This was a remake of *The Flame of New Orleans,* which had starred Marlene Dietrich. This time it was Yvonne De Carlo who, as Roxy McClanahan, battled her way to happiness and love during the mid-1800s in San Francisco.

It was more travel upon completion of the film, this time to attend the International Film Festival in Uruguay. Connie joined me in the group that included Alexis Smith, Rhonda Fleming, Merle Oberon, Robert Cummings, Evelyn Keyes, Reginald Gardiner, and many others. When the seemingly endless cocktail parties were behind me and the junket came to a close, Connie and I wanted to see something more of South America. With the help of friends made in Uruguay, we booked a flight to Buenos Aires, Argentina.

We were well taken care of in Buenos Aires and visited a film studio on our second day in the country. Connie and I were taken on a sound-stage where a scene was in progress. It held my interest more than it might have otherwise because of *him:* a six-foot-three, blond-haired, blue-eyed actor who, I would soon learn, was the Argentinian star Carlos Thompson. An additional tidbit was that he was then in the middle of a highly publicized love affair with Mexican superstar Maria Felix. I watched him work, so debonair in smoking jacket and pipe, and when we met after the scene I felt like a Hollywood talent agent.

"Have you ever thought of making pictures in America?" I asked.

"I think I would find Hollywood very interesting," he said, "under the right circumstances." He spoke with no trace of an accent.

"So, what you're saying is: you would come to Hollywood if you were to get the right role. Is that right?"

"Yes—of course."

Before his next scene, we exchanged addresses and phone numbers, and I promised to try to find something for him in Hollywood. I'm not sure if he believed me at the time, but I knew I would somehow deliver. This was a man I had to know better—and I wasn't about to move to Argentina to do it.

Before leaving Buenos Aires, I agreed to hold a press conference. Amid the questions and answers I made it known that I had great admiration for Argentina's First Lady, Eva Perón, and said that I would have been honored to meet her during my visit. Otherwise, I said, my intentions were to do some shopping, enjoy the convivial atmosphere, and in a few days return home.

When it came time to leave, Connie and I were at the airport awaiting our boarding call. There was some commotion, and we suddenly found ourselves confronted by a group of smartly uniformed military men. One of them, apparently the ranking officer, stepped in front of me, gave a heel-clicking salute, and said, "Are you Señorita De Carlo?"

"Why . . . yes, I am."

"You will please come with us."

I was terrified. "But our plane—it's ready to leave. There must be a mistake."

"Do not worry," he said more gently. "It will be detained."

I was trying desperately to figure out what I had done, recalling an incident in Iran when an irate hotel manager tracked me down for having taken a brass ashtray from my room. In the airport's main office I was given a smiling greeting by an officer who held a telephone in his hand. He handed it over to my military escort, who spoke into the phone in Spanish. In a moment, he handed it to me. "Señora Perón," he said to me in English. "She wishes to speak with you."

I recognized the famous voice, but couldn't understand a word. It was apparent that the First Lady had read the newspaper accounts of a few days earlier. Soon an interpreter came on the line to translate what she had said. She said she had always enjoyed my movies, especially *Buccaneer Girl.* It later dawned on me that she could identify with the character of Deborah McCoy, who capitalized on her position as a prostitute to move up into high society.

She also said that she had often considered bringing her life to the screen, and that I would be perfect for her role. During one of the translations a military officer instructed me to wish her a speedy recovery. After thanking her profusely for her kind words, I did just that. "I hear you have been ill," I said, "and I hope you will have a speedy recovery."

Her closing words were "Buena suerte."

Connie and I were returned to the airport but the plane didn't take off for another half hour. Then we saw an official-looking sedan come careening across the airstrip and screech to a stop beside the plane. Soon a military officer was in the plane and leaning over me.

"Señorita De Carlo," he said, handing me a carefully wrapped package. "Compliments of Señora Perón."

It turned out to be a copy of Eva Perón's biography, inside which she had inscribed in Spanish this message: "A remembrance of your passing through Argentina, with my gratitude for your kindness toward me. With my best wishes for your happiness always and a big hug—Eva Perón."

Within five months Eva Perón was dead. Her illness was cancer.

Chapter 24

I may have nurtured a lifelong fantasy of Nordic lovers, but when I think back over all the men in my life I had few who met those qualifications. Aside from the one introduced a couple of chapters further along, there is only Sterling Hayden, which was far from a meaningful relationship, as they say nowadays.

One of the most handsome men I ever met was through a publicity person, Helen Ferguson.

She had me over for dinner, mentioning that a friend might drop by, and sure enough there later came the sound of the doorbell. When she opened the door, I almost choked on my broccoli. Helen hadn't told me the name of her friend, and now she didn't have to. There with widow's peak and gorgeous blue eyes was the handsomest of all human males, Robert Taylor.

His rich voice and ready smile made him good company over dessert, and when it came time for both of us to leave he offered to walk with me to my car. In parting, he asked if it would be all right to call me sometime. I thought it over for the better part of a millisecond and scribbled out my number.

In the past I had wasted many hours or days awaiting telephone calls that never came, but my call from Bob Taylor was the very next day. We had an enjoyable dinner a few evenings later at Restaurant La Rue on the Sunset Strip, then moved across the street to the Mocambo for dancing.

It started out with dinners, movies, and riding at Circle J. We were very compatible and never ran out of interesting conversation. He was just about all a girl could want, and well . . . I had stars in my eyes. Things were developing nicely between us, when we were prematurely confronted by a turning point. He had to go away on location for an MGM Western at a crucial time in our relationship; that critical time when it can either flourish or evaporate to a memory. I was feeling dejected by the prospect of his leaving, but his timely suggestion saved the day. "Look, Yvonne," he said contemplatively, "you aren't on a picture just now. Why don't you wait a week or so and join me on location."

That sounded like a great idea to me, and I promised to try to work it out. A few days later he called from the location in Utah. I was going to tell him it was all set for me to join him, but he didn't give me the chance.

"I've talked to Helen Ferguson," he said hesitantly, "and she doesn't think it would be proper for you to come and visit me."

"Oh?"

"Yes, that's what she says. She's afraid it would get to the press and cause too much talk."

"I see."

"But I'll be back in a month . . . and I'll see you then."

I guess it was a matter of Helen Ferguson giveth and Helen Ferguson taketh away. The wind had certainly been taken out of my sails. I somehow sensed that our time had come and gone. The fact that he could be so easily manipulated by his press agent exacted a toll on my image of what he was, and my cool reaction probably affected his impression of me. Fortunately, however, we would remain friends for a long time.

All this was going on in early 1952, a winter unparalleled in Southern California for storms and mud slides. I was set to leave for New York but was advised to get out of my house the night before my departure—just in case. I got all my things together and booked a suite at the Beverly Hills Hotel for the one night. Just as I was leaving for the hotel, the phone rang. It was Bob, who had returned a week early from location.

He met me later at the hotel and we had dinner in one of the downstairs dining rooms. Afterwards he came upstairs and we talked into the night. He gave me a bit of advice, "Always set your sights high, Yvonne."

I listened and thought later: How much higher could a lady set her sights than on him—Bob Taylor! We got very little sleep that night, but it didn't seem to matter.

In the morning my cab was loaded with my bags, and Bob had to leave for his studio. There was a perfunctory kiss, and a bon voyage for me, but promises for our future were noticeably absent. I knew that this would mark the end of the intimate phase of our relationship, and I knew it would be a substantial loss.

I went to Europe, and Bob wrote me frequently while I was there. His letters were long, interesting, and very well written, but they weren't love letters. The name of Ursula Thiess came up a few times, and within a couple of years they would marry.

I was in Europe to attend the Fifth Annual International Film Festival at Cannes, and received a wire from Mario saying he was due to be in the south of France at about the time of the festival and wanted to know if he could meet me. I let him know I would be at the Carlton and would be happy to see him again. Mario arrived in time to escort me to a cocktail party at Prince Aly Khan's Château de l'Horizon. The party was in full swing by the time we arrived, and the international set had turned out in full complement. Aly was in a huddle with a pair of European starlets, but upon seeing us he left them to come over and introduce himself.

"Are you really as good a horsewoman as I have heard?" he asked me. "Is it true you prefer making films in Europe over Hollywood?" He also asked if I was that good a marksman, and any number of questions that established not only his charm but his interest in me. He had obviously done his homework, and my invitation from Elsa Maxwell, who was hostess at the party, was no accident. I was immensely flattered, and as we carried on our opening flirtation I was totally unaware of poor Mario standing silently at my side.

Aly eventually excused himself to greet some later arrivals and Mario and I strolled among the beautiful people with our glasses of champagne. Aly caught up with us again out on the terrace, where Mario and I were enjoying the view of the Mediterranean. Aly invited me to a reception he was having the next afternoon, and when I explained that my aunt Connie was arriving he said to bring her along. There was also an implied invitation for Mario, but I was grateful to him for not accepting it. Despite his narcissism, he was sensitive.

So began a week of wining and dining, hedonism, call it what you may, but it was a week of never-ending parties, glitter, and dissipation. It was a menu that Aly Khan seemed to thrive on, and with his flair and poise it seemed the only way to live. As I joined Aly in all the frivolity, the French and Italian press were close behind. Seeing me as "in the running" to catch Aly's affection they photographed us dancing cheek to cheek, and our pictures were in the papers all during the week. One caption read: WATCH OUT, RITA—I'VE GOT YOUR MAN. Aly knew that I had neither encouraged nor sought this kind of press, so he took it all in good humor. In fact he seemed to enjoy it.

Aly was a man of contradictions, savoring his playboy way of life yet feeling guilty for being so wealthy when his homeland was so impoverished. Strong ties welded him to the staid traditions of his birthplace. His father, the Aga Khan, had sown his wild oats with even more profligacy but remained intolerant of his son, and defiance would mean an end to Aly's income, so he was constantly walking a tightrope. All of this made Aly an enigmatic person to deal with.

Now that Aly and Rita Hayworth had definitely parted, I decided to make myself available—just in case. It was easy to see why Rita had found Aly Khan so attractive, because he was. He was charming, he had grace, status, and intelligence, and the more you saw of the man the more attractive he became. Then, of course, there was the matter of his money. I made it a point that Mario was only a friend, but I'd have been better off saying Mario was the love of my life. I would learn later that Aly loved to steal other men's women. The festival came to a close, but not my relationship with Aly.

Aly didn't drink much, but he came alive with the music and could dance the night away. He held his partners very close when he danced and I found myself getting jealous, but that was foolish, because there were always other women and he danced closely with all of them. The evenings usually ended at dawn or later, and he never ran out of energy. Aly was an expert lover, adept in every nuance of pleasure, and I doubt if there was ever a more attentive man when it came to pleasing a woman. He didn't take a woman, he tasted and taunted, making certain every move was perfect. There are no courses in such behavior —one either has it or not, and Aly had it.

What I could never fathom was his ability to function without sleep. I don't mean just "function." Aly did everything in a dead run, and he seemed to consistently do everything right. He once told me that sleep wasted precious time. He lived as though he had a lot of living to fit into a small niche of time.

Although his lovemaking was usually gentle, he sometimes had tastes for the exotic. We would go out on his motorboat for the ostensible purpose of fishing or snorkling, but we rarely got around to that. We would end up lying nude on deck sunbathing as the boat bobbed in the wave swells. There, exposed to the bright Mediterranean sun, oblivious to the intrusion of passing vessels, we would make animated love. It was in these highly individual ways that Aly would express his deeper passions, and under his careful direction the scene always played to perfection.

One of Aly's close friends, Elsa Maxwell, was always included in his functions. She was also a frequent house guest at the château. I was fascinated that this chubby little woman was able to keep up with Aly, to match his every step. Maybe it was this kindred quality they admired in each other—energy.

On occasion we would all go waterskiing, but as hard as I tried I never quite got the hang of it. What I appreciated most was the horseback riding, and we did lots of it. Aly was an expert horseman and treated his horses as gently as he did his women. He took special care of his thoroughbreds and personally supervised all their breeding procedures. One day, he took Connie and me to his Normandy farm to show us his studs and mares, including his prize stud, Tabriz. Would we like to see Tabriz doing his thing? Why not?

Tabriz moved in casually, taking friendly nips at his girl friend's neck and ears, and gave her a gentle nuzzle or two. I immediately thought of Aly and his brand of lovemaking. Then Tabriz got down to business —or maybe I should say *up* to business. He really gave his all to his lady fair.

"Now that's how a male is supposed to make love," I quipped. "Are you taking notes, Aly?"

"You must be kidding," said Aly. "How do you suppose I learned what I know?"

On a few occasions Aly confided in me about certain facets of his personal life, but only once did he bring up Rita Hayworth, saying he fell in love with her beauty and fame, only realizing after marriage how little they shared. She had no interest in horses or the races and was continually badgering him about his gambling. He had hoped she would be amused by redecorating their city houses and villas, and related sadly that she just didn't have an interest in decorating. He pleaded with her to learn French, but she didn't have the motivation. He said he would have given her the world if she had tried just a little to please him but she was unwilling, and after each quarrel their alienation grew.

I was perfect for him. I loved horses and liked watching them race, I enjoyed the outdoors and the partying. I imagined I could even learn to like gambling, especially if I was risking someone else's money. But I wasn't quite ready to open my heart to Aly. I shared his every enthusiasm—horses, houses, and languages. I think I might have been good for him.

Connie adored Aly, and when Cousin Ken turned up he admired him too. We went to the races, and Ken was handed ten thousand francs with which to make bets. Ken lost all of it, and felt obliged, embarrassing as it was, to show Aly all the losing betting slips. Aly wouldn't hear of it, saying he would be insulted if Ken made such an accounting and that it would be even more of an insult to Ken. Aly was always generous with his friends and treated them as the royalty he himself was.

When we were in Paris the Longchamps racetrack was a second home. Every night it was a party in one or the other exclusive restaurant. Aly basked in the limelight, amused by all of it, and I was having a good time too, but the carnival atmosphere was beginning to get to me. I think it was the thought of getting back to work that made the good times seem like sin.

I was back in Hollywood June 5 to begin work on an MGM picture with Ricardo Montalban, Cyd Charisse, and the Italian star Vittorio Gassman. It was *Sombrero,* in which I played Maria of the River Road. I played opposite Gassman and wondered when the fur would start to fly. I say that because Vittorio was then married to Shelley Winters; their spats had been broadly publicized. Shelley was around the set but kept herself fairly well sequestered in Vittorio's dressing-room trailer. The moment she was gone, Vittorio came to life, asking me to lunch, and as we had our sandwiches in a cafe near the studio I couldn't resist asking, "How is the marriage coming along?"

He studied the food on his plate and yawned. "It will be interesting to see if it works out," he said. Of course, it didn't work out at all.

One of the first questions I asked my agent after returning from Europe was "Any word from Carlos Thompson in Argentina?" My next picture after *Sombrero* would be *Fort Algiers,* and the lead in the picture was perfect for Carlos. I had wired Kohner from Paris to send for Carlos at my expense so he could try out for the part, but so far there had been no word from him. While I was pacing the floor I got a wire from Aly. He was coming to New York for a meeting with Rita to settle a dispute over their daughter Yasmin and asked if I could meet him there. The timing was right. I promised to stop in New York en route to London.

We had only a few nights together, and it was nothing like Paris, but life was never dull with Aly. One night we were asked for cocktails to the Essex House apartment of Judy Garland and Sid Luft. Sid met us at the door and made us a drink—then another. No Judy. Sid went into the bedroom several times in an effort to rouse her, but to no avail. He finally apologized and said that Judy wouldn't be joining us. We had one more drink and left. When we were outside, Aly told me that Judy was very ill but didn't go into detail. I didn't probe further, but the malady would become public knowledge a few years later. In 1952, Judy was well on her way to self-destruction.

I had arranged to go on to London from New York because it was there I would announce the founding of "Vancouver Productions," an independent film company to be headed by Paul Kohner and myself. In a carefully planned press conference I explained our confidence in the future of the film industry, and how our company would allow us the opportunity to choose worthwhile properties for development. We would produce a Biblical movie, we had a comedy planned, and we had also optioned a contemporary love story.

Whatever became of Vancouver Productions?

Nothing—absolutely nothing. It seemed like a terrific idea at the time, and we had great expectations, but unfortunately expectations are never enough. We couldn't get it all together, and our heralded corporation eventually faded into nothing more than a vague memory.

Chapter 25

I was back in London to begin work on *Sea Devils* and my costar would again be Rock Hudson. This assignment was something of a psychological victory because I was finally working in a Howard Hughes movie. Well, not exactly, I guess. It was an RKO movie and Howard owned RKO. This would be as close as I would ever come to career help from Howard. He had nothing whatever to do with my being cast in the role, of course, and probably didn't even know about it, but I liked the idea just the same.

I have never been anyone's protégée; I haven't had any special boosts from admirers or acquaintances. I'm not saying there wasn't help along the way, but that is what life is all about. One person leads to another —you are introduced to someone else who leads you to the next plateau. As in the case of Billy Wilder: he didn't give me a part in any of his movies, but it was Billy who set me up with a first-class agent. I would say that is the kind of help one gets along the way.

I've often wondered why I couldn't have married a practical man, a producer or businessman. After a certain age, it is difficult to maintain star status. Most actors and actresses need the influence of a faithful business thinker. I think I could have been a bit more pragmatic.

London had become a second home by this time, especially since Cousin Ken had married and was succeeding there as a photographer.

In fact, speaking of help from loved ones, Aly Khan hired Ken to photograph all of his thoroughbreds and gave him other jobs along the way.

Our director on *Sea Devils* was Raoul Walsh, whose specialty was action films. This film was a nineteenth-century spy story set mostly on the high seas, so the blustery Walsh with his black eyepatch was in his proper element. Walsh was the type of director who let his actors run free. I liked it fine, and didn't feel hurt when Walsh would end a take with a grunt rather than an accolade. With Rock it was more difficult. He was doing well by this stage of his career but he still wasn't the most secure actor in Hollywood, and he needed direction and personal nudges at times. Raoul started out by treating Rock almost as a son, but that situation changed. Raoul came to me one day and in his macho way said he didn't like the "birds" that were gathering around Rock.

"Birds?" I questioned.

"I don't like the birds he's traveling with," he said. "You know—birds of a feather?" We were filming in Guernsey and Jersey, the Channel Islands, and Raoul didn't care for the kind of men who followed Rock over to our location. I had nothing to contribute to Raoul's comments. I only knew that Rock was Rock, that he got his trick first name from agent Henry Wilson, and he was a very, very nice guy. Anything beyond that would be conjectural.

As I said, Raoul was a light-handed and sometimes puzzling director. The way he directed the bedroom scene is a good example. "Okay, Yvonne, let's get this over with. You've left Rock baby downstairs. Now, run to the bed, get into it, but before you do, look under it first for Errol Flynn. Okay, now, roll 'em." On another take he'd yell out, "Yvonne, don't forget, Rock is injured. Take out the cooking sherry and give him a good swig of it. If that don't work, get under the covers with him. That'll cure him. ACTION!"

After completing the scheduled work on the Channel Islands we moved on to Saint-Malo, France, for more location work. One morning as we worked in rough waters in an attempt to film the landing of some small boats, a huge wave capsized the boat that was carrying Raoul and the cameraman. The camera and our director went into the sea. Raoul was severely shaken and had to suspend work for a couple of days to recuperate.

I wished no harm to our good director, but I didn't mind the time off. Aly had just come to visit me and we used the free days to take a tour along the glorious Normandy coast, driving through Honfleur and

Trouville and abandoning the car to climb over the rocks and up the steep stone stairway to the monastery of Mont-Saint-Michel. Once the tide comes in, the only way out is by boat, and that was how we finally got back to the car. We went to the casinos of Bagnoles-de-l'Orne to lose some of Aly's francs and then made a stop at le Pin au Haras to see Aly's favorite stud farm. It was wonderful weather, and we made the most of every day together.

Back in Paris, we went to a popular cafe for dinner. As we were seated, the orchestra went into the strains of "Laura," the leader smiling toward our table. The song, of course, was the theme song of the famous Gene Tierney movie of the same name. Aly was embarrassed for me, because the band clearly mistook me for Gene Tierney, who had recently been romantically linked with Aly. I assured him I wasn't injured by the mistake—that I was, in fact, flattered.

That opened the way for a discussion of his affair with Gene, one I had been careful to avoid. I knew it would be a fatal error to become possessive with Aly Khan, and I was afraid he would mistake my curiosity for jealousy. That night, and many times over the months ahead, Aly would tell me more than I cared to know about Gene Tierney, until I was sorry that the subject had ever come up.

Aly said he regretted his inability to fulfill Gene's desires, which boiled down to marriage. At Aly's farm, he fanned through a stack of letters from Gene. He read a part of one to me, but I made him stop. I felt like a voyeur listening to such intimate and forlorn revelations. He put the letters away and told me: "We were so wonderful together, Gene and I. No sex has ever quite come up to ours." He said that as much as it saddened him, he had had to be firm in making the break. The Aga Khan had emphatically declared that if Aly should marry Gene Tierney, his door would be closed to him forever. Although Aly didn't say it, I assumed that all the money would remain behind the door as well. Gene wasn't taking the breakup well at all.

Since my love for Aly wasn't of the heartthrob variety, I didn't feel defeated by his romance with Gene or by the news of his father's decree: "No actress as a wife!" I settled then for remaining Aly's friend and lover for as long as it was convenient to both of us, happier with it that way because at least I knew where I stood.

After finishing *Sea Devils,* Rock Hudson and I were sent to Antwerp and Brussels to promote *Scarlet Angel.* I was accustomed to the ruthlessness of the foreign press, but since Rock was relatively uninitiated, I gave him a briefing and we devised a code. When I sensed a loaded question, I would give him a light kick in the shins. As they started to close in on questions about his love life, I let him have it, kicking him so hard he doubled over and said something like "Ooof!" It may not have been the answer the reporter wanted, but at least it wasn't something they could quote out of context.

An event of a lifetime lay ahead of me in London, so after the Belgian trip I went on to Paris to have an appropriate dress designed. It was of peacock-blue taffeta, studded with pea-sized rhinestones. In a few days I would be attending a royal film performance and be presented to Queen Elizabeth and Prince Philip.

I felt like a little girl awaiting Christmas, and, as with Christmas, the big night finally arrived. A huge crowd had gathered outside the Empire Theatre in Leicester Square to see the arrival of the royal party and the celebrities. I invited Denis, the Earl of Lanesborough, to be my escort, which I thought was a good insurance policy against protocol boo-boos, and having him at my side gave me confidence I might otherwise have lacked. Among the celebrities were Sir Laurence Olivier and Vivien Leigh, the Charlie Chaplins, Rock Hudson, John Mills, Margaret Lockwood, Gene Kelly, Doug Fairbanks Jr., Trevor Howard, and others. With great fanfare, the Queen and her entourage, including Princess Margaret, entered the theater. A little later, we all lined up for presentation in the reception lounge. Her Majesty looked far more elegant than I would imagine possible. She moved from person to person, stopping for a brief visit with each. She seemed to know exactly what was pertinent to say to each of the celebrities. When she stepped before me, I curtsied perfectly, just as I had rehearsed at least a thousand times. She asked if I enjoyed working in London.

"Oh, yes indeed, Your Majesty. I'm enjoying every minute of my stay here." I think she asked if I intended to stay a while, and I'm sure whatever I said was brief and to the point. I was warned that I should volunteer nothing, just answer the questions quickly and courteously. That was the way it was.

I was really impressed with her great dignity and spirit of authority. When Denis asked me what I thought of it, I said, "She's wonderful. She behaved just like a queen."

While still backstage, I became friendly with Douglas Fairbanks Jr., and asked if he would be kind enough to introduce me to Sir Laurence Olivier and his lovely wife. The introduction was made, and I asked the Oliviers to sign autographs for me. What a thrill! They were my all-time favorite screen couple. After this, we all watched the movie, Mario Lanza's new release, and a stage show, and then on to the Savoy Hotel for a lavish supper party. It was a night to remember. I do.

It was back to reality after the evening with British royalty, and that meant Hollywood—which, in contrast, didn't seem very stimulating.

Carlos Thompson had arrived in town in my absence, and through my agent's guidance landed the male lead in *Fort Algiers.* Our relationship was more or less a business arrangement at the outset, but it didn't take long for it to assume a new, more intimate dimension.

I was hoping I could introduce Carlos to the Peggy Middleton behind the façade of Yvonne De Carlo. It seemed that most of the men I had been dealing with were seeing me as the image they had seen on the screen, or the one they had read about in press releases and magazine articles. I wanted Carlos to know the real me. So with that in mind I planned small trips. I took him to Lone Pine, for instance, my haven in the High Sierra. We hiked, rode horseback, and communed with nature. I was enjoying it immensely, but it suddenly occurred to me that Carlos wasn't happy at all. He perked up immediately when we were back within the glittering boundaries of the film capital. That was where he was happiest.

The picture started, but we managed to get some time off during the Christmas holidays of 1952. We drove to Las Vegas, and during the several-hour trip, Carlos finally told me about his ill-fated romance with Maria Felix.

He said that they had made plans for marriage, and right up until the moment of taking their vows, all was fine. Then at the last second Maria jilted him—literally at the altar. He was so humiliated, and had suffered such a horrendous loss of face, that he broke his own arm. It was the only measure he could come up with at the moment that would account to his friends and the press for such a sudden change of wedding plans. I introduced Carlos to the right people in the industry and took him to special parties and screenings. We attended the premier of *Moulin Rouge* and the elegant party at the Mocambo afterwards. Practically every star was there, and Carlos was anxious to meet them all. I made sure he met the people who could best help in his career.

I was asked by the press if Carlos was signed to a personal contract. This was definitely on my mind. Paul Kohner, my agent, had been working hard for him, and I had invested some money. Carlos did sign up with Paul Kohner, but he did not sign a personal contract—not then.

With the completion of *Fort Algiers,* I had to hurry back to England to do *The Captain's Paradise* with Alec Guinness. I hoped Carlos would come with me. He waited as long as possible and then at the last moment announced his decision. "I will stay in Hollywood," he said. "I will be waiting patiently for your return."

So that was that. It didn't seem very romantic for new lovers, but it was his decision to make. I didn't press the issue, and I couldn't help but wonder about his behavior in London when I heard that Carlos had accepted an offer to do an MGM picture with Lana Turner. We had a gentlemen's agreement that we would decide his career moves together. After Carlos signed a long-term contract with MGM, our letters started to carry a slightly different tone. Carlos had made a prize fool out of me, and I was bitter. I felt as though I had been had. My misery was compounded when Carlos began dating starlets like Piper Laurie. He even had the audacity to write me about a lovely lunch he'd had with Marilyn Monroe—and how sweet and pathetic he found her, how vulnerable!

Finally, a letter came in which Carlos suggested that I should not include him in any future plans. I was furious. My Sicilian blood found me plotting all sorts of heinous deeds to get even. I even dreamed about how I could pick him off with a long-range rifle without anyone being the wiser.

It was years before I saw him again, and when I did there were practically no ill-feelings. As a matter of fact, there were no feelings of any kind. I should have asked him where the money he still owed me was, but I didn't. I only thought of Maria Felix, and what a wise move she had made all those years before when she left Carlos at the altar.

Chapter 26

 When the script of *The Captain's Paradise* was first sent to me, I could see only one person in the role of the captain. Anthony Kimmins, the director, then called from London to see if I wanted to do the film. I said I would be happy to do it, but only if they could get Alec Guinness for the male lead. Kimmins said he had Ray Milland or Michael Wilding in mind. "Alec Guinness," he said, "is so highly unavailable."

"Submit the script," I begged him. "I have a feeling he'll love it."

Kimmins did just that and Alec did love it. He accepted the role.

The script was a marvelous mixture of wit and broad comedy. The British captain of a ferry steamer crosses back and forth between Gibraltar and Ceuta in North Africa, and keeps a wife in each port. Celia Johnson played his very sedate English wife in Gibraltar, and I played the fiery Moroccan who goes on wild evening sprees with the Captain when he's in that port. The Captain has the best of both worlds until the women get wind of what's happening. Then they make his life less than a paradise.

On the first day of rehearsal in London, I found Guinness all alone practicing flamenco steps for one of our dance numbers. As we introduced ourselves, his expressive eyes seemed to be searching my face, as if trying to get a reading on me. His scrutiny made me uncomfortable. He was polite; too polite. That made me nervous. I wondered what he was thinking.

On the first day of shooting, Anthony Kimmins had us do a run-through of the first scene, and Guinness was as stiff and reserved as before. Was this the way the next months would be? I had never been more tense.

Then, "Places please." Our first scene had begun before the cameras.

When the scene was a wrap, I remained frozen in position as Alec approached me. He broke into a broad grin and embraced me. "Thank God!" he said jubilantly.

I had no idea what he was saying, but I had never welcomed anything more than that sweet grin. I soon learned that he had been terrified at the prospect of working in a picture with a "Hollywood glamour girl," and was delighted to see that I knew what I was doing as an actress.

We worked together in full harmony after that and became close friends. I was told that to gain the professional respect of Alec Guinness was to gain his friendship. He wasn't an outgoing person on the set; acting to him was a very serious business, and it required his total attention. But he was a warm friend, and one of the most valuable mentors I had ever had. I learned more about comedy from Alec Guinness than I had ever learned from a coach, and he wasn't even teaching. He was simply performing his skills, and I was fortunate enough to be able to watch.

I was sorry to see the picture come to an end; it had been such an exhilarating experience. Alec and I remained friends, and made contact with each other on several occasions. We tried to rearrange our schedules to do another picture together, but it simply wasn't to be.

Aunt Connie had come to England with me, and at the start of the filming we took a flat near Berkeley Square not far from where Kenny lived. We had lunch together one day and were going out afterward to do some shopping. I returned to the flat to get a warmer jacket, and while I was there I made the spontaneous decision to change my earrings. I took the small suitcase out of the trunk, and inside the locked suitcase was my jewel case, also locked. When I looked inside I knew at once that I had been robbed. Within an hour or so, someone had entered the flat, found the jewel case, opened three locks, and made off with nearly $150,000 worth of jewelry. I lost some pieces designed by Cocteau, diamonds and gold. They were made by Ruser in Hollywood, a set of brooch, necklace, and bracelet with stones given me by Dorez. There was also a choker made of platinum, diamonds, and pearls.

Scotland Yard sent a team of investigators who were courteous and seemingly efficient. They said that the jewels were probably already in Holland by then. There were no fingerprints, no sign of forced entry —and no arrests. That was one highlight of this trip to London—some highlight.

There was another incident that may have been minor in importance, but in terms of fun it was major. Ava Gardner and Grace Kelly were in town doing postproduction work on *Mogambo,* which had just been shot in Africa with Clark Gable. Ava asked if I would join them in an evening of ballet. Me, the Pavlova of Vancouver? Count me in. Ava loved champagne and had arranged for us to have plenty of it in our box. We sat in our box sipping champagne throughout the performance, getting more and more giddy as the show went on. It struck us as funny that here we were, three of the more glamorous Hollywood stars, attending an evening at the ballet without escorts. I guess the audience thought it curious as well, because we created quite a stir when we went to the lobby during the intermission.

Afterward, Ava's driver took us to a charming Soho restaurant for dinner. By now the drinks were starting to have a lugubrious effect. Grace began to lament over the short-term affair she had had with Gable. He gave her an expensive 16-mm movie camera, and she reasoned he must have loved her to have given her that. We agreed, of course.

That brought Ava to memories of the better times with Frank Sinatra and how despondent she was that their marriage was now in the process of breaking up. "I love that man," she told us. "But God how I hate him."

After hearing Ava's sad tale, her secretary joined in. She too was suffering from love's malady and broke into real tears in relating her story. So I guessed it was my turn. I thought and thought, feeling sure I could come up with a sad story to swap, but I couldn't. Despite all my abortive romances at this moment, I was free of romantic entanglement. I felt deprived in the atmosphere of such grand despondency. I started to sniffle.

"What's wrong?" said Ava. "You got it too?"

"No," I said. "I haven't got anybody to cry over—and it makes me sad."

Then everyone was laughing.

"Come on," Ava said. "We're all going to my place."

That's what we did. We went to her Mayfair flat and put on some flamenco records. By this time it was well after midnight, and I was worrying about Ava's driver. When I brought it up, she waved the problem away. "Forget it," she said. So I did.

I'd studied flamenco so I showed the girls some steps. That started it. Here we were, in the early hours of the quiet London morning, four slightly loaded young gals wildly pounding our heels into the floor. We had great fun improvising and flailing around. The funniest scene of the predawn bacchanal was Grace Kelly's solo. She was stomping, clapping her hands, a rose clenched between her teeth. "Guapa . . . guapa," she called out. "Olé . . . olé!" Somehow seeing this blond, dignified woman in such devil-may-care activity was hilarious. It was daylight when the party broke up, all of us not much worse for wear.

With *The Captain's Paradise* completed, Connie and I went to Paris to discuss possible film ventures. We stayed at Aly Khan's townhouse, and were treated as if we ourselves were royalty. When Aly returned, we drove to Château l'Horizon, but with Aly behind the wheel, "drove" is not really telling it. What we did was fly. His compulsion for speed seemed only to intensify with the passage of time. I love to drive fast myself, but I loathe being a passenger at high speeds, and with Aly I was in constant terror. To chide him, to tell him to slow down, brought only a grin and a harder push on the gas pedal. On one occasion, Rhonda Fleming was with us as a passenger in Aly's overpowered Chrysler. We were churning along the Grande Corniche at speeds in excess of one hundred miles per hour. She rode home with someone else.

At one of Aly's l'Horizon parties I had the pleasure of meeting Noel Coward, who was totally charming. He told me he had seen two women in films who stood out above all others. Marlene Dietrich was one, and I was the other. Whether he meant it or not, it was some compliment. He asked me what role I would like to do over all others. I answered, "Peter Pan."

"WHAT!" He couldn't believe what he was hearing. "You have what so few women have. Why would you want to disguise it? Would you like to see Marlene Dietrich as Peter Pan?"

What a great idea. "I'd love to see her as Peter Pan!"

He thought that was very funny, and we had a wonderful time together for the remainder of the evening. He said to me, "Keep that glamour at all times. Don't disappoint the public by giving them something they don't expect."

I continued to give them what they expected in America, whether I wanted to or not. It was almost becoming a standard routine; I would do the Technicolor action films on home ground and go to England to do the marvelous comedies in which I could play a variety of interesting roles. My good fortune in landing outstanding costars in England continued. In *Happy Ever After,* later called *Tonight's the Night,* my partner was David Niven.

I played an Irish widow, complete with accent, who is seeking romance and fortune with David Niven her prey. Barry Fitzgerald was in it, and the director was Mario Zampi, an Italian with a thick accent (directing a typically Irish script). Another cast member was the fine actor Robert Urquhart. We did all the shooting at Elstree Studios, forty miles from London.

By this time *The Captain's Paradise* had opened on both sides of the Atlantic to extremely favorable reviews, and I had been well treated personally by the critics. *Newsweek* and *Time* were both generous, but my favorite of all reviews came from the London *Star:* "She has a knack for tempestuous comedy which had been weighed down for years under the claptrap of a series of Hollywood costume pictures."

On *Happy Ever After* David Niven was his usual charming and witty self, always ready for a laugh or a good time. But it was Robert Urquhart for whom I tumbled romantically. At thirty-one he was quite attractive, but not overly handsome. He was masculine, talented in front of the camera, had a beautiful, trained speaking voice, and was a serious two-fisted drinker. Who knows, maybe that was the attraction. He came over like a Scottish Howard Duff. We started out as pals, then things steamed up in subtle gradations until we woke up one morning as full-fledged lovers. It wasn't long before I wondered what I was getting involved in. This was a time when I was trying to simplify my life, not make it more complicated.

September 1, 1953, was my birthday, and I had a small party in my Mayfair flat. Among those in attendance was Raymond Moore of the London *Sunday Dispatch.* He noticed several volumes on space travel, which were given to me by Cousin Ken, and when he learned of my interest in the subject he arranged for me to meet Arthur C. Clarke. He and his wife, Marilyn, visited me on the set, and Arthur gave me a copy of *Childhood's End.* I stayed up all night to read it. I had always loved his writing and was impressed with his unfailing ability to translate complex subjects into terms that anyone could understand.

We became close friends, and it was through Arthur that I became a member of the British Interplanetary Society. I didn't understand a word of the monthly bulletins they sent me, but it was fun pretending I did. I even wrote a screenplay, a comedy with interspace travel, and it attracted some studio attention, but never got off the ground.

I saw Aly on a brief visit to Paris, and while there, received a cable from my agent: "Come home at once. Robert Sherwood TV original. Top offer."

I returned to Hollywood and was signed to do the ninety-minute live-television production of Robert Sherwood's *Backbone of America.* For some reason, I didn't think I would be frightened by live-television acting. I was—*plenty.* Panicked is a better word. The day came to film the show—I remember glancing over the red light of the camera to the exit sign above the door of the studio. I was sorely tempted to make a break for it, but thoughts of Robert Sherwood in the control booth kept me going. I did the ninety minutes without a fluff, and was accepting all compliments offered at the postproduction party given backstage. Hedda Hopper came over and I expected an official accolade. All I got was, "You looked very large in the chest to be a business executive."

While I was back in Hollywood, Cecil B. De Mille returned to my life. It had nothing to do with the television performance or with his promise some ten years earlier that I would someday work in one of his pictures. But I *would* be working in a De Mille epic, and I had Henry Wilcoxon to thank for it.

Wilcoxon was De Mille's favorite actor and was also his assistant. Nina Foch was being considered for the role of Bithiah in *The Ten Commandments,* and to see some film on her they borrowed a clip from *Sombrero.* Wilcoxon ran the clip and saw me in a scene with Nina. When he reported back to C. B., it was *my* face he wanted him to see. I was told that as soon as De Mille saw the film he turned to his associates and said, "That is the face of Sephora. I have found her."

When I met with the "Great Presence," he was as warm and friendly toward me as he'd been when I was at Paramount. We joked about my (mis)adventures on *The Story of Dr. Wassell,* and he again complimented me on my "wonderful gray eyes." "But," he added, "you will need brown eyes to play a Jewess. Brown contact lenses will be made for you."

"Of course," I said hesitantly, dreading the very thought.

He then explained how Moses' wife, Sephora, shepherdess and eldest of Jethro's daughters, would fit into the drama. He lifted the heavy script, and instead of asking me to read he read to me. He read all of Sephora's scenes, including the one where she proposes marriage to Moses.

He reminded me of the prestige gained in playing a major role in a De Mille picture, which was worth far more than the twenty-five thousand he wanted to pay me. I purposely allowed a frown to cross my brow, just to see if he had still more charm to zap me with. But that was it. He paused to wait for my decision. Did I want the part or not?

I wanted it, I told him, even though he would be paying me about one-third my usual salary. What he didn't know was that I'd have done the part for nothing. Actually, that's probably why he got away with paying such low salaries. He *did* know that most dedicated actors would work for him for nothing.

At the door, he took my shoulders in his hands. "Well, my dear Yvonne," he said solemnly, "at last we are professionally married."

It was an unusual experience to be back on the Paramount lot after being away ten years. When I walked past Billy Wilder's former office, my heart still fluttered. I remembered my politicking days, the lunches at Lucey's and Oblath's, and the toddies after the day's work in Ray Milland's or Gary Cooper's dressing rooms. All the memories of those innocent days played back, and grasped my heart for a moment.

That was only ten years later, but recently I was in the area again, thirty years later than that. I discovered that Oblath's had closed, but that it had lasted until very recently. I couldn't find the original De Mille gate at Paramount that was once the main gate. Gone. That wonderful restaurant of long ago, Lucey's, has, of course, been gone for some time. Its sturdy Spanish façade is now a cemetery monument store. On this recent visit, it wasn't so easy to call up the friendly recollections. I felt as though I had entered hostile territory, made so by time and change.

There was one place that hadn't changed, and seeing it was quite an experience. On Melrose Avenue just a block east of Paramount there remains standing the Western Costume Company. I went there recently in search of a saloon-girl outfit for a personal appearance, and found myself lost in a labyrinth of movie costumes going back more than half a century.

When I came to the rack of women's period costumes, I spotted something that seemed familiar. My God—it was the gray and purple travel outfit I wore in *Frontier Gal,* my second movie. I looked at the tiny waist, sighed—and moved on. I didn't stay long: too many ghosts. It was an eerie experience, but I was glad that at least a few of the old Hollywood landmarks do still remain.

Chapter 27

Many times over the years I have said a word of thanks for the internal influence that impelled me to study and learn the French language. I was never an academic scholar, but by magic I developed a thirst for knowledge of the language my mother chose to forget. It must have been a divine directive of some kind.

One of the times I benefited from my language skills was in 1954 when I was chosen to play Napoleon III's mistress in the French film *La Castiglione.* It would be the first time a Hollywood actress did the lead in a film for which there was no English-language version. It was a distinction that made me feel proud.

Georges Combret was the director and cowriter of the film, and it was he who introduced me to Claude Boissol, his cowriter and associate. I found myself attracted to Claude even with his dark Gallic intensity. He wasn't my type, but I was always broadminded about such things. But first came somebody who was very much my type—my dream type, at last.

I saw him one evening when Connie and I were having dinner at a Montmartre restaurant. There he was across the room alone and handsome with his flaxen hair and cold blue eyes. There was a visible scar across one cheek. His icy eyes scrutinized me all during dinner, and after we had finished eating this tall man with a military bearing came to our table. "Baron Julian von Thuna of Köln," he said, thrusting two camellias our way. "At your service." He gave his heels a smart click and I could barely hold back a smile. I remember thinking that all he needed was a monocle.

I received a dozen long-stemmed pink roses the next day, and a phone call at the suite. Would I have dinner with him? I accepted, always in the mood for a new adventure, and this promised to be an interesting one. We had a wonderful dinner at the famous Maxim's and I learned quite a lot about this Nordic nobleman. He was an executive at the Ford plant at Köln; his father had been a German flying ace in World War I, and Julian had been a captain in the Panzer Corps during World War II. I was fascinated. I must admit to a secret fantasy I had in those days: I would be swooning in the embrace of a handsome German officer garbed in full uniform complete with black boots. Baron von Thuna must have been the personification of that fantasy.

I had a meeting with my director in my hotel suite and foolishly invited Julian to join us. The meeting wouldn't last long, and he and I could be together afterwards. Georges Combret arrived and I introduced him to the Baron. I didn't learn until afterward that Combret despised all Germans. Claude Boissol told me that most Frenchmen did. Combret suspected me of setting up the situation just to humiliate him, which I certainly had no intention of doing.

So the movie was off to a grand start, and from then on it got worse. Combret wouldn't speak to me, so Claude served as intermediary. There were myriad problems with the script, casting, and production. Nothing seemed to work. Then came a scene where I was working with a group of German soldiers. "This scene should make you very happy, Miss De Carlo," Combret shouted in French. "You'll be surrounded by Boches!"

As if there weren't enough trouble with the director, one of my co-stars, Rossano Brazzi, made his contribution. On the first day of shooting, hardly fifteen minutes had passed before Brazzi was declaring his undying love for me. After we had become better acquainted, his charm won me over and eventually I accepted his invitation to dinner.

We went to an Italian restaurant. He was extremely personable and I summed him up as a "nice guy." After dinner he walked me back to the Hôtel Georges V, where I was sharing a suite with Aunt Connie. It was getting late and Rossano and I both had to work in the morning. But suddenly I found myself flung onto the floor smack in front of Connie's bedroom door with Rossano on top of me cooing ardent words and breathing heavily. "Stop this nonsense," I muttered, "or I'll bang on this door and my aunt will come out." That did it. He was off me in a second, stood up, straightened out his shirt, bowed, bade me good night, and left. I wasn't offended, just amused.

It was at about that time that I started to consider Claude in a more romantic way. I had been attracted at the beginning, but the Teutonic presence of the Baron temporarily overwhelmed me. However, we ended up being only friends after the embarrassing incident in my hotel room at Georges Combaret. But now, with Claude as my only ally on the set, we started getting closer. In his old tin can of a car, a pre-war Renault, Claude showed me the true Paris, where the real Parisians live. Unlike Aly Khan, Claude was part of the masses, and the world that he showed me was more exciting and charming than the world I saw from the back seat of Aly's limousines and sports cars. With my growing affinity to Claude came the inevitable. We became closer and closer—I loved speaking French to him, and we met when we could in some very romantic spots along the Riviera.

Aly Khan, of course, popped into town when he learned I was there. I took the opportunity to have him set me up with his special jeweler, whom I hoped to have design a diamond necklace. I used fifteen thousand dollars worth of French francs, part of my salary from the film, to have it cut. The necklace, by the way, was brought to the U.S. by Aly along with many other gifts for friends of his—all legally declared. He was very proper in that way.

Aly hinted that there was another woman in his life, and since there always was, I didn't ask any questions. It was fairly obvious by now that he could never settle for any one woman, no matter how much he loved her at the start. My own relationship with him was pretty relaxed; I was his friend, his lover, and his confidante, but even so when we were together it was *very* romantic. Aly's attitude was "Vive la femme toujours!"

This meeting was in February, but I saw Aly again at the end of March when Connie and I went to the Cannes Film Festival of 1954, and we met for yet another week in June when we both attended the Berlin Film Festival. It was in Berlin that I met a relative newcomer to films, Sophia Loren. She was there to attract the press, and in her skin-tight evening gown was succeeding very well. Gina Lollobrigida was seated with the dignitaries, watching us like a tigress ready to pounce.

I was asked by the photographers if I would try to get Gina to pose for a picture with me and Sophia. As I had nothing to lose, I asked her the question in French. Her reply: "With that woman?" She did finally consent, and the picture of the three of us made all the papers the next day. We were all wearing exactly the same hairdo, the "Italian Cut," and we seemed to have almost exactly the same expressions on our faces. The caption in one paper read: NEED THEY LOOK SO MUCH ALIKE?

I went to Dublin for the opening of *Tonight's the Night,* then returned to Hollywood to play the leading lady in an independent Western called *Shotgun.* This would hardly be worth mentioning except that the male lead was my old Scandinavian dream man, Sterling Hayden. The man who served as his stuntman, Bob Morgan, was to play a principal role in my life, but I would only become well acquainted with him later.

Sterling enlisted in the Marine Corps early in the war and was decorated in battle. When he got out of the service, he seemed to be a totally different person. We got together at that time for a small party on his boat at Newport Beach. He had been a serious man before the war, but "somber"—or perhaps "bitter"—would describe him better now. All he seemed interested in was political arguments, and there was very little laughter that day. I had come to the boat hoping to rejuvenate an old romance, but soon realized how naive such feelings were. Now, eight years later, I felt not the slightest tinge of romantic interest in Sterling. He had long been divorced from Madeleine Carroll and was in the process of divorcing a woman named Betty DeNoon, by whom he had four children. On location in the sweltering town of Sedona, Arizona, we behaved like fellow actors and nothing more. I once asked if he'd like to go into town with me and have a steak. He said he had to be circumspect about dating because of his pending divorce case. And that was that. I remember thinking that sometimes things *do* work out for the best, although I loathe that cliche. Sterling was *such* a political activist and I know next to nothing about politics. What would we have had in common?

My next film was *Magic Fire,* a story of the life and loves of German composer Richard Wagner. It was a Republic production, but had a sizable budget by their standards. It was made on location in Munich, Germany, and one of the more interesting cast members for me was the actor who played Franz Liszt. It was none other than my old flame Carlos Thompson.

If you stay with me, you'll see that this was a period for cleaning out the debris of old love affairs. As for Carlos, we did our scenes together and went our separate ways. I didn't dare start in about the money he still owed me or I knew I would never be able to stop so it was just a matter of a couple of actors doing their jobs and getting it over with.

Connie and I stayed at the Hotel Fier Jahreszeiten, and within a couple of days Aly showed up in Munich. He had asked me to meet him at the airport but not to tell *anyone* that he was coming. I disguised myself with a big scarf, glasses, and false blond bangs so the press would not spot us. His plane arrived on time and off we went to my hotel. Aly checked into the royal suite on the floor above my room. I would sleep in Aly's suite and slip back down the back staircase to my own room early in the morning. In those days it was unacceptable to register together in a hotel. We did some shopping together, dined together, did everything as discreetly as possible, but the reporters always managed to find us. By this time we were hot copy as a romantic item.

REPORTER: "What brings Aly Khan to Munich?"
ME: "He came to see a man about a horse."
REPORTER: "Do you plan to marry? What about Gene Tierney?"
ME: "Aly and I are old friends. I met him before Gene Tierney did. Whenever we're in the same town we get together for dinner, that's all. Anyway, the Aga Khan doesn't want him to marry another actress."

The day Aly left Munich, I went with him to the airport. I should have been attending a press conference for *Magic Fire* and was severely scolded by the studio brass, but I didn't tell them I went to the airport to see off Aly Khan.

With Aly's departure, Claude Boissol flew in for a visit, and was on the set as I was playing a very old lady. The aging didn't spoil his enthusiasm, but I could tell he was impressed by the work of the makeup experts. Claude had a work assignment so didn't stay very long, which was just as well. When he had been gone from Munich one day, Baron von Thuna arrived. I was never lonely in Munich.

I had told Claude that I would stop over in Paris after *Magic Fire* was finished, and would give him a call when I arrived. He was so anxious to be with me that he drove his battered Renault all the way to the airport to drive me into town. The problem was that Aly also knew when I was coming in and had sent his chauffeur and custom-built Chrysler to pick me up. I finally elected to go in the Chrysler, not because of the status but because I didn't want to offend the Prince. After all, I had told Claude to wait for my call. When I explained, he accepted the explanation grudgingly, but not angrily.

I knew I would soon be returning to Los Angeles to begin a long work stretch on *The Ten Commandments,* so I wanted to have as much time alone with Aly as possible. Every night it was the same routine, with his rat pack clinging to him, so I specifically asked if we could spend my last night in Paris together. There was no acknowledgement one way or the other. When the night arrived, he told me we would be joining a group of people at the Place du Tertre. He said I should meet him there and all of us would go someplace for dinner.

I was hurt. I wouldn't be returning for a long time. Couldn't Aly spare me one night alone? In anger and injury I asked Claude out, and I brought Connie along for our dinner date at the Place du Tertre, a short distance from Aly and his entourage. It was my childish hope that Aly would see us and get jealous when he saw how much fun I was having with Claude. As you can see, I still hadn't grown up. The three of us had a nice dinner and returned home early. No sign of Aly.

Late that night Aly phoned my hotel suite. "Where were you, Yvonne?" he said angrily. "You embarrassed me in front of my friends."

I mumbled something in my defense, knowing I had committed what to Aly was an unpardonable sin. "Listen carefully," he said. "If you should ever meet me on the street, Yvonne, do not acknowledge my presence and do not speak to me. Everyone expected you tonight. You should have shown the courtesy to call or show up."

"But it was my last night in town." I guess I kind of whined it. "All I wanted was to be alone with you."

"Our friendship is over," he said. "Finished!"

"The trouble with you, Aly," I said, "is that you're not exclusive enough."

Somewhere in the closing moments of our final conversation, he said, "Why is it that anyone I've ever loved has never loved me?" Aly's ego had been irreparably bruised, and mine was crushed. I can never express how badly I felt over the loss of Aly's friendship.

A few months later Julian the Baron and I went to a lake resort together in Switzerland. By this time, I was getting weary of his cheapness and his demanding nature, so I wired Claude to join me on the day Julian was leaving. Since he was driving I expected Julian to leave early, but he kept staying on, talking about "our" future. It was getting late and still he lingered. What if Claude arrived and Julian was still there? In a real state of nervousness, I put on a nasty scene. I told Julian I thought it best if we ended our relationship then and there. My tantrum served its purpose. Baron Julian von Thuna drove off confused and dejected. Moments later Claude was being let out of a taxi. Whew! I shuddered as I thought of the possible embarrassment that would have resulted from that scene of "the changing of the guard."

Chapter 28

It was formally announced by Paramount that I would be playing Sephora in *The Ten Commandments,* but my scenes were still several months away. In September of 1954 C. B. De Mille went to Egypt to supervise the finishing touches of the massive set and to begin location shooting. For no good reason other than curiosity and my insatiable spirit of adventure, I went to Egypt.

I arrived with Cousin Ken in early December. De Mille had had a mild heart attack a few weeks earlier while inspecting the sets, but he looked fine now. I arrived on the set to see "the great man" standing in the desert with hand mike, instructing hundreds of extras and technicians. He bellowed his directions like a mighty dictator, and when he spoke everybody listened.

At lunch break I rode to his tent in a military jeep driven by an Egyptian captain of police and two other Egyptian policemen. "Hello, Mr. De Mille," I called, "Sephora here." He was astonished, and his expression showed it. Afterward, I was glad the shock hadn't brought on another heart attack. We embraced, and he led me to his lunch table, where he brought me up to date on the progress of the film. Then he took my hand. "Yvonne," he said, "your great-great grandchildren will watch this film one day."

I had seen some fairly spectacular sets in my day, but nothing could even remotely compare with this. The real shame was that once the filming was over, all the massive and magnificent structures would be torn down. Finally, the big day came: the filming of the Exodus. For the violent wind effect there were four small airplanes with propellers spinning. The wind would envelop the thousands of extras costumed as children of Israel as they came down the draw with their geese, ducks, pigs, and goats. Special effects would later make it appear as though the Red Sea had opened up to them.

During the rehearsal, the propellers were kept at minimal thrust, but, unknown to the extras, the engines would be on full thrust for the take. At De Mille's signal, Charlton Heston, as Moses, stood on a hilltop with arms raised, beckoning the masses of people through the parted sea. The steadily increasing winds actually threw me to the ground. The parade was led by an ox cart, and just when it appeared that everything would go in a single take, someone's Stetson hat blew into the scene and clung to the wheel of the cart in full view of the cameras. "CUT!" De Mille did some swearing and chastising, but back up the hill trudged the hordes.

Since I was in Cairo, RKO arranged for me to do a personal appearance at a special premiere of *Passion,* a film I had made with Cornel Wilde. Since Charlton Heston played Moses, De Mille kept him at low profile, but there was little danger of misconstruing an appearance at a movie premiere so Chuck came along as my escort. As we approached the Diana Theatre the streets were mobbed with fans awaiting my arrival. They hadn't recognized him in civvies, but when they did, the pushing, clawing, and tussling became a near riot. Chuck and I were separated for a time, and when we were finally reunited he was gasping for breath in an alleyway. "Never again!" he declared. "Parting the Red Sea was a cinch compared to throngs of excited Arabs."

As it turned out, I still had several months before my work was scheduled. There was, in fact, time for another picture, so I signed to do *Flame of the Islands.* Before doing that, however, I stopped in New York for the opening of *Tonight's the Night,* the David Niven picture which had originally been titled *Happy Ever After.* The reviews were very good and the reception was excellent in New York, as it would be a few days later in Minneapolis, where I also made an appearance.

I returned to Hollywood just in time to attend a reception at Paramount for the Shah of Iran and Queen Soraya, and was really looking forward to the reunion with Reza. I managed to say hello to the Shah, but just as I was about to inquire about Dorez we were interrupted by Barbara Stanwyck, who launched a monologue that carried on up the seating, and I was not near the Shah at the table. After dinner, I managed to get near the lovely Soraya, and said to her, "We all think you are just beautiful." Without expression, she gave a nod of her head that carried nary a spark of good feeling. The occasion ended with no further conversation.

Flame of the Islands was shot in the Bahamas, where I was given the same hotel cottage that had been occupied by the Duke and Duchess of Windsor during part of World War II. The film had four leading men, including my old flame Howard Duff, for whom I felt no lingering emotions. The others were Zachary Scott, Kurt Kasznar, and James Arness. I was given two numbers, "Bahama Mama" and "Take It or Leave It." Both were written by Nelson Riddle in his first movie assignment, and I choreographed the numbers myself since no choreographer had been assigned to the film. I was encouraged by Nelson to pursue a recording career, and he saw that the tunes from the film were later recorded and released.

With all of this completed, the time arrived for me to report for work with De Mille and company. I had spent many hours worrying about the contact lenses I was told to wear. I went to an ophthalmologist for the proper fitting, but no matter how I tried, they kept popping out. It reached the point where I dreamed that my *eyes* were popping out instead of the lenses. The other preproduction task was to learn ancient weaving. In the role, I had to weave as I spoke dialogue, which isn't as easy as it sounds.

My first day of shooting included the weaving scene and everything went without a hitch. Afterward, De Mille said I had naturally perfect timing, and coming from him it was a super compliment because he was never given to casual praise. He was also a stickler for perfection, but would not help with the reading of lines. An actor came to him and asked how he thought a line should be read. "Why are you asking me?" De Mille said. "You are being paid for knowing what you're doing."

One morning Bud Westmore approached me in the makeup department, confiding that De Mille had decided to forget the contact lenses. Sure enough, I was called into De Mille's office, and he gave me the news in the sweetest possible way: "I've decided that your main asset is your eyes," he said with a smile, "and I'm not going to change a God-given treasure." What a relief. I thanked him profusely and gave him a quick, hard kiss on the cheek. Then I left the office, on what I regarded as just the right exit.

We were about to shoot the six sisters' dance for Moses and several Arab guests. I remembered how the Arabs had reacted to my dance in *Hotel Sahara* by clapping in time, and they'd done the same thing when I danced in Cairo. I gathered up the courage to suggest this to Mr. De Mille, and he liked the idea. He put it in, and it worked.

I should have quit while I was ahead.

I saw a small lamb leaping into the air one day on a gentle hillock, such a peaceful and innocent scene that it seemed perfect for my entrance. Again Mr. De Mille liked my idea, and all other activity was halted while the assistants tried vainly to get the lamb to go through its paces. After several expensive takes, De Mille dropped the idea. That day I skulked off the set in embarrassment, and swore that in the future I would keep my bright ideas to myself.

I remember another time when an animal had the last laugh. De Mille was giving a speech to a couple of hundred extras in a voice that sounded like God himself. He was detailing the pattern they should follow in the next scene. As he was taking pains to give very precise directions, a twitter arose from his audience. C. B. was stunned. Then he looked behind him: he had left his script on a stool, and a goat was in the process of eating it. Laughing, he said, "Well, maybe that's where the scene belongs."

De Mille could be amusing and charming, but he could also be mean and belittling. Those close to him said he usually regretted his outbursts, and he certainly didn't like to hurt people's feelings, but he did it—often. I was somehow spared his wrath, which, I suppose, suggests that he respected me, and for that I have always been thankful.

He was such a perfectionist that he became impatient with his underlings, and there were times when ultimate patience was required from cast and crew. Vincent Price, Edward G. Robinson, and I used to sit in our dressing rooms hour after hour awaiting our turns before the cameras. The only person who seemed never to have to wait was Chuck Heston, who seemed to be always clambering up a mountain with his tablets, or being blown to shreds by the wind machines.

There was a scene where my sisters and I came to the Midian well for water, only to be confronted by the bad guys—the Amalekites. I'm knocked down by one of them, and Moses comes to the rescue, running the culprits off. Helping Chuck stage this scene was Bob Morgan, whom I had met on the set of *Shotgun*.

After the scene was completed, I walked over to Bob to say hello. When I asked how he had been doing, he told me that his wife, Helen, was very ill and things looked bad. I felt sorry for him; there seemed to be such an air of tragedy about him. His wife was supposed to be a very special lady and was then only thirty-three. I offered my sincere wishes for her speedy recovery.

I didn't see much more of him on the picture, but I found his image coming to mind more often than I could understand. It was shortly after we completed *The Ten Commandments* that I learned his wife had died.

It was mid-August 1955 when my part of *The Ten Commandments* was finished. On my last day of work, Mr. De Mille presented me with a leather-bound copy of my script. The inscription read:

Yvonne,
When you retrod the path of Sephora's life
"He Who Has No Name" surely guided your steps.

Thank you for your help.
Cecil B. De Mille

PART THREE

On the Road Again

I've gotten through Herbert and J. Edgar Hoover
Gee, that was fun and a half
When you've been through Herbert and
J. Edgar Hoover
Anything else is a laugh.

Black sable one day—next day it goes into hock
But I'm here.
Top billing Monday—Tuesday you're touring
  in stock.
But I'm here.

Been called a pinko Commie tool
Got through it stinko by my pool
I should have gone to an acting school
That seems clear.
Still, someone said, "She's sincere,"
So I'm here.

Chapter 29

I mentioned that I first met Bob Morgan on the *Shotgun* location, but we had actually met before that, as Bob reminded me, when Jocko Mahoney brought me to the Morgan home in the Valley. It was several years before, on a Sunday afternoon, and Jocko said he wanted me to meet a stuntman friend of his. Bob's wife was the former Helen Crlenkovich, National Diving Champion and performer in Billy Rose's Aquacade. It was surprising that I would have forgotten the occasion, but I guess it illustrates my total involvement with Jocko at the time.

It was strange of me to forget, because I remember finding Bob extremely attractive on the *Shotgun* location. He walked past me, shirtless and muscular, and I gave him a wolf whistle, to which he responded with a charming, toothy smile. Then we all became a family on the desert location, and had weekend get-togethers in our motel. It was during these parties that Bob introduced me to the martini cocktail, to his secret blend in which he substituted white wine for vermouth. It was great.

During this location, I learned that Bob hailed from Mount Carmel, Illinois, had spent five years in the Naval Air Transport Command during the war, and had once been a professional swimmer. His first job was doubling for Bogart in *Dark Passage.* After that, he doubled for many Hollywood stars and was rated among the top four men in the business.

This was one of the most arduous location assignments of my life: sheer desert, no shade, and on the move from dawn to dusk—so I had little further contact with Bob. After a quick dinner, sleep was what everybody was interested in. With the picture behind us, Bob and I had dinner a couple of times at the Wild Goose Restaurant in the Valley. Then, one afternoon he knocked on my front door. It was then that I told him it was time we curbed things before they burst into flame. He was married and had a child, and I had no interest in a secret love affair. He agreed, and we stopped seeing one another.

After *The Ten Commandments* my thoughts of Bob faded. Then one day I heard from him. He had been away on location, and now that he was a widower, he again thought of me. We attended a few small dinner parties and had great fun in our mutual interest in outdoor living. It was more of a friendship than anything at this time, as it was a slow adjustment for him after the death of his wife, and most of his efforts were now devoted to succeeding as single parent.

By Halloween of 1955, we had gradually grown closer to each other. It wasn't the skyrocketing kind of love that I was accustomed to; it was based more on mutual respect and interests. I had never experienced anything quite like it. At a costume party at the Circle J Ranch, the site of so many memories, Bob and I made our commitment. I was dressed in a multicolored Pierette costume and Bob was a Swiss yodeler in lederhosen with feathers in his cap.

"It's time we got married, Yvonne."

That was it; it wasn't even given in the form of a question. "You're right, Bob," I replied. We got up then to dance and I guess you could say we were engaged.

Marie hadn't met Bob yet, so a few days after his proposal I brought him home. She gave her blessing, which relieved me, but there remained one more difficult obstacle. All through my rise as an actress, I had a constant adviser and confidant, my acting coach George Shdanoff. He was like an unpaid manager, and a man whose judgment was usually unassailable. I gave him the news, and the frown appeared. The more I explained, the worse his reaction.

He did not approve and he gave me his reasons. He said Bob hadn't achieved enough stature in the business; he was nothing more than a "cowboy." Why must I always insist on muscles and brawn? As far was George was concerned, I was throwing my life away. His response hurt me deeply but it didn't change my mind. I wanted to be married. I longed to be loved and cared for; I wanted to love and care for one man.

We planned a relatively secret wedding and chose Reno as the place for it. The wedding party consisted of my lifelong pal, Pat Starling, and her husband, Geo Schweiger, Pat Newcomb, my publicist, Rory and Lita Calhoun, and stuntman Chuck Hayward. I mentioned earlier that Rory and I had our differences, but he had settled down to a more stable way of life following marriage to cute and vivacious Lita Baron. He and I had just finished a film together called *Raw Edge* and were much closer now than before.

The morning of the wedding I was in an almost uncontrollable state of nerves. I remember a half-eaten breakfast, fixing my face and hair, and getting dressed in my ivory and pink wedding dress. I pinned the little lace skullcap in place, picked up my pink beaded purse, and gathered in a bouquet of pink roses that somebody handed me. I told the girls I was ready. It was nine forty-five A.M., and en route to the Reno Episcopal Chapel I started to do battle with doubt. One inner voice told me to run like hell. Another voice said, "You're committed now, and you'll see it through. You're in love, and nothing else matters." The second voice won out.

It was a crisp and sunny day on November 21, 1955, when the Reverend Kirsteder pronounced us man and wife. Bob slipped the ring on my finger, we kissed, and off we went. We drove to nearby Virginia City, where our entourage saw that every bar in the town did a good off-season business. That night we had dinner at the Mapes Hotel Show Room. While we were celebrating, some of the wedding party slipped away and decorated our honeymoon suite. We found exploding light bulbs, vitamins for Bob in the medicine chest, and a cowbell cleverly attached and hidden under the bed. Discovering the bell, we called the suite where we knew the perpetrators of the mischief would be gathered. Lita answered the phone and hung up.

We drove off the next morning for one of the briefest honeymoons since World War II, because Bob felt compelled to be back in Los Angeles in time to spend Thanksgiving with his daughter Bari, who had been living temporarily with relations. I was in no hurry to get back. I had already seen the newspaper headlines announcing our marriage to the world, and knew that as one of Hollywood's best-known bachelor girls, I would have to face the press. But more importantly, I just wanted to be alone with my new husband. I wanted to stay away forever. Well, Bob got his way. We returned to my house on Coldwater Canyon, arriving in the middle of a cold November night. We were famished and there was no food in the house. The furnace decided to break down, so we just decided to climb into bed. Bob got up to get a glass of water and managed to hit his leg on my glass coffee table. He let out a loud yelp and a string of curses. Our first night in our future home was far from idyllic.

Before we could ease into our domestic roles, we had a round of congratulatory parties to attend. Producer Benedict Bogeaus and his wife, Dolores Moran, gave us a lovely reception in their Bel Air home. There were a number of celebrities present, but it was mostly a party of close friends among whom were Yura and Elsa Shdanoff. Elsa was as talkative and friendly as ever, but Yura sat in a corner with his hands clasped as though in solemn prayer, sending searing glances whenever Bob came his way.

I had been totally free for many years, but now I had to become domesticated in short order. Bob's daughter made me an instant mother, and I was soon pregnant myself. This restricted the roles I could take, but the shooting schedule made it possible for me to accept the part of Bridget Kelly in *Death of a Scoundrel.* It was the role of a prostitute devoid of scruples, a fun part to play. George Sanders was the scoundrel, and his wife, Zsa Zsa Gabor, also had a part, but they had been separated before the film began. When George learned I was pregnant, he became something of a pest in his ardor, confessing that he loved the "aura" of pregnant women. Later, Luther Adler said he had similar fancies. And I thought then I had heard everything.

Bob and I saw a lot of the Vincent Evanses and Cliff Lyons and his wife, Betty. Margie Evans and I soon learned that we had much in common, although I suspect that what we had most in common was our macho husbands. Vince, a writer, liked to get boisterously drunk with Bob and they would sometimes get into public quarrels. If they weren't quarreling among themselves, then Margie and I would become targets. On more than a few occasions, Margie and I took off alone, leaving our husbands to hash it out.

At that time, there still remained the delightful game of making up after a quarrel—and when I was working, I didn't have much time to brood. Even with a protruding tummy I was given the opportunity to make a longplay recording on the Imperial label, and fairly leapt at it. The album was called "Yvonne De Carlo Sings," and it turned out very well. I had some difficulty breathing properly, being eight months pregnant, but it wasn't noticeable on the recording.

Toward the end of my pregnancy, the seclusion was beginning to get to me. Bob went to San Diego for a horse show, and I came up with the bright idea to pay a surprise visit. I went by train, a bumpier ride than I'd expected, and by the time I arrived that evening I had swollen ankles and labor pains. We called my doctor, who said I should get back to the hospital in Santa Monica immediately. By now the pains were six minutes apart and before the drive was completed the pains were coming at two-minute intervals. Dr. Weinberg was waiting for me at the hospital, and all of us were sure the baby would be delivered within moments. It actually took fifteen hours.

I had always heard about expectant mothers screaming in pain during labor, but for me the pain was so severe I could only grunt. The screams of the other women in the small cubicles were horrible to hear. I just gritted my teeth and wondered if it would ever be over. At seven o'clock on the morning of the seventh day of the seventh month Bruce Ross Morgan was weighed in at seven pounds seven ounces. We had our share of lucky sevens on that summer morning of 1956.

The birth of my son was the greatest moment of my life thus far. To give birth to a healthy child was an accomplishment I was terribly proud of. To round out my happiness, Cecil B. De Mille offered to be the baby's godfather and Bob and I accepted with gratitude.

With Bruce only a few months old, I should probably have been focusing on his well-being, but I still had a career. *The Ten Commandments* had openings in Los Angeles and New York in early November and cast members were required not only to make appearances at the premieres, but also to contribute heavily to the film's promotion. The De Mille epic was a hit of the magnitude that C. B. had envisioned, and all the cast benefited from it. Almost concurrently with the positive reviews of the film, I was offered the leads in two Warner films: the musical biography *The Helen Morgan Story*, directed by Michael Curtiz, and *Band of Angels*, to be directed by Raoul Walsh. When I learned that Clark Gable would star in *Band of Angels*, that became my choice. "The King" had long been one of my idols and I thought I would be a fool to pass up a chance to work with him.

Bob came with me on location, Baton Rouge, Louisiana, in early 1957. We left the baby in the able hands of two grandmothers and a nurse. I had been coached for weeks on the characterization of Manty the Mulatto and felt well-prepared for my work. I knew Raoul Walsh from *Sea Devils*, so anticipated no problems in that quarter, and since Kay Gable and I hit it off from the start, the only question mark that remained was her husband. He was friendly enough before the start of the picture, so I looked forward to working with him.

Kay and Clark addressed each other as "Ma" and "Pa," and seemed to have fun with it. The same pet names had been shared between Clark and Carole Lombard, and Kay was like Carole in many ways. She was blonde and classy, and loved to use earthy language. Clark liked to tease Kay. She had a heart condition that required medication, which she was constantly forgetting to take. Clark would say to her, "You take that medicine, Ma. If you don't do what I tell you, I'll give you a kick in the ass." She retorted, "You kick me in the ass, and you know where I'll kick you."

The local fans were constantly on the lookout for interesting pictures of Clark or me. Every time I came out of the trailer toilets, I'd see somebody aiming a camera to catch me zipping up the back of my slacks. One day Clark was going in as as I was coming out. "Say, Clark," I said, "better make sure your dingus is tucked in before you come out of there. Those shutterbugs are just dying to catch you zipping up your fly." He grinned, making some sort of retort, but that broke the ice. Clark liked regular joes and welcomed me into the down-to-earth club.

It rained a lot, and many dreary afternoons were brightened by cocktails in the Gables' hotel suite. Clark was one to pour man-sized drinks, and this endeared him considerably to Bob.

Despite all my careful efforts, I eventually ran afoul of Clark. We had been called for a morning photo session and on the appointed day, I woke up feeling ill, so I phoned the publicity department and asked if I could come in later. I was told that would be perfectly all right. However, at precisely 9:10 A.M., Clark's agent phoned and told me to get to the studio—fast! Clark did not like to be kept waiting. I didn't realize what a no-no it was to be late for a Gable appointment. I wanted to explain the reason, but all I got from Clark was ice. Much later, Kay told me that Clark's fatal illness was aggravated because of Marilyn Monroe's unfailing lateness on the sets for *The Misfits.*

Band of Angels was rushed into release because they wanted to beat another Civil War drama being prepared by MGM. Our picture made the theaters first, but MGM's *Raintree County* was far more successful. *Band of Angels* made money, but it was not the hit we all hoped it would be. It was said that the timing wasn't right to deal with racial issues.

I learned I was pregnant again during the shooting in Baton Rogue, and Michael came along on November 14, 1957. This time the pregnancy and the birth were much easier and I was thinking that after the fifth or sixth, I might really get the hang of it. While I was pregnant with Michael, C.B. De Mille again asked me for a picture, this one to be directed by his son-in-law, Anthony Quinn. I told him about my pregnancy and he said they would not be able to wait, so I missed getting the role of the lady pirate in *The Buccaneer.* As it turned out the film was not really a hit and nipped Tony's directing career in the bud. It also turned out to be the last picture produced by Cecil B. De Mille. He would die in 1959 at the age of seventy-eight.

Before I pass the year 1957, I must chronicle another death that came as a terrible shock to me and the others who loved him. On April 21 in Las Vegas a taxi was moving through rush hour traffic when it was struck from behind by another car. The passenger in the cab was Nils Thor Granlund. "Granny," my dear friend for so many years, was critically injured. The year had started out well for Granny. His book, *Blondes, Brunettes* and *Bullets,* had been published, and it gave him a new flash of recognition after some very lean years. Granny also won ten thousand dollars on a TV quiz show, but the IRS snatched that for back taxes. Things were looking good again, though, because Granny was about to sign a deal that would bring him back as a nightclub MC— this time in Las Vegas—and on that fateful day in April, Granny was headed for a law office on the Vegas strip to sign the contracts.

It was my friend Hal Belfer who let me know what had happened. He was working in Las Vegas as a show packager and choreographer and hurried to the Nevada Memorial Hospital when he heard about the accident. The hospital people were trying to locate Granny's family and Hal thought I might be able to help, but I knew nothing about his family. He had been abandoned by just about everyone. I was trying to decide what to do when I received another call from the hospital: Granny was dead. The nurse told me that even if he had lived, he might have been a vegetable due to the extensive brain injuries. When the nurse asked me who would claim the body, I said I would.

Pat Starling and I saw that Granny had a decent funeral and burial, choosing Forest Lawn not for its prestige but because this was where Granny, Pat, and I used to ride horseback years ago. We had the body shipped from Las Vegas and got in touch with as many of the Florentine girls and acquaintances as we could. It was a small gathering. The floral arrangement on the casket read, To Granny From All of His Gals. . . . Love.

After the services, some of us Florentine gals got together for a wake of sorts, talking about all the people who owed Granny for past favors. Several of his buddies who had accepted his hospitality and food and drink for years just ignored their friend's death. Many others of Granny's old male friends couldn't seem to make it to the funeral.

No man has ever been kinder to me. As I look back over the years, I wonder if my search for a substitute father didn't end that August evening of 1940 when I walked into the Florentine Gardens. May God rest your sweet soul, Granny, wherever you are.

Chapter 30

In April 1959 I did a "Playhouse 90" television show called "Verdict of Three" that brought kind words from the critics, and I then signed for *Timbuktu,* in which I co-starred with Victor Mature. It was my first picture in more than a year. Then, thinking that work abroad always enhanced my career, I took the offer for an Italian movie, *La Spade e la Croce (The Sword and the Cross).* It would give Bob and me a second honeymoon in Rome in late August, but more importantly it would provide added income. In the months before the location I attended the Pacific School of Languages for private lessons in Italian.

While I was in New York City early in August I took the opportunity of auditioning for a potential Broadway musical, *Destry Rides Again.* It was a David Merrick production of the successful Western movie, and the part I wanted was Frenchy the saloon hostess. Unfortunately, nerves got the better of me, my voice was a bit shaky, and the audition wasn't as good as it might have been. I learned much later that Dolores Gray was hired for the part. However, there was no time to become depressed, because the very next morning Bob and I left for Europe.

We stayed at Claridge's for a few days, then went on to the Venice Film Festival. One of the big American entries that year was *God's Little Acre* and we attended a glittering party by the company at the Excelsior Hotel. Bob and Rosemary Stack were there and we had great times as a foursome around town. From there it was off to Rome, where William Wyler was directing Chuck Heston and Stephen Boyd in *Ben Hur*. It was party time for several days, and then to work.

I can take all kind of hardships as long as I'm properly prepared, but I can also be hard to get along with when I'm given surprises. The Italian press had apparently been told that I would be available for interviews throughout our stay in Italy. Traveling by train to the director's villa on the Italian Riviera for a weekend, I was accosted by the press. Bob and I barricaded ourselves in our compartment and refused to come out. The producer was angry at me, I was angry at him, and the entire production got off to a difficult start. I was glad when shooting was completed.

After a Mediterranean cruise, Bob and I returned to New York, where we picked up a car and drove back to L.A., stopping on the way in Mount Carmel, Illinois, to see Bob's family. The relatives were all very nice, and this leg of the journey was all right. But I think there was a quarrel for every mile of the trip. By the time we reached St. Louis, if Bob had left the hotel room for even ten minutes I'd have packed my suitcase and caught a plane for Los Angeles.

I wanted so much to see the children and was especially anxious to see how much Michael had grown. When he was brought to me, he cried and pulled away. To him, the nurse was his mother. I was dejected and guilt-stricken about leaving my baby in favor of work—and now that I saw the results, my guilt came into sharper focus.

Despite these feelings, I went back to work harder than ever. Since I hadn't gotten the Broadway show, I tried to think of another way to get in some singing and came up with the idea of putting together a nightclub act. With the encouragement of friends and family, I got started. Edith Head agreed to design the costumes. We then contracted for two boys and two girls to sing with an authentic Spanish guitarist and my musical conductor, Emilio Baffa. I found a great flamenco dancer to teach me a dance for the finale, which was an operatic rendition of "Habanera" from *Carmen*. The program was expensive and I realized some of the difficulties of being a producer. We opened the act in July of 1959 at the Chaudiere Club in Ottawa and appeared later in Los Angeles at the Coconut Grove. Nothing went smoothly. It was chaos from beginning to end. At dress rehearsal the girls discovered they couldn't get into their bikini panties because the crotches had been sewn too small. And the straps on their jeweled harem bras were too long. Aunt Connie became the Fastest Needle in the West to save the day, but we ended up having to cut that number, which was too bad because it was the comedy element of the show. On the same bill was

Buddy Hackett, and because his feelings were injured by the size of the blowup shot of me in the lobby and my top billing, he didn't show up for rehearsals, arriving just when it was time to go on.

It pleased me that several friends were in the audience applauding generously for the flamenco number: the Charlton Hestons, Tony Martin and Cyd Charisse, and Walter Wanger with his wife, Joan Bennett. From Los Angeles we went to the Tropicana in Las Vegas, where we shared the bill with bandleader Ted Lewis. He also objected to my life-sized cutout in the lobby, but he didn't just sulk. He dragged the cutout from the lobby and stashed it God knows where.

By the end of the tour in mid-November, I had grossed $53,500, but I had unfortunately spent $47,027.13, which didn't make this the most lucrative investment of my life. But I did sing and dance, showing my operatic voice to people who had no idea I possessed it, and for that reason I considered the venture a success.

I recall telling a reporter once, "I'm afraid of only two things—death and failure. To me, divorce is failure and I want no part of it." Those words played back to me hundreds of times over the years, and I wondered how I could have been so certain the marriage would succeed. I dreaded the thought of my sons being brought up in a broken home but there were many times when I could see no way to avoid it. Bob had an outlet in his physical-type work, his golf, and his drinking bouts with his buddies, but my anger was kept inside, so when I did let loose, it was with one hell of a bang. The explosions were coming with regularity after a time, and several times I walked away. Once I left home with Bruce in tow and wound up at Lake Tahoe with divorce papers in hand. Another time, I stormed off with some luggage and both boys and went to stay with my friend Pat. I rented a house another time, a mile from my own, when the atmosphere at home was impossible to bear. We seemed incapable of compromise; we just kept knocking our heads together against a wall of incompatibility.

There was a time when making up after a quarrel was sweet and exhilarating, especially in bed. But that feature had long since failed to serve. I'm not sure if I would have wanted additional children, especially under the prevailing circumstances, but I would like to have had a vote in the matter. Bob had a vasectomy without even telling me about it.

I went on tour to South America with Bob, and it was then that everything bad about our marriage intensified. First of all, I should never have accepted the tour without knowing more about the booking people. It turned out that I'd be playing in second-class establishments. The bad luck started on the very first night when some shrimp gave me a severe case of food poisoning. It was agony to try to do my act in the Rio nightclub with stomach cramps, but Bob was on the side of the impresarios, so I couldn't cancel out. To keep going I had to spend the night in a hospital after each night's work. From Rio it was São Paulo, where I appeared in a huge theater and had a doctor standing by to minister to me between numbers. After surviving this horror, we moved on to the new capital of Brasília, where we played in an unfinished auditorium.

I was still sick, but I think Bob believed I was faking. I was never so relieved as when we were finally on a plane heading toward home. First we flew to Lima for a one-night stopover, where my stomach problems flared up even worse than before. Bob went to a pharmacy and brought back some recommended medicine. Then he went off to do the town. My reaction to the medicine was violent; it only aggravated the condition and I had to crawl to the phone to call for the house doctor. I was told he was out to dinner but that they would try to locate him. I had still had no attention when Bob returned several hours later.

I wanted to recuperate in Lima and fly home when I felt better but Bob vetoed the idea of postponing the long flight home. We boarded the plane and all I could think of was home and my own comfortable bed but this dream too was shattered. The plane developed engine trouble and was forced to land near the jungle town of Manaos, Colombia, where we were stuck in a primitive hotel for more than twenty-four hours. I, of course, recovered soon after returning to Los Angeles but what was even worse than the physical discomfort I suffered was the realization, during this trip, that whatever had once been positive between Bob and me was now a lost cause.

The South American tour was in the winter of 1961. The following summer, in 1962, I had a belated opportunity to finally do *Destry Rides Again* when it was released for summer stock. The engagement was for the famed Papermill Playhouse in Milburn, New Jersey, and it proved a good break-in experience for my first musical—a tough show with dance numbers and ten songs. I was very happy with the way the show turned out and did a repeat of it later on at the Dallas State Fair theater, with Tom Poston playing the title role. Virgil Miers of the *Dallas Times Herald* wrote:

> Miss De Carlo, it turns out, has been hiding an admirable musical theater voice in a screen career of playing harem beauties and adventuresses. This is not the movie queen playing here-I-am theater, but a vibrant actress with a singing voice that projects, and with fine comedy timing.

In retrospect, it occurs to me that this was when my agents and managers should have been pushing for musical stage assignments for me. It would take too many years before I would make my own success in that medium.

In the early spring of 1962 I decided to break in an entirely new club act, a one-woman show. Connie drove with me to Hesperia, where I opened at the Apple Valley Inn. The show went fairly well, and I was feeling encouraged about resuming a nightclub career in spite of the fact that I hated that phase of show business. I had to make money. I *had* to pay the bills. Shortly after returning home, the telephone rang. It was Bob's stunt buddy, Chuck Hayward, calling from Arizona, where they were on location for the *How the West Was Won.*

"Yvonne," Chuck said, "are you sitting down?"

"Uh . . . why?" I asked.

"Well, there's been an accident, and Bob's broken up pretty bad."

I braced myself. "How bad?"

"Pretty bad," he murmured. "It was a train accident."

I caught my breath and waited.

Chuck continued, "He was run over and he's in bad shape. I've been with him since it happened. You'd better fly on over here as soon as you can."

He told me no more. The shock settled in after I hung up.

Chapter 31

My emotions following that fateful call play back like the changing designs in a kaleidoscope. I recall that I tried my best to convey the urgency of the call to Connie, who was in the kitchen. I hastily packed some clothes and within minutes a car from the MGM production department arrived to take me to the airport.

Somehow we made the trip to Phoenix, and an MGM production manager and I went to the Good Samaritan Hospital, where Bob was in the intensive care unit. So far no one had specified the extent of Bob's injuries, but my intuition told me it was something horrendous. Before I entered the intensive care ward, one of the nurses called me aside. "Now, Mrs. Morgan, your husband's in pretty poor shape. You're not going to faint on us, are you?"

"It's that bad?"

"He has tubes practically everywhere on his body," she said, "and his left leg is suspended. We've been too busy to clean away all the blood."

"I won't faint," I told her.

Bob, bandaged and still bloody, was coming out of the anesthetic as I entered the room. He immediately asked me what happened, and I said something to the effect that he would be fine. I didn't know what

I could tell him, because I knew nothing. After he slipped off to sleep I met with the doctors.

The sphincter was lacerated; the coccyx was dislocated; the right eyeball had been dislodged but could probably be saved; the femur was dislocated. "His finger was dislocated?" I asked. I had misunderstood them, and they explained that it was his femur, a much more serious dislocation than a finger. In this case it certainly was: they warned that there was a good chance he would lose the leg because of it.

Bari, Bob's daughter, had joined me by now and we checked into a motel, where I learned from Chuck Hayward more details of Bob's accident. The scene, staged near Globe, Arizona, called for George Peppard to wage a gun battle with the outlaws on top of a moving train. Bob, doubling for Peppard, was directed to cling to a log stacked on a flatcar and dangle over the coupling that joined the cars. The chains holding the logs were designed to be released hydraulically at a given signal. As a result of a miscommand they were released too early, and Bob, still with cameras turning, was smashed by part of about fifteen tons of timber. The impact thrust him into the path of the train and a pair of flatcars and the caboose passed over his body as he lay between the rails. One of the flatcars, they said, had been derailed by the impact.

Gushing blood, Bob was rushed to the hospital in Superior, Arizona, in a station wagon. En route, Bob asked Chuck, "How am I?" "Not bad—just a little lost skin," Chuck said, taking some gauze from a first-aid kit and holding the right eyeball in place. The hospital in Superior wasn't equipped for traumatic emergencies, so Bob had to be driven all the way to Phoenix.

Bob's mother, one of the bravest women I have ever seen, arrived soon and helped keep vigil during the critical hours. She adored her son but not a tear was shed, nor a complaint made. Bob was taken to surgery in a special hospital bed, and I managed to get a couple of hours' sleep curled up on the floor in the now vacant room. I was wakened by a doctor who let me know that Bob was out of surgery and was in I.C.U. Bob's mother and I were allowed only a peek inside, where Bob was now sleeping. He was hooked up to some special machine, and I.V. tubes were seemingly everywhere. We could tell very little by our peek, but at least we could see that he was breathing.

I did a lot of thinking during those marathon hours in the hospital about how fickle fate could be. Just days earlier I had been seriously planning divorce. Now, nothing mattered but for Bob to survive this catastrophe. My friends praised me for standing by Bob during his period of crisis, but to have done anything other than what little I did would have been unthinkable.

Enormous amounts of blood had been pumped into Bob, and several local radio personalities campaigned for blood donors over the air. Some of the stunt people formed their own programs to promote much-needed transfusions. As Bob slowly began to mend, other considerations came to mind. Bob's fairly good income had helped keep us afloat, but it now appeared that I would be the sole breadwinner for some time to come. Bob would need successive surgery to repair each part of his mangled body. Some of the costs would be paid by insurance, but far from all. I could see that I could no longer be choosy about the jobs I took. I advised my agent not to turn down any club date, no matter how small.

One of those small jobs put me into a club across the street from Disneyland in Anaheim, doing three shows nightly, trying to be funny, and singing. I did it, but it wasn't easy. Then one night I was signaled from offstage to come to the telephone—an emergency. The call was from the doctor in charge of Bob's case. "I'm sorry," he said, "but it looks like you'll have to come immediately. Your husband's leg is gangrenous, and we'll need you to sign for an amputation. Otherwise, we're sure to lose him."

I flew to Phoenix and signed the necessary forms. Bob's mother wouldn't take responsibility for amputation. Then I started to wonder if Bob would later blame me for his loss. When he was cogent, he steadfastly refused to permit the amputation, but he had deteriorated to the point where he was no longer rational enough to make his own decisions.

Bob actually died for a moment, but was brought back. It took two hours before they could proceed with the operation and even afterwards the toxemia remained and there was a stretch of time when his prognosis was not good at all. But he did survive, and finally started to regain his strength. Bob dealt with his missing leg by denying it was gone. The surgeon tried to tell him, but Bob wouldn't listen and finally a psychiatrist had to be called in to deal with it. It took the psychiatrist three visits but Bob eventually acknowledged that the leg was no longer there. He was somewhat appeased when the hospital psychiatrist assured him that he would not have to give up golf.

Once Bob was well on the road back, we could start to survey our situation. He felt he had a good case against negligence and that we should sue. But then we learned that we were playing in the big leagues. When Bob was still suffering in the hospital under medication, someone had sneaked into his room and had him sign a document. There had been so many documents, Bob only vaguely remembered it. But that signature, along with the disappearance of a key witness and the displacement of crucial evidence, would close out any case he might have had. Mortgaging my house ballooned our monthly payments, but there was no choice. Many months it seemed as though the house would go, but somehow we managed to hang on.

Bob was going through a special hell with constant pain, agonizing hours of physical therapy, and the shattering knowledge that he had to depend on others for survival. But he hung in.

I was working the nightclub circuit, but I couldn't bear to be away from the boys and I finally started taking them with me. The hours were terrible and the incessant travel maddening. I was finally offered the lead in a straight play for summer theater in Ohio, and I grabbed at it. The comedy. *Third Best Sport,* was successful in Ohio and was booked into the Drury Lane Theatre in Chicago for late August, which gave Bob a goal to shoot for. He was determined that he would be there to see the show and to celebrate my birthday with me on September 1. We all encouraged him, but none of us really believed he would make it. He did.

This would be the first time we would be alone together since the accident, and the doctors had already warned me that Bob could have recurrent emotional problems and might not be able to function sexually. I made up my mind just to take it frame by frame and hope for the best.

On the night of my birthday, sure enough, wheelchair and all, Bob made an appearance backstage. After the performance we had a birthday celebration together with dinner and cocktails, and once we started feeling comfortable in each other's company we tried our luck in bed. "Hallelujah!" Bob cried out. "I made it. This ole country boy is back in business again." I thanked God that night, as I had so many nights before.

Next came a two-week stint in Sydney, Australia, where I did my one-woman show, and while the pay was good I needed more, a good film role. The day I returned home our good pal, Duke Wayne, offered me a costarring role in his Western comedy, *McLintock!* Before I could even say thanks, the Duke said: "I want you in my picture, Yvonne, not because of Bob or the accident, but because I need you for the role." This would be my first feature in four years, and did it ever feel good to be back in front of the camera. And it was a class production. My part as John's lusty housekeeper was a solid one and I enjoyed every second of it.

My luck began to change for the better with my role in *McLintock!* When I had finished I landed a cameo role in *A Global Affair* with Bob

Hope. This was set for June, and I fitted in another film in the interim, the Western *Law of the Lawless* with Dale Robertson.

Bob was recuperating well and progressing measurably in his therapy. He had been fitted with an artificial leg, and his enthusiasm for prosthetics led to his invention of a metal leg that swiveled. Within a few months he was playing golf in a tournament in San Diego and trying to market a new golf cart. He induced me to invest in the scheme, which sent my inner warning bells ringing furiously, yet I did invest ten thousand dollars, losing it all. We ended up with practically an acre full of inoperative golf carts.

I went to Madrid in July of 1963 to perform my nightclub act, taking along Connie and my two sons. It turned out Duke Wayne was there filming *Circus World*, and he and a group of friends came to see my show. Wayne had been asked to make an appearance at Torrejón Air Base nearby to greet U.S. servicemen stationed there. He asked if I would do something with him, and I, of course, agreed. We did a variation of the comedy routine I had done with Bob Hope in *A Global Affair*. The G.I.s were thrilled to see their hero, John Wayne, and shouted as the Duke and I cavorted our way through our comic dialogue, finishing with a sexy Spanish dance.

The Spain trip started out as a joyous event until an incident spoiled everything. A European rag of a newspaper wrote a totally erroneous article about me, in which "ex-movie star Yvonne De Carlo" had been reduced to doing stripteases and belly dancing at stag affairs, garbage that was picked up by some American periodicals such as *Confidential.* I was ready to kill. I always did a class act, only spoofing occasionally with an imaginary striptease in which I'd unhook my skirt to reveal my legs, Mitzi Gaynor style. I considered suing, but was advised it would only add fuel to the fire.

After returning to the United States I was booked on Johnny Carson's "Tonight Show," and foolishly used that forum to complain about the injustice of the foreign press. I learned a lesson: never try to be serious and philosophical on a talk show, with the possible exception of "Donahue." My appearance was a flop and on all future Johnny Carson spots I made a point of being as witty and lighthearted as possible. I did four more Carson shows in the following years and was very successful.

Back home, I found myself with more time on my hands than I really wanted. I had hoped to spend more time home with the boys, who were now five and seven, and that was exactly what I was doing. But, regrettably, Bob wasn't. He'd never been the traditional father; he was more of a casual spectator. Having been deserted by my own father, I may have been hypercritical, but I was fixated on the necessity of fatherly guidance. I was the one to take the boys fishing or camping, and when we went to the High Sierra it was the motel owner, Frank Perry, who played surrogate father: baiting hooks, giving lessons in patience, and generally performing many other paternal tasks.

I did guest acting appearances on "The Virginian" in November of 1963, and was on "Burke's Law" in December. That was it until early spring of 1964, when an offer came along that I couldn't refuse: to take over Vivian Blaine's vamp role of Angela in Carl Reiner's hit Broadway comedy *Enter Laughing.* I played the role on Broadway for a week— a first for me—and then they took the show on the road. This was the kind of prestige and exposure I needed.

I've never watched a performance of someone I expect to replace in a stage role, because I prefer always to give a role my own interpretation. During rehearsals with Alan Arkin, who had been doing the show for a year and was bored to death, he began to come alive and seemed to enjoy himself, saying that my original interpretation of Angela brought a new meaning to his role.

After closing in New York, we went to Boston and later to Los Angeles. I was in my dressing room at the Biltimore Theatre when my agent called. "Yvonne," he said, "how would you like to play a vampire in a CBS television series?"

"A vampire?"

"That's right, but there's something else I should tell you."

"So there's a hitch," I said.

"Well, the part calls for you to wear green makeup, black fingernails, and long black hair with a silver streak in it. But it's a comedy and you love comedy."

"You've got to be kidding."

"No, it's true. And you never know, Yvonne. This series could run a long time, and could be very lucrative for you."

Sure, I thought—a likely story.

Chapter 32

Some of my friends thought it was insane that "The Most Beautiful Girl in the World" would consider playing a century-old vampire with floor-length black wig, sunken cheeks, and green makeup. I'll admit to some misgivings of my own at first, but the money was good, and it was comedy—that was what really clinched it for me. I needed all the money I could get, and as I thought about it, a change from the glamour role might open the minds of the casting people. Above all, with a series in the works I would no longer have to travel to earn a living.

The day came for my test at CBS Television City. When I arrived, an usher swept me into a small dressing room, where a makeup man did his "worst" on my face, and a hairdresser pinned on a long black Indian wig. I was given strict orders to remain where I was until I was called for. It occurred to me later that I was only one among several potential Lily Munsters who were trying out.

After waiting about an hour, my turn came. I was taken through deserted corridors to a small set, where I met an actor who would read Herman Munster's lines with me. I had very little time to study the script, so had no firm interpretation of the role, except that I was told to think of Lily as a Donna Reed type of housewife. But it must have been all right, because I received the job offer a few days later.

"The Munsters" debuted on Thursday, September 24, 1964, and

was an instant hit. The viewers seemed to love the blend of outrageous comedy, satire, and horror. New scripts were ordered and we all settled into a daily routine. My routine was no simple matter, by the way, since my makeup took three hours to apply. The producers believed the bile-green color of the makeup set the proper mood, even though the viewers would see the show only in black and white.

At first I was timid about being seen off camera in my makeup, but that didn't last. It was the makeup, in fact, that helped me become friends with Marlon Brando. We filmed at Universal, and it was here that Marlon was making *The Appaloosa.* I wandered on the set one day during my break and stayed to watch the scene they were shooting. After a time, Marlon spotted Lily Munster in full regalia and asked who I was. He came over and introduced himself, and offered me his set chair. We had a long conversation, mostly about makeup and characterization. We could have gone on for hours, but it was time for me to get back to my own set.

When I returned a few days later I was cornered by some of the crew, who asked if I was game to pull a prank on Brando. I agreed. They took me into a confessional booth of a church set, where Brando was about to make a confession to the priest. When his speech started I was instructed to open the curtain and let him see me. I did it at the appointed time, and Marlon's reaction was priceless: he fell off the stool and pretended to walk off the soundstage. But he loved it.

Starring in a series allowed me to bring together members of my old Universal family, Marie Bodie and others, but it didn't really seem like old times. Now the studio was part of a huge conglomerate and was cold and impersonal. It was the new Hollywood that every actor had to deal with, like it or not.

The public adored the Munsters, and Fred Gwynne (Herman Munster), Al Lewis (the 378-year-old Dracula), and I did whatever was necessary to keep the Munster image alive. We did personal appearances and interviews, and I even customized my Jaguar Mark X with coffin handles, spiderweb hubcaps, and the Munster family crest (ten semiprecious stones shaped like drops of blood) on the doors. I was twice elected honorary mayor of North Hollywood, and at my first installation told my boosters: "As mayor of North Hollywood, I'm happy to say that I will have the counsel and advice of a typical American family—the Munsters; a group that has its feet in the ground, and its fangs on the pulse of the people."

While in costume and makeup, I also enjoyed the gibes I would get on the Universal lot. One crew guy yelled to me, "What's wrong, Yvonne, did you eat in the commissary?" I wandered onto the Milton

Berle set one day. Berle spotted me and said, "Hi, Yvonne. Working today?"

"The Munsters" was doing extremely well in the ratings battle, and the ruling powers had until June to renew the cast's options. It was announced that a color feature of the series, *Munster, Go Home,* would be rushed into production, and that if it was successful the series would enter its third season. The movie did well at the box office, but "The Munsters" was still dropped from the fall lineup—why, nobody seems to know. Judging from the continuing high ratings of the show in syndication, it was a mistake. But we were dead after just two seasons.

What could possibly come next? I wasn't sure, so I went with the options that presented themselves, doing *Pal Joey* at Melodyland in Anaheim and then agreeing to separate engagements of *Catch Me If You Can.* In early 1968 I joined Donald O'Connor for an extended run of the musical *Little Me.* Ten weeks of the run were spent at Harrah's Club in Lake Tahoe and another five at the Sahara in Las Vegas. There were no nights off during this time except for the travel time between the two cities. We did two shows a night until two-thirty A.M., and rarely did I get to sleep before five A.M. Which meant I would get up around three or four in the afternoon, eat, and rest a little before going back to work at eight. It was a grind that only a fellow gambling-den performer would understand.

When I was working so hard in strange towns, I could only think about getting it over with and returning home, but once I was all the horrendous wrangling started up again with Bob. Leaving the broken ashtrays and vases behind me, I scooted off again, this time with Bruce, who had turned twelve. We went up to my old sanctuary in the High Sierra, where I took some time to sort things out, concluding that there was no way for my marriage to continue. I looked up an attorney in Bishop and started proceedings. On the way back I discussed the divorce with Bruce and his reaction was not what I expected. He didn't want to have the family separated, and was afraid I would cart him off to the mountains somewhere and expect him to live in an A-frame cabin. I was so afraid my sons would despise me that I cancelled the divorce proceedings before they even got started. Ironically, years later when I told Bruce what had transpired that day, he said, "Mom, why did you listen to me? After all, I was only twelve." Nice to know a decade or so later.

I went back to the boards again in December of 1968, this time in *Hello Dolly.* I had Bruce with me for the opening in New Haven, Connecticut. You may remember my mentioning that I have family in New Haven. I certainly remembered when the show played there; the theater was seemingly filled with D'Amatos, Castigliones, and De Carlos, most of whom I had never even heard of.

I chose to play the part of Dolly with an Irish accent. Why not—wasn't her name Dolly Gallagher? Judging from the reviews, I must have pulled it off. Whoever planned the five-month tour must have been either drunk or sadistic, because we criss-crossed and hopscotched all over the country, with no date in sensible proximity to the next. Michael was with me on this phase of the tour trip, and he was delighted by what I decided to do. I chartered a small plane and pilot to hop us to the remainder of the dates. It cost more than I could afford, but there was no other way I could have completed the tour. We finally closed in Phoenix in April, and on our final curtain call the entire cast went into embraces with sobs and hugs, the audience witness to it all.

By now my marriage was in a state of suspended animation, so almost immediately I went out again, this time with John Vivyan in *Cactus Flower.* It went on from there, a show here, a show there, a nightclub stint or two, and a few movies thrown in. None of it was very prestigious, but it was a way of keeping busy and a way of paying the bills in a home I rarely saw.

Then a lucky connection occurred which carried me into a world of considerably higher artistic potential. I signed a contract with Ruth Webb, a theatrical agent, who almost immediately set me up for an important musical comedy interview. She invited me to New York, put me up in her own apartment, and set about to present me in a proper way to Hal Prince, Stephen Sondheim, and Michael Bennett, who were assembling a cast for their new musical, *Follies.* We hired the best accompanist and coach, Ron Clairmont, who helped select my audition numbers and then coached me in them. Ruth thought I was right for the major lead in the show, and wanted everything to be done right.

I did the audition and was as nervous as I have ever been in my life, especially with the cold reading that was done onstage with the stage manager cueing me. Then I sang "Ten Cents a Dance," and "Before the Parade Passes By." I felt good with the songs but I knew I wouldn't be right for the leading role, a sophisticated society type. They let me down easily, but it was rejection just the same and I was terribly disappointed. The only consolation lay in the fact that there were plenty of others who were also rejected, among them Roberta Peters.

I was surprised a couple of weeks later when Ruth told me Harold Prince wanted to see me again. I met with the trio a second time to learn that they had liked my audition very much, and had, in fact, written in the part of Carlotta especially for me. There had also been a specialty number added for Carlotta to dance and sing.

Alexis Smith was the one to win the role I had tried for, and she was perfect for it. Dorothy Collins (she, Alexis, and I were all Canadians) joined the cast, along with Gene Nelson, John McMartin, and Mary McCarty. The irony of the plot line didn't take long to sink in: three ex-Follies showgirls return to their theater for a final grand reunion before the building is torn down. Each girl reveals her past and present, and projects into her future. Alexis and Dorothy are having marital problems, a major theme of the show, which reminded me how far gone my own marriage was. Strangely, my character was the most upbeat in the group.

A song show, *Follies* was also a dance marathon, and with a perfectionist such as Michael Bennett doing the choreography there was no such thing as just getting by. I've worked all my life and I'm used to discipline, but I have never felt more like I was back in school than in those two months of rehearsal. I have always hated tap dancing, and there was plenty of it in the show. People thought I could dance, so I danced. But when you're dealing with the Broadway stage, there is no way of faking it. It's the real world of dancing, and I learned it the hard way.

Since I had joined the *Follies* cast, James Goldman and Stephen Sondheim tried to give my character a special lilt of optimism in a generally downbeat story, and by the time I started rehearsing in New York, Stephen was working on my special musical number. The song he wrote was called "Oh Boy Can That Boy Fox-trot." It had a three-octave range, and a gimmick in which I used three different voices while whirling around the stage. The trick was to wind up with enough breath to do an effective vocal finish. Since I wasn't as studied a musician as many of the principals, I rehearsed endlessly. Hal Hastings, the musical conductor, was a paragon of patience.

The wonder of a new show is watching the creative process take shape, in this case Prince, Goldman (the author of the book), Sondheim, and Bennett bringing their spectacular ideas to life. Out go entire numbers, and new numbers are forthcoming. Then, the actors, dancers, and singers have to start again with something completely new. It was one of the greatest learning experiences of my life, and I grew to share their spirit of perfection. I only wish I had been introduced to Broadway theater a few years earlier.

I had done my first audition for the show in late October of 1970, was signed and in rehearsal by early December, and we were in Boston for our opening road performance in February 1971. After it was over we gathered together to await the critics' reactions. The consensus was that *Follies* was a great show when it sang and danced, but when it talked it was overlong and morose. Only one member of the cast was singled out for raves: Alexis Smith. As for the show, it needed work.

I thought it would be impossible to retain the theme of the show if everything were revamped, but the team went back to work. One night after the performance, Stephen came into my dressing room. Without preamble, he said, "Yvonne, we're dropping your 'Foxtrot' number. It just doesn't work."

Devastation! I broke into sobs even before Stephen finished what he was saying. "I'm sorry I let you down," I wept. "I did the best I could."

With my reaction so demonstrative, Hal Prince and Michael Bennett showed up. "This sort of thing happens all the time," one of them said. "It's how the musical theater works."

I was told by Stephen that he had liked the warm quality I showed in the audition and that the "Foxtrot" number made me come over too brassy. Stephen told me that the specialty song was a "one-joke number." But he also added, "We're going to write a more suitable song for you."

The song Stephen came up with was "I'm Still Here," and it was indeed a big improvement. We were in New York, with opening night coming up soon and reams of rewritten material to learn. We were rehearsing downstairs in one of the rooms off the lobby of the Winter Garden Theatre, and I was doing my new number for the approval of Stephen and Hal. Pleased, they asked me to read back the dialogue to make sure the changes had all been covered. I looked at it and didn't recognize a single word. "Is this dialogue new?" I asked.

The stage manager, Fritz Holtz, gave me a strange look. "No, those are the lines you've been rehearsing all morning."

I looked at the words again, but nothing registered. I looked up to see the trio in a whispering conference. Then Hal said, "Let's take ten." Off he went with Stephen.

When we were alone, Fritz explained that it wasn't at all uncommon for actors to become disoriented when too much is thrown at them. The tension under these circumstances had been terrific, and it had taken its toll. When he was convinced my mind was clear enough to do so, he sent me home to rest. In only a few hours the scary episode of partial amnesia had passed, and I was back on track.

After twelve New York previews, the show opened at the Winter Garden Theatre. We were all nervous but the show played well and the audience seemed pleased. After the show we went to the Rainbow Room for the big cast party. When the reviews came in, Hal Prince began reading them aloud. The critics considered our show "brilliant," "wonderful," "intelligent," and "breathtaking." There was some doubt expressed as to whether the show's melancholy theme would have mass appeal, but nearly all the critics insisted it was a must-see show. All, in fact, with the single exception of the *New York Times*.

My personal reviews were generally as upbeat as the character I played. *Newsweek* said that I did a "moving and witty song of survival," and *Variety* said that my debut on Broadway "rates as attractive . . . plenty of poise and charm."

The impact of my role came from the song "I'm Still Here." It was a remarkable creation, filled with sharp biographical touches that could almost be mine. Establishing my stage character as a champion survivor, it told of a former showgal who became a film star and then went on to become a television personality. The Sondheim lyrics catalog each decade of a life in which riches, love, and career have seesawed relentlessly. Each section of the song ends with, "I'm still here." The number always rated a big audience reaction. Thank you, Stephen!

Chapter 33

As I became better acquainted with the *Follies* people, I let it be known that my marriage was in a shambles. One night after the show I was in Stephen Sondheim's room, and the subject came up. "You'd better end it," he said. "It looks as though your marriage is going nowhere but down." That was the sort of advice I was getting from all friendly sectors by this time, and of course, I knew they were right. The boys had reached an age where they could deal more easily with family crisis, and with them coming into their own it would be easier for me to deal with a community property settlement. For the moment, however, I settled for the status quo.

When I say "status quo," I refer to the state of the marriage; there were other matters that were due for change. I had known only one man sexually for sixteen years—*that* was what would change. My sexual furnace had been banked for a long time, but that didn't mean the fire was out.

Unlike Los Angeles, New York is an easy place to meet desirable men. With the show a hit, the members of the cast were in constant demand for newspaper, radio, and television interviews, and we were invited to all the top-drawer parties. I loved to give interviews, and enjoyed being outspoken, or "good copy," openly discussing my survival instincts and admitting my to-the-right-of-right politics. I said also that I liked to shoot firearms. Hal Prince and his liberal pals named me the "right-wing Fascist" of the company. Once, in keeping with my title, I came to a rehearsal with a gun belt strapped to my waist, bullets and all. It was good for a laugh. Another time I had my dressing room door decorated with a poster of Whistler's Mother—with a machine gun on her lap. Hal loved it.

My popularity with the press took on personal meaning at a cocktail party on Thanksgiving Day 1971. It was there that I met a middle-aged, extremely attractive newsman whom I will call "Jeff." He was successful, and lived in a comfortable residential section that overlooked the Hudson River. He owned a home in Connecticut, where he would go weekends to be with a long-term wife whom he no longer loved. (Sound familiar?) This arrangement presented obstacles, but for the time being I was willing to live with it—taking one day at a time.

The romance started with a trip to the Catskills, with fresh air, a roaring fire in the cabin fireplace, and a multitude of soft touches and whispered words. Back in the city, we attended movies, explored museums, and talked by the hour about each other's lives and dreams. And we made love. We felt alive again, like teenagers. We even held hands in restaurants.

Things were off to an idyllic start, but there were signs I should have read: the broken dates with inadequate explanation, the daring and uninhibited incidents of his past, and, not incidentally, the mandatory porno movies before we made love. I found these titillating and fun at first, but not forever.

It turned out that my new "Mr. Right" had many things wrong with him, but while it played it was nice, and it was he who let me know I could still have romance in my life. He proved to me that I could still give and receive affection, which was immensely important.

In time, when I discovered he was much more committed to his Connecticut life than he admitted, we came to the end of the line, and, in retrospect, one of our final battles was more comical than tragic. By this time the live-for-today philosophy had gone by the boards, and the old familiar horns of jealousy had once more begun to sprout.

Jeff had lied to me in breaking a date, and I called him on it. We were having dinner when I accused him of being with his wife on that particular evening. He rose from the table in anger and shouted, "How dare you accuse me of sleeping with my wife!" With that, he stormed out of the restaurant. To be frank, it was Jeff who gave me the old heave-ho. He did it via a "Dear Joan" letter that he dropped off at the Winter Garden stage door. My emotional pain lasted well beyond the closing of the play.

One night early in the play's run a group of us were having a late sandwich at Reuben's. We were into our own conversation, but I was suddenly distracted by a nearby presence. I turned to see a tall, rugged-looking gray-haired man, standing next to the maître d'. The maître d' smiled and said, "Miss De Carlo, I'd like you to meet . . ." The name was mumbled, and I didn't ask for it to be repeated.

The tall, steely eyed man pointed out his table with his long cigar and asked if I would join them for champagne and caviar. I was intrigued enough to say I would have a drink with them, which hit me hard after a tough day. Someone suggested we go to the famous Copacabana. I was all for it. There was quite a group of us gathered there, and it grew as if by magic. There were suddenly men I hadn't seen earlier, and pretty girls seemed to come out of the woodwork. Before long someone in the party spirited me into the lobby, where I was introduced to a stocky man whose name I recognized at once. It was Joe Colombo. The meeting was innocent enough, with Colombo closing the visit with a gift: a small pin with an *I* on it for *Italy.* Inscribed beneath the letter were the words, "Capo Numero Uno."

Before the evening progressed much further, I was aware that I was mingling with *the* organization, and a man named Tony was a ranking member. A swarthy, bullnecked man called "Chief" was the top man in charge of the entire New York area. I had met people from all walks of life, and my discovery was not an earth-shaking matter to me. In fact, I must admit I was intrigued.

Tony called a week or so later and asked me out to dinner. Thus began a round of innocent but sobering encounters with the mob. It soon became obvious that the unattainable could usually be attained quite easily by Tony or his pals, so when I could find no other way to get tickets for *Jesus Christ Superstar* I turned to Tony. We planned to see the musical together, but Tony didn't last long. He didn't feel safe in an enclosed place with so many strangers.

Another time I went with Tony to a real "family" reunion somewhere deep in the bowels of Greenwich Village. We went through the door of a plain-looking building, and entered a gaily decorated hall filled with festive people who had gathered to honor the coming of age of "Sonny." Tony took me to a long table and seated me beside the Chief. There were at least a dozen people at the table, many of whom were, by now, on a "foist" name basis. The Chief's girlfriend was there too, dripping with ice: two diamond brooches, one rock-sized ring, three bracelets, and earrings. As I looked around, I could think only of the wedding scene from *The Godfather.*

I had never seen so much food, nor had I tasted better. There was shellfish diavolo and caviar for starters, and six courses after that, all types of wine, anything and everything a person could think of.

Later, upon returning from the ladies' room, I was met by several teenagers who asked for autographs and wanted to hear all about my movies and Lily and Herman Munster. I joined them at their table and really enjoyed their company. But I couldn't get those youngsters out of my mind. What would be their fate? Would any of them ever escape family influence? I wondered if they would be allowed the luxury of freedom and self-expression. It kind of worried me.

Even though the power of my new friends was awesome, and it was apparent that they could have just about any material thing they wanted, it was not a way of life that I could envy. They existed in a state of constant fear, never going anywhere without watchdogs and protectors. I remember a night that Tony and I had dinner with Jayne Turner, the prima ballerina in the show, and her boyfriend in an East Side restaurant where I recognized several men whom I had seen before with Tony. They were bodyguards sprinkled strategically throughout the dining room.

Tony was very solicitous of my safety, which I really didn't mind. When he learned that I had to walk three-and-a-half blocks from the garage to the theater, he posted lookouts along the way to see that I made it safely.

A few close friends were really concerned about my associations with mob characters, and I finally come around to agreeing that it might be judicious to break things off with Tony. He was understanding but asked that we have one more dinner together. We crossed the George Washington Bridge into New Jersey and had dinner at a chic, private suburban restaurant. I paid no attention to it at the time, but Tony paid for the expensive evening with a credit card—a credit card stolen from a superior court judge known for his hanging ways.

A few weeks later, a young and handsome detective from the district attorney's office paid me a visit. He seemed to know that I had been dating Tony, and that I was with him at the restaurant in New Jersey. I admitted knowing Tony, as I knew many people in show New York. I explained that celebrities meet many people via the stage door. I knew I had to be careful with my wording, because I was stuck in the middle.

The detective said they wanted Tony in the worst way and asked me for his address and phone number. Luckily, I didn't know his address or even his phone number. I wasn't lying—and I was grateful that I knew so little.

A few days after that I heard from the Chief, who insisted that I meet him. I told him he could come to my Riverdale apartment the following

Sunday. He arrived with a pair of his lieutenants, and we had a brief talk regarding the "borrowed" credit card. He offered the services of an attorney if it should turn out I needed one, but I told him I would hire my own attorney if necessary. He asked if he and his friends could at least buy me dinner. Since I had no other plans, I accepted. But this time I chose the place, an Irish restaurant near the apartment. We drove there in the big, black, standard-issue sedan and got out in front of the restaurant. Just ahead of us inside were a pair of burly red-haired men, each with a pair of handcuffs dangling from his back pocket.

"Jeez," said one of the Chief's men after we were seated. "She brings us to an Irish place full of cops. We could get arrested just for eatin'."

It was said as a joke, but I could tell that the Chief and his "boys" weren't having much fun that night eating their corned beef and cabbage.

Chapter 34

The final curtain for the Broadway company of *Follies* was on July 1, 1972, and the house was stacked with friends of the show, people who had seen it many times and knew every nuance of plot and business. The great roars of audience approval rang all the way up into the third-floor dressing rooms. At the end of the show, the applause was still going on after we had started packing up.

Jayne and I went off to a late dinner, becoming so sentimental that afterwards we returned to the theater to watch them load the trucks with props, costumes, and sets. It's always a sad time when a show closes, but it was especially so for me on this occasion; it had been my first Broadway experience and I hated to see it end.

The show was too unwieldy to take on tour, but the producers did agree to a week's run at the outdoor Municipal Opera House in St. Louis, and then a longer run in Los Angeles at the newly opened Shubert Theatre in Century City.

St. Louis remains memorable to me because of "the night of the bug." Dorothy Collins was singing her lovely song, "In Buddy's Eyes," when a bug—a moth, I think—flew right into her open mouth during a high note. She swallowed the beast and went right on singing. That, to me, is professionalism.

I had been away from Los Angeles for nearly nineteen months. I was homesick for friends and familiar surroundings but dreaded a resumption of the every-night-at-the-fights with Bob. It was even more difficult now since I had broken my personal pledge of marital fidelity and had decided on divorce. I was thankful that I was busy with rehearsals for the Los Angeles opening.

The show, with the complete Broadway cast, was scheduled to open July 22, and it was chaos. Workmen were hammering away; the downstairs garage was only half finished; the lobby carpet was being installed as we did our dress rehearsal.

Opening night was a benefit for the Actor's Fund, and there was a party afterwards for 1,700 guests, in what they then christened "Shubert Alley West." Helen Hayes served as hostess and chairwoman for the event. It was an elegant occasion with dozens of Hollywood's top names in attendance.

It made me feel proud to perform well in a successful show in front of so many old friends. My big song held special personal meaning. It was important to me to let the gang know that "I'm Still Here." Just in case they had forgotten.

As thrilling as it was to play in Los Angeles before my peers, it was in many ways anticlimactic. When the show closed eleven weeks later, it was time to look ahead.

I had spent a lot of money in New York on my apartment and on my dressing room. Those expenses in addition to the monthly bills in L.A. brought back the all-too-familiar money worries. When I was invited to take over a musical role from Cyd Charisse in Australia, I responded affirmatively. She had been in Australia doing a revival of *No, No, Nanette* for six months and was ready to come home. The tour had been intended for Betty Grable, who fell ill—fatally, as it turned out—and Cyd covered for her. Now I would take over for Cyd, and would leave for down under within just two weeks after the close of *Follies.* I wasn't anxious to hit the road again, but I really had little choice.

At the airport I told Bob exactly how I felt. I had serious misgivings about having to leave home again so soon, to leave my boys, and to go so far away for so long—six months. "Why," I asked, "should I have to be the breadwinner all the time? This job is the last straw!"

I was so distressed that I was almost glad when the airline clerk found no prepaid ticket for me. I was about to walk off and forget it when they called me back. There was a ticket after all, but in the name of Peggy Middleton. I'd forgotten that I'd asked to have the reservations made in my former name. So I made the nineteen-hour flight reluctantly— I hadn't wanted to leave the children. Thankfully, this was one occasion when the negative bells of my mind would ring untrue.

Upon arriving in Sydney, there were droves of reporters on hand and I had no opportunity to freshen up before facing them. The questions were, for the most part, variations on old themes, questions I had answered hundreds of times before. But one of them was a perfect match for my mood.

"What's the secret of your seventeen-year marriage, Miss De Carlo?"

"Separation!" I replied.

Four days and several television and radio interviews later, I arrived in Melbourne with only two weeks to learn my lines and the music, not to mention the complicated tap-dance choreography. Good Lord, more tap dancing! For someone who hated it, I was getting my share. So it was back to work, intensive bone-wearying work.

At last, with the help of a wonderful cast, things started to jell. Paul Wallace, who had played Tulsa in the Broadway and movie versions of *Gypsy,* was my leading man, and the cast included Bobby Limb and Jill Perryman. Although I had never been much for nostalgia, I was beginning to feel good about *Nanette.*

On November 6, I joined the cast at Her Majesty's Theatre, and I was treated as if it were a fresh opening night. When I finished my big tap routine, the audience loved it. What really turned them on was a fluke. Cyd always completed her version of this show-stopping number with a high kick and a fast exit. I had tried that in rehearsal, but in doing so I tore a tendon. With the kick out of the question, I chose to improvise. I closed the number with a raw and rumbling burlesque "bump." The audience almost fell into the aisles.

Once the show became routine, I began to brood about Jeff, my newsman lover in New York, but mostly I missed my sons. There was also the subconscious fear aroused by death-threat notes that some kook had sent to Cyd, and now to me. Even Liberace got them when he was in Melbourne. Nothing happened to anyone, but it was still disturbing.

One night between entrances I was in my dressing room reading a science fiction novel when my mind went blank. I would think of a past event, then wonder if it had really happened or if I was imagining it. I was so disoriented that when I saw these young men backstage wearing Roaring Twenties sweaters, I couldn't figure out why. I looked out at the orchestra, at Bobby Limb—nothing looked familiar. I went up to a nearby showgirl and asked, "Am I in *Follies?*" She must have thought I was making a bad joke.

By some miracle, I entered at the right cue for the big tap number, "I Want to Be Happy," and did it the same as always. Then I exited at the right time, but I had to ask afterward if I had. I was told it was okay. I felt shaky and almost fainted, and had to sit down. I lowered my head to regain my concentration but nothing helped. It went on this way for the entire show. Later, I realized this was the second visit of the frightening "partial amnesia" that had happened before in *Follies.*

With all of these matters compounding my loneliness, I invited my sons to come and visit me during their Christmas holidays. They arrived December 17.

In New York, I had found it worked out best if I alternated one boy at a time. This time both came. Bruce's big interest then was swimming, and he was good at it. I arranged for him to be coached by one of Australia's best coaches, Otto Son Lightner. Michael's big thing was motorcycle racing, so I arranged to have a bike waiting for him when he arrived. To do this, I agreed to go on a TV giveaway show in which one of the prizes was a Yamaha 90 trail bike. I won it. Then, as I stood there awaiting Michael, I couldn't stand it. I took some lessons myself.

When my sons arrived I became their tour guide, and they loved Australia. Bruce was soon involved in his swimming program, and Michael made immediate contact with the motorcycle dealers about racing bikes. One of them gave him a choice of street or dirt bikes to ride in competition. It frightened me to death to watch him leap through the air on his brute of a bike, but I didn't let him know it. He loved to have me watch. He was only fifteen then but qualified to enter a trials race competition, in which he competed against older, more experienced riders. Another time he competed in motorcross. After the event, one of the officials came to me, "Is Michael Morgan your son?"

I said that he was.

"He is a very talented young rider," said the man.

Secretly I would have preferred that Michael like tennis or something sensible, especially when I learned that one of his Australian buddies crashed his bike and broke his arm. He was strapped up by the ambulance attendant and watched the remaining races without a single complaint of pain. A strange breed, bike racers—not unlike stuntmen in their disregard for pain.

The boys, now both into their teens, had been acutely aware of the gravity of their parents' domestic problems, but it was on this Australian holiday that I made it a point to treat them both as young adults and not try to cover up the fact that I was dating other men. I think they accepted the situation much better than I.

Much too soon, the Christmas holiday ended and the boys had to return to Los Angeles. It was agreed before they left that when school was out in the spring, they would join me in New Zealand, where the show was next scheduled.

Meanwhile, the show packed up in Melbourne and was shipped off to Adelaide in South Australia, where we opened January 18 for a four-week run. It was so incredibly hot that some of the dancers fainted backstage after their extremely strenuous dances.

I had a lovely house just a fifteen-minute drive from the theater, but I was lonely, and once again thoughts of Jeff came back to taunt me. When a short vacation came up, I wondered where to spend it. I asked about the Barrier Reef, but the Aussies laughed: it was even hotter there than in Adelaide. I followed their suggestion and settled for a hop to Tasmania. The travel agent told me I'd be staying in a brand-new hotel in Hobart, and as a bonus Jerry Lewis would be performing there. Oh boy, gee—all the way to Tasmania to wind up with Jerry Lewis?

I stayed in Tasmania long enough to cool off and thoroughly enjoyed it, telling the press that if a nuclear holocaust came I would try to get to Tasmania, because who could bomb a place that was this beautiful? I also said I would like to return and become "Queen of Tasmania." I said the usual nonsensical things that I had always said to the press, but I hadn't bargained for their lack of sophistication. Everything came out as straight information. Hey, can't you take a joke? Even so, Tasmania was fascinating—at least one hundred years behind the times, or so it seemed, and that was okay.

Before proceeding to Sydney I had the Yamaha crated and sent to Los Angeles via freighter. It was too much of a temptation to have it around. After a couple of spills I thought it best to keep my tap-dancing legs intact for the show. After a long run with wildly enthusiastic audiences, I started to seek a social life. The first person I called was my old friend Lee Liberace, who was performing in the city. We met for dinner and had a lovely evening reminiscing over the good old days when we were both at Universal. I always marveled at Lee's warm disposition, especially in his dealings with the public, and wished that I could have been more like him in the early days of my career instead of being so introverted and shy.

It has only been in relatively recent times that I began to change. It's hard to pinpoint, but I think it was in the early 1960s that my attitude went through a curious metamorphosis. I began to take a genuine interest in others—members of movie crews, strangers at parties. It turned out that life was more fun and infinitely easier when you helped put smiles on the faces that surround you. I even managed to soften a bitter New York cab driver once while on a mad hop crosstown. He was swearing at other drivers, using expletives to describe the police. He was as mean as could be. I started to commiserate with him, and chatted in a friendly manner until he turned into a pussycat. As he let me out, he was actually smiling. "Watch it, ma'am," he said. "Right side, left side—left side suicide." He even wished me a good day.

Lee and I had lunch on occasion, and dinner several times as well. I visited him at his apartment, which was fabulously decorated in white, black, and red. But that was friendship, not romance.

I had had a nice romance in Melbourne just after arriving. He was called "Champ," because he was a champion auto racer in Australia. I met him while I was learning to ride the Yamaha. One of the racing clan took me to a meet in which Champ was driving. He was one of the handsomest men I had seen in a long while, and he had eyes of the purest blue. I was hooked. We walked through the pit section and I felt the electricity between us. Then I think I was especially endeared to him, when we neared the area of the pits. "Would you like to see my equipment?" he asked. Talk about a straight line. I felt like saying, "If you show me yours, I'll show you mine"—but I didn't. I knew he was referring to his racing car, which I wanted to see as well.

That started a round of parties with wild, fun-loving, and beautiful people, and all was well for several weeks. But soon the time came when it was important to Champ to spend some time with his wife.

One day I was asked to make an appearance at a horse race, the Cup Race, and a reporter I had met introduced me to many of the society types who were on hand. Among them was "Dinkie Die." That was what his friends called him because of his quaint way of expressing himself: with "dinky die this; dinky die that." Almost every statement had to be accompanied with a "dinky die." It makes him sound like a lunatic or an eccentric at the least, but understand this is Australia, and they have their own way of talking.

Dinkie Die was an extremely wealthy sheep rancher, who loved horseflesh and having fun. After he saw me in *Nanette* he said, "Ah, Yvonne m'luv, you have the legs of a thoroughbred. Just look at those slim ankles."

"How do you like my mane?" I asked him. "Or maybe you prefer palominos."

Dinkie Die turned out to be an inveterate romantic, and his first letters from the outback proved it: "Love is not just for today. Love is for tomorrow and tomorrow is forever. . . ." He became so serious about me that it started to frighten him, so we chose to cut it off neatly and say goodbye. He, of course, was married, and had three young sons and little hope of changing his life. When we parted he gave me "a fair dinkum crown," which stands for "a good-looking Australian hat." He told me that I had been his first affair while married and would be his last. I believed him—why not?

After closing in Sydney, we moved on to Auckland, New Zealand, for a July 13 opening. Time had passed so quickly, it seemed impossible that *Follies* had closed in New York only one year ago, but just one year had passed. It was a year of younger men for me and it turned out to be a badly needed ego boost. I was feeling good about myself and having a good time. The good feelings were only increased with the arrival of my sons for the remainder of the summer vacation.

One matter of seeming significance came with a newspaper story. It was a front-page account of a woman who claimed that her teenage son was my half-brother. My long-lost father was alleged to have come to Wellington in 1948, married this woman with whom he had the child, and then died in 1963. It was something to think about, I admit, but my conclusion was that if the woman were telling the truth she would have contacted me rather than going to the press. Intuition told me that nothing could be gained by further inquiry, so I let the matter lie. I never met the young man.

When the boys arrived, I made sure that they saw something of a variety of living styles, as well as taking part in their favorite activities, like bike racing and swimming. They had a wonderfully enriching summer as a result.

When they returned for school it was time for the show to move on to Christchurch, where we played for the month of September. We opened in Wellington October 5 and remained there until the show closed six weeks later.

I arrived in Los Angeles after a year's absence with a new, stronger attitude. I could interest men, and I could hold an audience. I was determined to break from the marriage. I wanted to explore the new and exciting world of which I had had only had a small taste.

Chapter 35

Not long after my return I convinced Bob that our marriage was over and that I was serious about getting a divorce. I don't think he believed it even then until he received the papers from my attorney. Then he hired an attorney, and most of the further discussions were carried on between them. I hated the idea of dragging intimate problems through the courts, and it was this dread that had made me put off the inevitable until now. Another factor that made all of it easier was a new law that allowed couples to divorce because of "irreconcilable differences." That was how I filed. It meant that we could settle out of court if we split our community property fifty-fifty. And that meant Bob would get fifty percent of what I had earned and owned, and I would get fifty percent of . . . Well, I'd get my freedom.

I knew I would be forced to sell the home on Coldwater Canyon to bail myself out, but it wasn't that easy at the time. In 1974 there was a slow economy, and to sell a large house with five-and-a-half acres of land meant finding someone with prime qualifications. Then another idea occurred to me. I still owned my first house in North Hollywood; it was where my mother lived. Marie had become arthritic and it was difficult for her to care for herself and a full house, so I probed to see if she would be interested in an apartment. She said she would be glad to move, especially if it meant her grandsons would not have to be uprooted from their family home.

I put the North Hollywood house on the market and began the search for an ideal place for my mother. But at about this time, the boys and I began to notice that Marie was not acting just right. She became reclusive and suspicious of her neighbors. Not even Bruce, who had always been close to her, could seem to get through. That's when we began to become really concerned. It seemed reasonable to me that she was reacting to the potential loss of her security. Plainly and simply, she was afraid, but her fears, normal enough, had become an abnormal paranoia. I halted the ads for the house and told her to relax and try to resume her regular routine; the house was hers as long as she needed it. But now, she became adamant; she wanted no part of the place and began to pack her things. To shorten the account of a rather long and depressing episode, it ended up with Marie having to be admitted to the Camarillo State Hospital, a mental facility deep in the San Fernando Valley.

With all of these terrible things happening, I couldn't take time out for a nervous breakdown of my own—I had to work. The San Bernardino Civic Light Opera Company asked me to play the role of Margo Channing in a musical version of *All About Eve.* It was not an easy show to do, and there were times I believed I couldn't go on with it, but my agent, Ruth Webb, who was now on the West Coast, gave me the necessary encouragement. I also had the professional and moral support of my old friend and designer Don Marshall, who made me up some glamorous clothes, real morale boosters. I'm glad I accepted, because the end result was success. The reviews were good, and I mastered the challenge.

All during this time, I was in daily contact with the doctors at Camarillo. They kept reassuring me that Marie would eventually come out of her funk, which I am glad to say she eventually did. She was released after a year, and took a comfortable duplex apartment not far from the hospital.

With my own stress and tension during these times, it was a wonder I didn't fall off the deep end, and maybe for a time I did. I was doing *Decline and Fall of the Entire World As Seen Through the Eyes of Cole Porter* in San Diego. It was a doubtful project from the start, a musical using Cole Porter's rejects—songs like "The Little Oyster." But that only meant we had to try harder.

One night after the show, I signed a few autographs as usual, and got into my car. I turned on the cassette player, which had a number of other Cole Porter songs I had to learn. The first song to play was "I Love Paris." I didn't recognize it at all; it meant nothing to me. I played it over and over with the same results. Then I tried to remember where I was staying. Blank. I just kept driving and through some sort of instinct made it to the hotel, located my door, and went inside. I had a list of production people staying in the hotel and studied it. None of the names was familiar. I looked up the room number of the producer and had the operator ring his room. When he answered I said, "This is Yvonne. You won't believe this, but I'm having a lot of trouble remembering things." What I finally managed to convey to him was that I would not be able to keep my appointments for the next morning's press interviews. I'm sure he thought I was shirking my responsibilities, but there was nothing else to do.

I then managed to get to bed, and with sleep the condition disappeared. This was the third and I hope the last siege of my own special "partial amnesia." I can only say that in each instance it showed up at times of extreme stress. Maybe I'll hire a psychiatrist someday to explain the whys and hows of these phenomena.

As for my stage or film roles, there was a period of time when I was less selective than I might have been. If a job was offered, and if the price was right, I took it. I needed the money. I had my first experience with dinner theater during this time. It was in St. Petersburg, Florida, and I did a translated French farce called *Nina,* which just didn't jell. Next, I went to Toronto to star with Anthony Newley in a feature film, *It Seemed Like a Good Idea at the Time,* which it did, and which it wasn't. The film had been sold to me as a lighthearted robbery caper, but something went awry. I think it remains buried there in the Canadian snow.

I did a television movie, *The Girl on the Late, Late Show,* which turned out all right, and another feature called *Arizona Slim* that was never released. I put on the tap shoes again to do the musical satire *Dames at Sea* in Windsor, Ontario, and segued to *The Sound of Music* in Dallas, Texas. That was the way it was as I tried as a bachelorette to rear two growing sons and pay off one former husband.

I finally sold the house on Coldwater in 1975, but I signed the papers with the agreement that we would not have to move out for a full year. When the year was up, I made a deal with the purchaser to assume the mortgage on a smaller house that he owned. I regretted making a deal on a house without a pool, since swimming is the only strenuous exercise I enjoy, but it was an easy transaction to make.

These times were difficult at best, and my constant prayer was that there would be no further nightmares. I could deal with the everyday exigencies of life; I just didn't want things to get worse. But then, almost inevitably, they did.

I was with my son Michael as he raced at Indian Dunes, California. He was doing very well in his motocross racing and wanted me to see him perform. I was very interested, of course, but I also felt a deep dread. I felt uneasy about motorcycle racing, because I was always aware of the attendant dangers. Yet it would have been ridiculous to admonish him for speeding when I had always been a female Andretti on the highways. Well, it happened. Michael took a terrible spill and was then struck on the lower back by another bike as he lay on the dirt track. We hurried him to the Riverside Hospital, about ninety miles away, and he was almost immediately sent to surgery. Afterwards, the doctor said that his injuries were severe, but an inch deeper would have meant permanent impairment. This was his first and only accident, and I'm thankful that his interests changed from bike racing to music after his recuperation.

I went out again in *Dames at Sea* in January of 1976, a merry odyssey that carried me from chilly Oklahoma City to the frigid climes of Ontario, Canada. Then I survived the equatorial heat of Buenos Aires to costar with John Gavin in a movie thriller, *House of Shadows.* By September I was in Salt Lake City playing the mother-in-law in *Barefoot in the Park.* Next, to Bucks County, Pennsylvania, where I was scheduled to do *You Never Know,* Cole Porter's musical version of *By Candlelight.* Before I arrived, the director had been fired, so he absconded with all the scripts, which gave us a frantic week of putting everything together before opening night. The only happy note here was meeting the diminutive actor Don Potter, who has done impressive musical comedy work for years. We became the closest of friends and performed together in *Cancan* in Atlantic City.

In a later version of *Dames at Sea* in Oklahoma City I became friends with a local matron of the arts. She was full of laughter and slightly perverse, which cemented our friendship. Realizing I was kind of lonely, she had an immediate idea. She knew a "real purty and tall, tall, tall policeman." She had met him when he was part of a security team for one of her parties. Would I like to meet him? Well . . .

After a couple of telephone calls, we made a date for lunch, and from my apartment door I saw this gorgeous hunk draw up on a huge black motorcycle—helmet, dark glasses, gun belt, black boots. Mercy me! I had to step back into the hallway to catch my breath. I finally steeled myself and went out to meet him. He stood up, up, up, all six-foot-six feet of him. I was so overwhelmed I could only comment on his great bike, the size, the make, its power. After obediently answering my stupid questions, he suggested that I follow in my car to a restaurant, which I did.

He waited until we were inside the restaurant before removing his dark goggles, and I could then see that his eyes were blue. That did it. We had a lovely visit over lunch, during which I learned the biggest factor of all. He was divorced and free as the wind. That night he saw the show and afterwards came home with me. There was no question that I had some years on him, but I had been with younger men before. We started seeing each other a lot, and it was weeks later on a trip together in New Mexico that I learned the exact disparity in our ages. I was thinking he was thirty-seven or eight. It turned out he had just turned *twenty-*seven.

"You seem shocked," he said.

"I am."

"Do you want me to turn this car around and go back?"

"Does the age difference matter to you?" I asked.

"Not to me."

"Keep driving," I said.

He visited me on five occasions in various locations in the United States: twice at my Westlake home and one time each in Missouri, Maryland, and Canada, where I was working. I fell. In thinking about it now, I must have bored my friends to death as I droned on about my undying love for this gorgeous man. The problem was his commitment and ties to his young son, whom he loved more than life itself.

We traveled everywhere, even doing the Hollywood nightclub scene together. The most romantic times were in his mobile trailer outside Oklahoma City. I cooked for him, helped him get off to work, even insisting on pinning the insignia on his uniform shirt. Every day and night together made the domestic scene that much more agreeable. For a time it was almost a "marriage" of the happiest type.

Then came some changes. After hearing about me, his ex-wife decided to make a second bid for him. She would come to the trailer, knowing I was inside, and sometimes even had the small son come to the door. "Daddy—daddy!" he would cry, his tiny fist beating on the door. His father would sit grimly silent waiting for the boy to leave. We both knew that to open the door would cause a scene neither of us wanted to face.

Our idyll lasted a while longer, but with all the extraneous tugs and pulls the fun part of it was drying up. I returned to California, and a couple of weeks later I received the big call from him. I sensed it was coming, because I knew how much he loved his son. He had decided to remarry his ex-wife.

It seems that each romance becomes just a bit harder to give up. I was destroyed when my young police officer went out of my life. I had severe stomach pains, couldn't sleep, and all my thoughts wrapped right around him and the wonderful times we'd had together. In short, I was a mess. The "mess" was slowly cleaned up by the most certain elixir of all—hard work, and thank God some of that continued to come my way.

In August of 1978 I was in Oakland, California, rehearsing *Gypsy* for a run at the Woodminster Summer Theatre. I had always wanted to play the role of Mama Rose, and this was my opportunity. but during the two weeks of rehearsal in the outside fog of Oakland, I came down with terrible bronchitis. It's one thing to sing through a cold, but it's impossible to sing through laryngitis, and I had it bad. I tried the show for a week, but my voice became progressively weaker, until I had to bow out on the last night's performance. My agent, Bob Hussong, was able to find a replacement for me by some miracle, because there was no understudy. No one subscribes more than I to "the show must go on," but the only way I could have continued this time would have been in Braille.

Later in 1978 I was invited to join a big cast of "Hollywood Jubilee" for television. The show was taped except for two very big live sections, one mine. I was to sing "I'm Still Here," from *Follies,* and on the last long "heeeaar" the brand-new H-O-L-L-Y-W-O-O-D sign would be lit up, and a huge fireworks display would be set off behind it.

Well, it rained. There I was in my gorgeous gold-beaded gown designed especially for me, holding an umbrella over my head. I slipped and slid my way through the number on a tiny stage, and all went pretty well until it came time for the fireworks. After an anemic sputter or two all was silent.

In 1979 I played a public-relations woman for the deranged Jim Jones in the movie *Guyana: Cult of the Damned,* shot in Mexico City. In this grisly film I ended up like so many others—dead. I was afraid the condition was going to be real when at five one morning Mexico City was hit by a medium-sized earthquake. I ran out on my balcony on the second floor and saw the water in the pool below sloshing like ocean surf. It may have been "medium" in their books but for that moment, at least, it scored about *ten* in mine.

At about this time, a series of losses colored my life. For years, hairdresser Bob Ross had been a close personal friend. We first met in a wig shop when I was preparing for my one-woman show, and he later toured with me in *Hello Dolly.* We saw a lot of each other until Christmas of 1975, when Aunt Connie and I had holiday toasts with him.

Then, after cutting all business ties, he simply vanished. No one that I know of has ever heard of him since that time.

Not long after that my dear friends Joe Connelly and Bob Mosher, creators and producers of "The Munsters," both suffered massive strokes within a month of each other. Bob died, and Joe became a partial invalid.

Connie's health was failing during the late seventies, and on my son Michael's birthday, November 14, in 1979 she was rushed to the Riverside Hospital. All through her lingering illness I had been severely affected by her suffering, almost as though I had a sympathetic illness of my own. I called Cousin Ken in London to inform him of his mother's condition, and to suggest he come home to be with her. It was then I learned the sad truth about Kenny. He had contracted multiple sclerosis, and was not well enough to travel, but in any event, he could not have reached her in time. My dear aunt Connie, as much a mother to me as Marie, died on November 16. I miss her to this day.

In mid-1979 I met author Hector Arce, who wanted to collaborate with me on my autobiography. We agreed on terms and started working together. Over the months we became more than collaborators, we became close friends. I took some time off in April of 1980 to concentrate on material for the book and chose June Lake in the High Sierra as the place to do the work. I called Hector to keep him informed of my progress, and he told me casually that he would be entering a hospital that day for minor surgery. I wished him well and said that I would call in a day or two. A day later I called my home and Michael answered the telephone. He said he had been trying to reach me. Hector had passed away just before they could get him into surgery. It was impossible; I couldn't believe it. But, of course, it was true. I put away all the research and believed that I never wanted to see or hear of the book again.

I kept in fairly close touch with my friends Vince and Margie Evans, who lived in Solvang. I would either drive all the way up to visit them there or we would meet in Santa Barbara, about thirty miles south of their home. It was Margie who influenced me to get closer to religion, and we attended Bible classes together. In early 1980 I phoned the Evans home to see if Margie could meet me for lunch. A secretary came on the line and gave me a halting account of what had happened to my dear friends. Margie, Vince, and their daughter Venetia had all been killed in the crash of their private airplane. The news came as a terrible shock to me and I was devastated.

It had been Margie who had seen me through the hard times after my divorce and, later, helped me accept the breakup with my young policeman. Margie had become a born-again Christian several years earlier, and told me I needed something new in my life. I immediately agreed, thinking she meant another man. What she prescribed, however, was Christ. "You need Jesus," she said to me. "You need to take him into your life and lean on him."

Actually, there have been many times in my life when a problem I was facing seemed beyond me and beyond Grandma's theory that God helps him who helps himself. I would go to a secluded spot—I'd pray for a solution. I'd also never forget to thank God for my blessings, whatever they were at the time. God has saved me and mine from some pretty sticky situations. For me, religion is a little like being a Republican or a Democrat. It's not the party that counts, it's the man. Therefore, I care not what house of worship I enter, be it Moslem, Catholic, Presbyterian, or Baptist. I elected God a long time ago and I'll stick with him, because I don't think his term will ever be up.

These days interviewers may ask me once in a while, "Are you afraid of growing older? Does it distress you?" The obvious answer is, everyone is distressed a little at the idea of age creeping up on them—but fear? No, I'm not afraid of getting older, unless, of course, it brings illness. As for being alone, I've coped with that all my life. I've known women who simply cannot handle being alone for any period of time, so they settle for something worse, any kind of mate. If I can't have the best, I'll be content to do a single.

I'm deeply grateful that I'm still able to work. I prefer musicals when it comes to stage or theater work. My club act is forty-five minutes of witty chatter and song—nostalgia. I receive a great deal of fan mail every day, considering I no longer have a TV series, and I love living where I live, on a ranch in the center of an Arabian horse area in the Santa Ynez Valley. I have a Rottweiler (remember the dog in *The Omen?*). She recently gave birth to eleven puppies and I kept one male.

Of course, I see a good deal of my two sons. Bruce, the eldest, is currently producing and directing his first movie; Michael is producing an album of his own compositions. Marie is still perky and rambunctions at eighty-two and I guess that just about covers everything. So— as Stephen Sondheim puts it in the song he wrote for me: "I'm almost through my memoirs and I'm here. . . ."

> *I've gotten through "Hey, lady aren't you whoozis?*
> *Wow! What a looker you were."*
> *Or, better yet, "Sorry, I thought you were whoozis.*
> *What ever happened to her?"*
> *First you're another sloe-eyed vamp*

Then someone's mother—then you're camp
Then you career from caree-eer to career
I'm almost through my memoirs
And I'm here
Good times and bum times
I've seen 'em all
And, my dear, I'm still here
Plush velvet sometimes
Sometimes just pretzels and beer
But I'm here.
I've run the gamut, A to Z.
Three cheers and dammit
C'est la vie
I got through all of last year
And I'm hee-eere
Lord knows, at least I was there
And I'm here—look who's here
I'm still here.

Filmography

Harvard, Here I Come (Columbia, 1942) 64 min. Director: Lew Landers; story: Karl Brown; screenplay: Albert Duffy. With: Maxie Rosenbloom, Arline Judge, Stanley Brown, Don Beddoe, Marie Wilson, Larry Parks. YDC as a bathing beauty in this comedy about Neanderthal-type Rosenbloom going to college.

This Gun for Hire (Paramount, 1942) 80 min. Director: Frank Tuttle; based on the novel *A Gun for Sale* by Graham Greene; screenplay: Albert Maltz, W. R. Burnett. With: Veronica Lake, Robert Preston, Laird Cregar, Alan Ladd, Tully Marshall, Marc Lawrence, Pamela Blake. Taut suspense thriller of a hired killer seeking revenge on those who double-crossed him. YDC as a showgirl in a nightclub scene.

The Road to Morocco (Paramount, 1942) 83 min. Director: David Butler; screenplay: Frank Butler, Don Hartman. With: Bing Crosby, Bob Hope, Dorothy Lamour, Anthony Quinn, Dona Drake, Vladimir Sokoloff. In the third of seven *Road* comedies, YDC is one of princess Lamour's harem hand-maidens.

Lucky Jordan (Paramount, 1942) 84 min. Director: Frank Tuttle; story: Charles Leonard; screenplay: Darrell Ware, Karl Tunberg. With: Alan Ladd, Helen Walker, Mabel Paige, Sheldon Leonard, Marie McDonald, Lloyd Corrigan. Comedy involving racketeer Ladd being drafted into the Army. YDC as a crowd-scene extra.

Youth on Parade (Republic, 1943) 72 min. Director: Albert S. Rogell; screenplay: George Carleton Brown. With: John Hubbard, Martha O'Driscoll, Bruce Langley, Ruth Terry, Charles Smith, Nana Bryant. In this campus musical set at Cotchatootamee College, YDC is a coed.

Rhythm Parade (Monogram, 1943) 70 min. Directors: Howard Bretherton, Dave Gould; story-screenplay: Carl Foreman, Charles Marion. With: Nils T. Granlund, Gale Storm, Robert Lowery, Margaret Dumont, Chick Chandler, Cliff Nazarro. In this musical of career-minded vocalist Storm, YDC appears in the Florentine Gardens club revue.

The Crystal Ball (United Artists, 1943) 81 min. Director: Elliott Nugent; story: Stevan Vas; screenplay: Virginia Van Upp. With: Ray Milland, Paulette Goddard, Gladys George, Virginia Field, Cecil Kellaway, William Bendix. Enterprising Goddard wins debonair Milland away from his conceited fiancée (Field) by pretending to be a crystal-ball gazer. YDC seen briefly as a secretary.

Salute for Three (Paramount, 1943) 75 min. Director: Ralph Murphy; story: Art Arthur; screenplay: Doris Anderson, Curtis Kenyon, Hugh Wedlock Jr., Howard Snyder. With: Betty Rhodes, Macdonald Carey, Marty May, Cliff Edwards, Minna Gombell, Dona Drake. Life and high jinks at a servicemen's canteen in Manhattan. YDC as one of singing Quartette girls.

For Whom the Bell Tolls (Paramount, 1943) 168 min. Director: Sam Wood; based on the novel by Ernest Hemingway; screenplay: Dudley Nichols. With: Gary Cooper, Ingrid Bergman, Akim Tamiroff, Arturo de Cordova, Vladimir Sokoloff, Fortunio Bonanova, Katina Paxinou, Joseph Calleia. The famous story of the American engineer (Cooper) caught in the midst of the Spanish Civil War and finding a great love (Bergman). YDC as a patron of the village cantina.

So Proudly We Hail! (Paramount, 1943) 126 min. Director: Mark Sandrich; screenplay: Allan Scott. With: Claudette Colbert, Paulette Goddard, Veronica Lake, George Reeves, Barbara Britton, Walter Abel, Sonny Tufts. Patriotic salute to the brave Allied nurses at Bataan. YDC as a spectator in the opening crowd sequence.

Let's Face It (Paramount, 1943) 76 min. Director: Sidney Lanfield; based on the musical play by Dorothy and Herbert Fields, Cole Porter, and the play *Cradle Snatchers* by Norma Mitchell, Russell G. Medcraft. With: Bob Hope, Betty Hutton, Dona Drake, Eve Arden, Zasu Pitts, Marjorie Weaver. Hutton supervises a fat farm with Hope as her zany boyfriend, based at an adjacent Army camp. YDC as an extra.

True to Life (Paramount, 1943) 93 min. Director: George Marshall; story: Ben Barzman, Bess Taffel, Sol Barman; screenplay: Don Hartman, Harry Tugend. With: Mary Martin, Franchot Tone, Dick Powell, Victor Moore, Mabel Paige, William Demarest, Clarence Kolb. Radio writer Powell finds plentiful ideas on the typical American family from Martin and her family. YDC as a walk-on extra.

The Deerslayer (Republic, 1943) 67 min. Director: Lew Landers; based on the novel by James Fenimore Cooper; screenplay: Harrison Derr; adaptor: John W. Krafft. With: Bruce Kellogg, Jean Parker, Larry Parks, Warren Ashe, Wanda McKay, Addison Richards, Phil Van Zandt. Based on the classic Leatherstocking Tale of American pioneers versus the redskins, with YDC as Princess Wah-Tah betrothed to Indian Parks and sought after by a Huron brave (Van Zandt).

Standing Room Only (Paramount, 1944) 83 min. Director: Sidney Lanfield; story: Al Martin; screenplay: Darrell Ware, Karl Tunberg. With: Paulette Goddard, Fred MacMurray, Edward Arnold, Roland Young, Hillary Brooke, Anne Revere. In overcrowded World War II Washington, D.C., visiting executive MacMurray and his secretary (Goddard) are hard pressed to find sleeping accommodations. YDC as a secretary.

The Story of Dr. Wassell (Paramount, 1944) 136 min. Director: Cecil B. De Mille; based on the real-life story of Dr. Wassell, and also the story by James Hilton; screenplay: Alan LeMay, Charles Bennett: With: Gary Cooper, Laraine Day, Signe Hasso, Dennis O'Keefe, Carol Thurston, Carl Esmond, Paul Kelly, Elliott Reid. The heroic account of a courageous physician (Cooper) helping to evacuate the Allied wounded from Java in 1942. YDC as a native girl.

Rainbow Island (Paramount, 1944) 98 min. Director: Ralph Murphy; story: Seena Owen; screenplay: Walter De Leon, Arthur Philips. With: Dorothy Lamour, Eddie Bracken, Gil Lamb, Barry Sullivan, Anne Revere, Reed Hadley, Olga San Juan, Elena Verdugo. A spoof of sarong films with Lamour as the shipwrecked miss who became princess of a South Pacific atoll. YDC as one of the royal handmaidens.

Kismet (Metro-Goldwyn-Mayer, 1944) 100 min. Director: William Dieterle; based on the play by Edward Knoblock; screenplay: John Meehan. With: Ronald Colman, Marlene Dietrich, James Craig, Edward Arnold, Hugh Herbert, Florence Bates, Joy Ann Page, Harry Davenport. Yet another remake of the popular story of the Bagdad beggar involved in royal intrigue. YDC as part of the queen's (Dietrich) retinue.

Practically Yours (Paramount, 1944) 90 min. Director: Mitchell Leisen; screenplay: Norman Krasna. With: Claudette Colbert, Fred MacMurray, Gil Lamb, Cecil Kellaway, Robert Benchley, Jane Frazee, Rosemary De Camp. Frantic wartime comedy of publicized pilot MacMurray returning from aerial duty to find Colbert expecting to marry him. YDC as an office worker.

Here Come the Waves (Paramount, 1944). 99 min. Director: Mark Sandrich; screenplay: Allan Scott, Ken Englund, Zion Myers. With: Bing Crosby, Betty Hutton, Sonny Tufts, Ann Doran, Noel Neill, Mae Clarke, Minor Watson.

Wartime romantic comedy as crooner Crosby joins the Navy and copes with twins—one frenetic, one quiet, and both played by Hutton. YDC as an extra.

Bring on the Girls (Paramount, 1945) 92 min. Director: Sidney Lanfield; story: Pierre Wolff; screenplay: Karl Tunberg, Darrell Ware. With: Veronica Lake, Sonny Tufts, Eddie Bracken, Marjorie Reynolds, Grant Mitchell, Alan Mowbray, Porter Hall. In hectic Miami, golddigging cigarette girl Lake sets her romantic sights on multimillionaire Tufts, now of the Navy. YDC as a club hatcheck girl.

Salome, Where She Danced (Universal, 1945) 90 min. Director: Charles Lamont; story: Michael J. Phillips; screenplay: Laurence Stallings. With: Rod Cameron, David Bruce, Walter Slezak, Albert Dekker, Marjorie Rambeau, J. Edward Bromberg, Abner Biberman. In her first starring vehicle, YDC as a famous Viennese ballerina who flees the Austro-Prussian war, stops over in an Arizona desert town to romance a bandit (Bruce), and travels on to San Francisco's Barbary Coast for more adventure.

Frontier Gal (Universal, 1945) 84 min. Director: Charles Lamont; screenplay: Michael Fessier, Ernest Pagano. With: Rod Cameron, Andy Devine, Fuzzy Knight, Sheldon Leonard, Andrew Tombes, Beverly Sue Simmons. In the frontier town of Red Gulch in 1900, YDC is a French dance-hall hostess, Lorena Dumont, who marries and battles with outlaw Johnny Hart (Cameron) and has his child (Simmons).

Song of Scheherazade (Universal, 1947) 103 min. Director-screenplay: Walter Reisch. With: Brian Donlevy, Jean-Pierre Aumont, Eve Arden, Philip Reed, Charles Kullman, Terry Kilburn, Elena Verdugo. The life of composer Rimsky-Korsakoff (Aumont), who is a naval cadet when the Russian fleet docks in Morocco. Exotic YDC as the fiery dancer named Cara de Talavera who inspires his great melodies.

Brute Force (Universal, 1946) 98 min. Director: Jules Dassin; story: Robert Patterson; screenplay: Richard Brooks. With: Burt Lancaster, Hume Cronyn, Charles Bickford, Ann Blyth, Ella Raines, Anita Colby, Sam Levene, Howard Duff, John Hoyt. A hard-hitting depiction of prison life and the men behind bars. In a flashback sequence, YDC is Gina, the Italian girl who murders her racketeer father and allows her soldier boyfriend (Duff) to take the blame.

Slave Girl (Universal, 1947) 79 min. Director: Charles Lamont; screenplay: Michael Fessier, Ernest Pagano. With: George Brent, Broderick Crawford, Albert Dekker, Lois Collier, Andy Devine, Arthur Treacher. In nineteenth-century Tripoli, a beautiful dancer (YDC) becomes involved with an American diplomat (Brent). The narrator is a talking camel with a Brooklyn accent.

Black Bart (Universal, 1948) 80 min. Director: George Sherman; story: Luci Ward, Jack Natteford; screenplay: Ward, Natteford, William Bowers. With: Dan Duryea, Jeffrey Lynn, Percy Kilbride, Lloyd Gough, Frank Lovejoy, John

McIntire. Lola Montez (YDC), the Continental favorite, comes to old California on a dance tour and encounters bandit Duryea.

Casbah (Universal, 1948) 94 min. Director: John Berry; based on the novel *Pepe le Moko* by Detective Ashelbe and the original screenplay by L. Bus-Fekete, Arnold Manoff. With: Tony Martin, Peter Lorre, Marta Toren, Hugo Haas, Thomas Gomez, Douglas Dick, Katherine Dunham. The musical remake of *Algiers* cast YDC as Inez, the native girl friend of jewel thief Pepe le Moko (Martin), who in turn loves the stranger-to-the-bazaar, Gaby (Toren).

River Lady (Universal, 1948) 78 min. Director: George Sherman; based on the novel by Houston Branch, Frank Waters; Screenplay: D. D. Beauchamp, William Bowers. With: Dan Duryea, Rod Cameron, Helena Carter, Lloyd Gough, Florence Bates, John McIntire. As Sequin, who runs a gambling boat, YDC seeks to win the love of a lumberjack (Cameron).

Calamity Jane and Sam Bass (Universal, 1949) 85 min. Director-story: George Sherman; screenplay: Maurice Geraghty. With: Howard Duff, Dorothy Hart, Willard Parker, Norman Lloyd, Marc Lawrence, Milburn Stone. Calamity Jane Canary (YDC) sets her romantic sights on well-meaning outlaw Sam Bass (Duff), who is involved with another (Hart).

The Gal Who Took the West (Universal, 1949) 84 min. Director: Frederick de Cordova; screenplay: William Bowers, Oscar Brodney. With: Charles Coburn, Scott Brady, John Russell, Myrna Dell, Clem Bevans, Houseley Stevenson. Opera star YDC appears on the Arizona scene of old and becomes enmeshed with the feuding grandsons (Brady, Russell) of Coburn, a Civil War veteran.

Criss Cross (Universal, 1949) 87 min. Director: Robert Siodmak; based on the novel by Don Tracy; screenplay: Daniel Fuchs. With: Burt Lancaster, Dan Duryea, Stephen McNally, Richard Long, Esy Morales, Percy Helton. Ex-criminal Lancaster is pushed back into a life of crime by double-crossing YDC, his former wife, who has a hankering for tough guy Duryea.

Buccaneer's Girl (Universal, 1950) 77 min. Director: Frederick de Cordova; story: Joe May, Samuel R. Golding; screenplay: Harold Shumate, Joseph Hoffman. With: Philip Friend, Robert Douglas, Elsa Lanchester, Andrea King, Norman Lloyd, Jay C. Flippen, Douglass Dumbrille, Henry Daniell, Verna Felton, John Qualen, Connie Gilchrist. Bostonian Deborah McCoy (YDC) is captured by a pirate (Friend) and becomes entangled with Lanchester and her "fancy" girls.

The Desert Hawk (Universal, 1950) 77½ min. Director: Frederick de Cordova; screenplay: Aubrey Wisberg, Jack Pollexfen, Gerald Drayson Adams. With: Richard Greene, Jackie Gleason, George Macready, Carl Esmond, Marc Lawrence, Rock Hudson, Frank Puglia. Princess Scheherazade (YDC) becomes involved with the magician Omar (Greene) and Oriental splendor.

Tomahawk (Universal, 1951) 82 min. Director: George Sherman; story: Daniel Jarrett; screenplay: Silvia Richards, Maurice Geraghty. With: Van Heflin, Preston Foster, Jack Oakie, Alex Nicol, Tom Tully, Rock Hudson, Susan Cabot, Arthur Space, Dave Sharpe. Scout Jim Bridger (Heflin) rescues wagon train, singer Julie Madden (YDC) from the rampaging Sioux Indians.

Hotel Sahara (United Artists, 1951) 87 min. Director: Ken Annakin; story-screenplay: Patrick Kirwan, George H. Brown. With: Peter Ustinov, David Tomlinson, Roland Culver, Albert Lieven, Mireille Perrey, Ferdy Mayne. British-made comedy with YDC as Yasmin Pallas, who during World War II connives to protect her husband's (Ustinov) desert hotel from the invading German, French, British, Americans.

Silver City (Paramount, 1951) 90 min. Director: Byron Haskin; based on a story by Luke Short; screenplay: Frank Gruber. With: Edmond O'Brien, Barry Fitzgerald, Richard Arlen, Gladys George, Edgar Buchanan, Michael Moore. YDC is Candace Surrency, working to exploit a silver mine with her dad (Buchanan).

The San Francisco Story (Warner Bros., 1952) 80 min. Director: Robert Parrish; based on the novel by Richard Summers; screenplay: D. D. Beauchamp. With: Joel McCrea, Sidney Blackmer, Richard Erdman, Florence Bates, Onslow Stevens, O. Z. Whitehead. In 1850s San Francisco, Adelaide McCall (YDC), the mistress of politician Blackmer, becomes infatuated with enterprising McCrea, the man she once horsewhipped.

Scarlet Angel (Universal, 1952) 80½ min. Director: Sidney Salkow; story-screenplay: Oscar Brodney. With: Rock Hudson, Richard Denning, Bodil Miller, Amanda Blake, Henry O'Neill, Henry Brandon, Dale Van Sickel. A remake of *The Flame of New Orleans* with YDC in the Marlene Dietrich role as Roxy McClanahan, a saloon singer in 1860s San Francisco, battling her way to success and love.

Hurricane Smith (Paramount, 1952) 90 min. Director: Jerry Hopper; based on the story "Hurricane Williams" by Gordon Ray Young; screenplay: Frank Gruber. With: John Ireland, James Craig, Forrest Tucker, Lyle Bettger, Richard Arlen, Mike Kellin, Henry Brandon. In the 1850s, Polynesian beauty Luana (YDC) is linked with grasping treasure seekers.

Sombrero (Metro-Goldwyn-Mayer, 1953) 103 min. Director: Norman Foster; based on the novel *A Mexican Village* by Josefina Niggli; screenplay: Niggli, Foster. With: Ricardo Montalban, Pier Angeli, Vittorio Gassman, Cyd Charisse, Rick Jason, Nina Foch, Kurt Kasznar, Walter Hampden, Thomas Gomez, José Greco. A multi-episode story of old Mexico, with YDC as Maria of the River Road, a peasant girl in love with aristocratic Gassman, himself dying of a brain tumor.

Sea Devils (RKO, 1953) 91 min. Director: Raoul Walsh; suggested by the novel *The Toilers of the Sea* by Victor Hugo; story-screenplay: Borden Chase.

With Rock Hudson, Maxwell Reed, Denis O'Dea, Michael Goodliffe, Bryan Forbes. In the nineteenth century, British spy Droucette (YDC) adventures as a countess and is protected by British naval officer Hudson.

Fort Algiers (United Artists, 1953) 78 min. Director: Lesley Selander; story: Frederick Stephani; screenplay: Theodore St. John. With: Carlos Thompson, Raymond Burr, Leif Erickson, Anthony Caruso, John Dehner, Robert Boon. French spy Yvette (YDC) masquerades as a nightclub singer and is saved by legionnaire Thompson.

The Captain's Paradise (Lopert, 1953) 80 min. Director: Anthony Kimmins; story: Alec Coppel; screenplay: Coppel, Nicholas Phipps. With: Alec Guinness, Celia Johnson, Charles Goldner, Miles Malleson, Bill Fraser, Sebastian Cabot, Ferdy Mayne. The classic English-made comedy of ferryboat captain Guinness with a staid British housewife (Johnson) in Gibraltar and an exotic Moroccan spouse (YDC) across the Straits in Ceuta.

Border River (Universal, 1954) 80½ min. Director: George Sherman; story: Louis Stevens; screenplay: William Sackhiem, Stevens. With: Joel McCrea, Pedro Armendariz, Howard Petrie, Alfonso Bedoya, George J. Lewis, Erika Nordin. Confederate soldier McCrea crosses into the free zone of Mexico in search of gold and finds romance with Carmelita (YDC).

Passion (RKO, 1954) 84 min. Director: Allan Dwan; story: Joseph Leytes, Beatrice A. Dresher, Miguel Padilla; screenplay: Leytes, Dresher, Howard Estabrook. With: Cornel Wilde, Rodolfo Acosta, Raymond Burr, Lon Chaney Jr., John Qualen, Anthony Caruso. In old California, YDC appears as twins: the gentle Rosa, the soon-to-be-murdered wife of Wilde; the tomboyish Tonya, who teams with her brother-in-law in his bid for revenge.

Tonight's the Night (Allied Artists, 1954) 88 min. Director: Mario Zampi; story-screenplay: Jack Davies, Michael Pertwee. With: David Niven, Barry Fitzgerald, George Cole, Robert Urquhart, Eddie Byrne, A. E. Matthews. Serena McGlusky (YDC), an enterprising Irish widow, weds Niven, the lord returning to his ancestral estate. Shot in England and Ireland. Original title: *Happy Ever After.*

La Castiglione (Radius-Taurus, 1954) 89 min. Director: Georges Combret; screenplay: Combret, Claude Boissol, Pierre Maudru. With: Georges Marchal, Paul Meurisse, Rossano Brazzi, Lucienne Legrand, Lea Padovani, Lisette Lebon. Italian YDC helps patriot Marchal escape the Austrian police. She later weds a count and in Paris meets Napoleon III. Filmed in Paris.

Shotgun (Allied Artists, 1955) 80 min. Director: Lesley Selander; screenplay: John Champion, Clark E. Reynolds, Rory Calhoun. With: Sterling Hayden, Zachary Scott, Robert Wilke, Guy Prescott, Lane Chandler, Angela Greene. Half-breed singer Abby (YDC) teams with a marshal (Hayden) and a bounty hunter (Scott) and deals with an Apache ambush in the desert.

Flame of the Islands (Republic, 1955) 90 min. Director: Edward Ludwig; story: Adele Comandini; screenplay: Bruce Manning. With: Howard Duff, Zachary Scott, Kurt Kasznar, Barbara O'Neil, James Arness, Frieda Inescort. Rosalind Dee (YDC), a girl with a past, becomes an investor in a Nassau nightclub, which leads her into dealing with club manager Scott and a fisherman (Arness).

Magic Fire (Republic, 1956) 95 min. Director: William Dieterle; based on the novel by Bertita Harding; screenplay: Harding, E. A. Dupont. With: Carlos Thompson, Rita Gam, Valentina Cortesa, Alan Badel, Peter Cushing, Frederick Valk. The life and times of composer Richard Wagner (Badel), with YDC as the actress Minna, who becomes his first wife.

Raw Edge (Universal, 1956) 76 min. Director: John Sherwood; story: William Kozlenko, James Benson Nablo; screenplay: Harry Essex, Robert Hill. With: Rory Calhoun, Mara Corday, Rex Reason, Neville Brand, Emile Meyer, Herbert Rudley. As Hannah Montgomery, YDC is the gal in the Oregon territory wed to villainous Rudley, who, in turn, had Calhoun's brother lynched.

Death of a Scoundrel (RKO, 1956) 119 min. Director-screenplay: Charles Martin. With: George Sanders, Zsa Zsa Gabor, Victor Jory, Nancy Gates, Coleen Gray, John Hoyt, Tom Conway. YDC is Bridget Kelly, a devious tart, who becomes Sanders's cohort in various shady business enterprises.

The Ten Commandments (Paramount, 1956). 221 min. Director: Cecil B. De Mille; based on the novels *Prince of Egypt* by Dorothy Clarke Wilson, *Pillar of Fire* by Reverend J. H. Ingraham, *On Eagle's Wings* by Reverend G. E. Southon, in accordance with the Holy Scripture, the ancient texts of Josephus, Eusebius, Philo, the Midrash; screenplay: Aeneas MacKenzie, Jesse L. Lasky Jr., Jack Garris, Fredric M. Frank. With: Charlton Heston, Yul Brynner, Anne Baxter, Edward G. Robinson, Debra Paget, John Derek, Sir Cedric Hardwicke, Nina Foch, Martha Scott, Judith Anderson, Vincent Price, John Carradine, Edward Franz, Douglass Dumbrille, H. B. Warner, Henry Wilcoxon. In this epic remake of his 1923 silent version, De Mille cast YDC as Sephora, the eldest daughter of Jethro, who weds Moses (Heston) and helps him to deal with the trials of the wilderness.

Band of Angels (Warner Bros., 1957) 127 min. Director: Raoul Walsh; based on the novel by Robert Penn Warren; screenplay: John Twist, Ivan Goff, Ben Roberts. With: Clark Gable, Sidney Poitier, Efrem Zimbalist Jr., Rex Reason, Patric Knowles, Andrea King, Torin Thatcher, Juanita Moore, Roy Barcroft. Amantha Starr (YDC) is the daughter of a Kentucky planter who in the days of the pre-Civil War learns she is a mulatto and is sold at auction to slave trader Hamish Bond (Gable).

La Spada e la Croce (The Sword and the Cross/Mary Magdalene) (Liber, 1958) 105 min. Director: Carlo Ludovico Bragaglia; screenplay: Alessandro Continenza. With: Jorge Mistral, Rossanna Podestà, Massimo Serato, Mario Girotti, Andres Aureli. An Italian-made Biblical spectacle with YDC as Mary Magdalene.

Timbuktu (United Artists, 1959) 91 min. Director: Jacques Tourneur; screenplay: Anthony Weiller, Paul Dudley. With: Victor Mature, George Dolenz, John Dehner, Marcia Henderson, James Fox, Leonard Mudie. During the hectic days of World War II in French Sudan, Natalie Dufort (YDC), the wife of the French local commandant (Dolenz), becomes intrigued with a gun-runner (Mature).

McLintock! (United Artists, 1963) 127 min. Director: Andrew V. McLaglen; screenplay: James Edward Grant. With: John Wayne, Maureen O'Hara, Patrick Wayne, Stefanie Powers, Jack Kruschen, Chill Wills, Jerry Van Dyke, Edgar Buchanan, Bruce Cabot, Strother Martin. In this comic Western romance, YDC is Louise Warren, the comely housekeeper at Wayne's ranch, where life and love take chaotic turns daily.

A Global Affair (MGM, 1964) 84 min. Director: Jack Arnold; story: Eugene Vale; screenplay: Arthur Marx, Bob Fisher, Charles Lederer. With: Bob Hope, Lilo Pulver, Michelle Mercier, Elga Andersen, Miiko Taka, Robert Sterling, Jacques Bergerac. When United Nations worker Hope becomes the custodian of a fifteen-month-old girl, many nations wish to adopt the infant. YDC as Dolores, a member of the Spanish UN delegation out to vamp Hope and win the child.

Law of the Lawless (Paramount, 1964) 87 min. Director: William F. Claxton; screenplay: Steve Fisher. With: Dale Robertson, William Bendix, Bruce Cabot, Barton MacLane, John Agar, Richard Arlen, Jody McCrea, Lon Chaney Jr., Donald "Red" Barry. Saloon singer Ellie Irish (YDC) becomes enamored with hanging judge Robertson in the old West.

Tentazioni Proibiti (Wonder Film, 1964) 88 min. Director-screenplay: Osvaldo Civirani. With: Dolly Bel, Christine Keeler, Brigitte Bardot, Alberto Sordi, Claudia Maiolini, Anna Maria Mareglia, Renato Rossini. A documentary of Continental nightclub acts, with YDC seen in excerpts from her Madrid club date.

Munster, Go Home (Universal, 1966) 90 min. Director: Earl Bellamy; screenplay: George Tibbles, Joe Connelly, Bob Mosher. With: Fred Gwynne, Al Lewis, Butch Patrick, Debbie Watson, Hermione Gingold, Terry-Thomas, John Carradine. In this feature film version of TV's mock-horror series "The Munsters," YDC was again Lily Munster, the 156-year-old vampire involved with her family in a visit to high-toned England and their conniving British relatives.

Hostile Guns (Paramount, 1967) 91 min. Director: R. G. Springsteen; story: Sloan Nibley, James Edward Grant; screenplay: Steve Fisher, Nibley. With: George Montgomery, Tab Hunter, Brian Donlevy, Leo Gordon, James Craig, Richard Arlen, Donald "Red" Barry. Dancehall girl Laura Mannon (YDC) shoots a man and is one of those being transported to jail in a prison wagon by sheriff Montgomery and his deputy (Hunter).

The Power (MGM, 1968) 108 min. Director: Byron Haskin; based on the novel by Frank M. Robinson; screenplay: John Gay. With: George Hamilton, Suzanne Pleshette, Michael Rennie, Nehemiah Persoff, Earl Holliman, Arthur O'Connell, Barbara Nichols, Aldo Ray, Richard Carlson. In this science-fiction thriller, YDC is Sally Hallson, who after the death of her scientist husband (O'Connell) turns into a good-time gal.

Arizona Bushwackers (Paramount, 1968) 87 min. Director: Lesley Selander; story: Steve Fisher, Andrew Craddock; screenplay: Steve Fisher. With: Howard Keel, John Ireland, Marilyn Maxwell, Scott Brady, Brian Donlevy, Barton MacLane, James Craig, Roy Rogers Jr., James Cagney (narrator). During the Civil War, YDC is Jill Wyler, a seamstress and a Confederate spy.

The Delta Factor (American-Continental, 1970) 91 min. Director: Tay Garnett; based on the novel by Mickey Spillane; screenplay: Garnett. With: Yvette Mimieux, Christopher George, Diane McBain, Ralph Taeger, Sherri Spillane, Ted De Corsia. In this spy melodrama, George is a private detective on a CIA mission to rescue an imprisoned scientist, with YDC involved in the caper as Valerie.

The Seven Minutes (20th Century–Fox, 1971) 116 min. Director: Russ Meyer; based on the novel by Irving Wallace; screenplay: Richard Warren Lewis. With: Wayne Maunder, Marianne McAndrew, Philip Carey, Jay C. Flippen, Edy Williams, Lyle Bettger, Charles Drake, John Carradine. In the exploited obscenity trial concerning a sex-oriented novel written by an anonymous author, YDC is Constance Cumberland, the surprise witness.

The Girl on the Late, Late Show (NBC-TV, 1974) 74 min. Director: Gary Nelson; teleplay: Mark Rogers. With: Don Murray, Bert Convy, Gloria Grahame, John Ireland, Ralph Meekers, Cameron Mitchell, Van Johnson, Walter Pidgeon. Video producer Murray is seeking a famous ex-movie star (Grahame) and in the course of his pursuit meets Lorraine (YDC), a restaurant owner.

The Mark of Zorro (ABC-TV, 1974) 78 min. Director: Don McDougall; teleplay: Brian Taggert. With: Frank Langella, Ricardo Montalban, Gilbert Roland, Louise Sorel, Anne Archer, Robert Middleton. Yet another remake of the swashbuckling classic with YDC as Isabella Vega, the wife of ousted governor Roland and the mother of Don Diego (Langella).

Arizona Slim (Two Diamonds, 1975) (unreleased) Director-screenplay: Chuck Wein. With: Sean Walsh, Michael DeBarre, Judith Cohen, Pamela Meller, Joseph Cortese. In this account of pool hustlers on the prowl in New York City, YDC is the Contessa.

It Seemed Like a Good Idea at the Time (Ambassador, 1975) 106 min. Director: John Trent; story: Claude Hars; screenplay: David Main. With: Anthony Newley, Stefanie Powers, Isaac Hayes, Lloyd Bochner, Henry Ramer. A comedy shot in Canada with YDC as Julia, a nearsighted gun-toting mama with a divorced daughter (Powers) and a demented artist ex–son-in-law (Newley).

Blazing Stewardesses (Independent International, 1975) 85 min. Director: Al Adamson; story: Sam Sherman; screenplay: Sherman, John D'Amato. With: Bob Livingston, Don "Red" Barry, the Ritz Brothers, Connie Hoffman, Regina Carrol. A racy comedy about a really enterprising lady (YDC) who teams with a rancher's (Livingston) foreman (Barry) to rustle the man's cattle and force him to sell the ranch to them. Three voluptuous stewardesses come to the rancher's rescue.

Won Ton Ton: The Dog Who Saved Hollywood (Paramount, 1976) 92 min. Director: Michael Winner; screenplay: Arnold Schulman, Cy Howard. With: Dennis Morgan, Madeline Kahn, Bruce Dern, Art Carney, Virginia Mayo, Rory Calhoun, Henry Wilcoxon, Ricardo Montalban, Johnny Weissmuller, Joan Blondell, Ethel Merman, Dorothy Lamour, Phil Silvers, Ann Miller, George Jessel, Rudy Vallee, Tab Hunter, Ron Leibman, the Ritz Brothers, Zsa Zsa Gabor, Fernando Lamas, Alice Faye, Milton Berle, Walter Pidgeon, Guy Madison, Patricia Morison, John Carradine. A Rin Tin Tin–type dog star of 1920s Hollywood has many (mis)adventures. A cast of veterans. YDC as the Cockney washerwoman involved in a chase sequence.

La Casa de las Sombras (The House of Shadows) (Pino Farina, 1976) 89 min. Director: Ricardo Wulicher. With: John Gavin, Leonor Manso, Mecha Ortiz, Amelia Bence, Nora Cullen, Duilio Marzio. Argentinian-made melodrama with YDC as a wealthy woman living in a memory-laden mansion, where a crime was committed in 1908 and not yet solved in 1930.

Satan's Cheerleaders (World Amusement, 1977) 92 min. Director: Greydon Clark; screenplay: Clark, Alvin L. Fast. With: John Ireland, Jack Kruschen, Sydney Chaplin, Jacqueline Cole, Kerry Sherman, Hillary Hores. A horror-thriller focusing on a group of revengeful cheerleaders, with YDC as the coach.

Fuego Negro (Black Fire) (Film Mexico, 1978) 85 min. Director: Raul Fernández; screenplay: Rex Rayter. With: Roland Ferlini, César Imbert, Susana Kamini, Aliscya Maxwell, Aurora Clavel. In the plantation era, YDC is among those witnessing the slaves' revolt and the influence of a voodoo cult.

Nocturna (Compass International, 1979) 82 min. Director-screenplay: Harry Tampa; With: Nai Bonet, John Carradine, Tony Hamilton, Brother Theodore, Sy Richardson, Ivery Bell, Adam Keefe. A sexy spoof of the vampire theme, with Count Dracula (Carradine) and his granddaughter (Bonet) leaving Transylvania and rendezvousing in New York City for fun and games. YDC as Jugula, who has been Dracula's lover for hundreds of years.

The Silent Scream (American Cinema Releasing) 87 min. Director: Denny Harris; screenplay: Ken Wheat, Jim Wheat, Wallace Bennett. With: Rebecca Balding, Cameron Mitchell, Avery Schreiber, Steve Doubet, Barbara Steele,

Brad Rearden, Julie Andelman. Thriller focusing on a mother (YDC) and her son (Doubet) who rent rooms in their large home to college students, knowing that the woman's insane daughter (Steele) is kept a prisoner in the attic. The deranged girl escapes and embarks on a killing spree.

Guyana: Cult of the Damned (Universal, 1980) 90 min. Director: Rene Cardona Jr.; screenplay: Carlos Valdemar, Cardona. With: Stuart Whitman, Gene Barry, John Ireland, Joseph Cotten, Bradford Dillman, Jennifer Ashley. A dramatic re-creation of the last days of fanatic Reverend Jim Jones (Whitman) and the slaughter of his followers. YDC as Susan Ames, the public relations officer.

Sam Marlow, Private Eye (The Man with Bogart's Face) (20th Century–Fox, 1980) 111 min. Director: Robert Day; based on the novel *The Man with Bogart's Face* by Andrew J. Fenady; screenplay: Fenady. With: Robert Sacchi, Franco Nero, Michelle Phillips, Olivia Hussey, Herbert Lom, Misty Rowe, Gregg Palmer, Mike Mazurki, Henry Wilcoxon, George Raft. A comic paean to *The Maltese Falcon* and the great detective thriller movies of the 1930s and 1940s, with Sacchi as the Humphrey Bogart lookalike sleuth solving a complicated caper in deadpan style. YDC is Teresa, involved in the chase for the coveted "Eyes of Alexander," a pair of priceless sapphires.

The Munsters' Revenge (NBC-TV, 1981) 100 min. Director: Don Weis; teleplay: Don Nelson, Arthur Alsberg. With: Fred Gwynne, Al Lewis, Sid Caesar, Howard Morris, K. C. Martel, Jo McDonnell. Reprising their "The Munsters" TV series roles, Lily (YDC), Herman (Gwynne), and Grandpa (Lewis) are the ghoulish family who must cope with diabolical Dr. Diablo (Caesar), who has masterminded a plot using robot wax-museum figures (including those of Herman and Grandpa) for a crime spree.

Liar's Moon (1981) 105 min. Director-screenplay: David Fisher. With: Matt Dillon, Cindy Fisher, Hoyt Axton, Richard Mull. A teen love story set in a small town in Texas in 1949. Dillon plays a boy from the wrong side of the tracks who falls in love with a rich girl home from boarding school. Their families are opposed to the match, which ends in tragedy for the young girl. YDC has a supporting role as the mother of one of the teenagers.

Yvonne De Carlo will be appearing in a horror film along with Rod Steiger and Michael J. Pollard. Produced by John Quested and Chris Harrop and directed by John Hough, the story centers around an American couple who decide to raise their children on an isolated island and not allow any outsiders to intrude. Those who do are dealt with severely.

Index

5